CONTEXTUAL PRACTICE

▌ ASSEMBLAGE AND THE EROTIC

IN POSTWAR POETRY AND ART ▌

STEPHEN FREDMAN

STANFORD UNIVERSITY PRESS ▌ STANFORD, CALIFORNIA

Stanford University Press
Stanford, California

This book has been published with the assistance of the Institute for the Scholarship in the Liberal Arts, College of Arts and Letters, University of Notre Dame.

Library of Congress Cataloging-in-Publication Data

Fredman, Stephen, 1948-
  Contextual practice : assemblage and the erotic in postwar poetry and art / Stephen Fredman.
    p. cm.
  Includes bibliographical references and index.
  ISBN 978-0-8047-6358-5 (cloth : alk. paper)
  1. American poetry--20th century--History and criticism. 2. Assemblage (Art)--United States--History--20th century. 3. Erotic poetry, American--History and criticism. 4. Erotic art--United States--History--20th century. 5. Poetics. 6. Art--Technique. 7. Aesthetics, Modern. I. Title.
  PS323.5.F69 2010
  811'.54093538--dc22   2009046361

Designed by Bruce Lundquist
Typeset at Stanford University Press in 10/14 Minion

■ FOR BARBARA ■

CONTENTS

FIGURES

PREFACE

We began to see ourselves as fashioning unnamed contexts,
contexts of a new life way in the making, a secret mission.

Robert Duncan

This book makes the argument that some of the most innovative works of
poetry and art in the postwar period (1945–1970) engaged in a "contextual
practice." The term refers both to a way of making art, for which the mag-
pie art of assemblage is the most vivid representative, and to a new relationship between art and life, which can be called "erotic poetics." In a time that
seemed evacuated of meaning by the devastating experiences of the Great
Depression and World War II, contextual practice involved drawing together
discarded or unremarked fragments (whether visual or verbal) from daily life
in order to reveal "secret" meanings and to insist on the regenerative potential
of everyday experience. In rejecting the grand, sweeping gesture in favor of a
vernacular vocabulary composed of the near-at-hand, poets and artists turned
particularly toward the body as a repository of unrecognized cultural potential. Basing their work in the body and its erotic energies, they created an art
of daily life that reveled in sexual display and drug experimentation, espoused
an anarchist politics and a communal sociality, and encouraged mystical and
shamanistic excursions. Contextual practice informed all of the branches of
the New American poetry; the writing, art, and filmmaking of the Beats; the
performance of happenings, events, and dance theater; the underground film
movement; and currents of assemblage, collage, junk art, and pop art. Having
never been looked at together before, the central figures treated in this book—
poets Robert Duncan and Robert Creeley; artist Wallace Berman; and filmmaker, artist, and folk music anthologist Harry Smith—form a constellation

that illuminates the theoretical and practical stakes involved in a contextual practice. Taking this artistic mode as a lens allows us to look back and see the first stirrings of a countercultural ethos that was to have a profound effect on society at large.

More than the other books I have written, this study has grown up within a context of shared exploration and conversation. Nearly all of it was originally written for conference panels, symposia, and lectures, or commissioned as chapters for edited collections. I am particularly grateful to the following people, whose interest in my work provided the occasions for its earlier manifestations: Gerald Bruns, Ronald Bush, Stephen Collis, Thomas Crow, Michael Duncan, Johannes Göransson, Scarlett Higgins, James Maynard, Steve McCaffery, Kristine McKenna, Peter Middleton, Robert Rehder, Rani Singh, Raymond Spiteri, Patrick Vincent, and Timothy Yu. For conversations about the topics treated in this book, I want to thank, in addition to these people mentioned, a much larger circle of friends and acquaintances, whose names I hope to list faithfully (knowing I will inevitably fall short): David Antin, Charles Bernstein, Marcia Brennan, Robert Cantwell, Joseph Conte, Michael Davidson, Steve Dickison, Sandra Dijkstra, Johanna Drucker, Clayton Eshleman, Al Filreis, Albert Gelpi, Graham Hammill, the late Burton Hatlen, Romana Huk, Lisa Jarnot, Nicholas Jenkins, Louis Kaplan, Robert Kaufman, Kevin Killian, Jeffrey Kripal, Nathaniel Mackey, John Matthias, David Meltzer, Thomas Merluzzi, Peter O'Leary, Michael Palmer, Andrew Perchuk, Marjorie Perloff, Herman Rappaport, Brian Reed, Jerome Rothenberg, Diane Rothenberg, Maeera Shreiber, Philip Smith, Stephen Vincent, Geoff Ward, Henry Weinfield, John Wilkinson, and Ewa Ziarek. Undergraduate and graduate students in my courses have had a hand in making this a clearer and, I hope, more compelling book. Thanks also to an anonymous reader for Stanford University Press, whose suggestions helped to bring the argument into crisper focus.

Through the generosity of Steve McCaffery, Ewa Ziarek, and the Humanities Institute at the University at Buffalo, I was able to spend two weeks as a David Gray Chair Library Fellow in the Poetry Collection. For hospitality, conversation, and material assistance during visits to Buffalo during 2006, I thank the two of them, along with Michael Basinski, Robert Bertholf, Harvey Breverman, Matt Chambers, Joseph Conte, Marilyn Dunlap, Susanne Hall, Lisa Jarnot, James Maynard, Kyle Schlesinger, Joseph Syracuse, and Krzysztof Ziarek. I have also benefited greatly from research leaves bestowed by the

University of Notre Dame. The publication of this book is made possible in part by support from the Institute for Scholarship in the Liberal Arts, College of Arts and Letters, University of Notre Dame. Thanks to Scott Smith and Marion Rohrleitner for able research assistance. For help gathering images, I am indebted to Shirley Berman, Tosh Berman, Ben Blackwell, Victor Coleman, Thomas Crow, Brian Graham, Scott Hobbs, Kristine McKenna, Virginia Mokslaveskas, Kathleen Pyne, Rani Singh, Margaret Sloan, and Christopher Wagstaff. My gratitude to the many skilled and conscientious people at Stanford University Press: Norris Pope, Emily-Jane Cohen, Mariana Raykov, Ariane De Pree-Kajfez, Tom Finnegan, Sarah Newman, David Jackson, and Puja Sangar.

ABBREVIATIONS

The following abbreviations are used for works frequently cited.

AM   Igliori, Paola, ed. *American Magus: Harry Smith—A Modern Alchemist.* New York: Inanout, 1996.

BB   Duncan, Robert. *Bending the Bow.* New York: New Directions, 1968.

CG   Duncan, Robert. *Caesar's Gate: Poems 1949–50.* Mallorca: Divers Press, 1955; 2nd ed., Berkeley: Sand Dollar, 1972.

CPAG   Ginsberg, Allen. *Collected Poems: 1947–1997.* New York: HarperCollins, 2006.

CPJS   Gizzi, Peter, and Kevin Killian, eds. *My Vocabulary Did This to Me: The Collected Poetry of Jack Spicer.* Middletown, CT: Wesleyan University Press, 2008.

CPRC   Creeley, Robert. *The Collected Poems of Robert Creeley, 1945–1975.* Berkeley: University of California Press, 1982.

FC   Duncan, Robert. *Fictive Certainties: Essays by Robert Duncan.* New York: New Directions, 1985.

GW   Duncan, Robert. *Ground Work: Before the War / In the Dark.* Eds. Robert J. Bertholf and James Maynard. New York: New Directions, 2006.

OF   Duncan, Robert. *The Opening of the Field.* New York: Grove, 1960.

PNY   Lorca, Federico García. *Poet in New York.* Trans. Greg Simon and Steven F. White. Ed. and intro. Christopher Maurer. Rev. ed. New York: Farrar, Straus and Giroux, 1998.

RB   Duncan, Robert. *Roots and Branches.* New York: Scribner's, 1964.

Self   Singh, Rani, ed. *Think of the Self Speaking: Harry Smith—Selected Interviews.* Seattle: Elbow/Citiful , 1999.

SP   Duncan, Robert. *A Selected Prose.* Ed. Robert J. Bertholf. New York: New Directions, 1995.

CONTEXTUAL PRACTICE

INTRODUCTION

"A Secret Mission"

In 1957, at an exhibition at the Ferus Gallery in Los Angeles, Wallace Berman displayed three large works that would be called today assemblages or installations. One of them, *Temple,* consisted of a rough black shed, open on one side and large enough to contain a life-sized figure robed in white, its head twisted 180 degrees away from the viewer and with an enormous key around its neck. On the floor of this inverted confessional or magician's parlor were tossed sheets from the first issue of *Semina,* a loose-leaf journal Berman published to showcase the art and poetry of a circle of friends. One of the sheets came to the attention of a policeman who had been called in to close down the show as obscene. The sheet contained an ink drawing by (Marjorie) Cameron, purportedly from a peyote vision, which portrayed two humanoid figures engaged in intercourse (Fig. 1). The confiscation of this drawing resulted in Berman's arrest and conviction for indecency, as he reported in *Semina 2:* "the righteous judge, Kenneth Holiday [*sic*], . . . taking the allegorical drawing in question out of context, declared me guilty of displaying lewd and pornographic matter" (Duncan and McKenna 52).[1] Commenting on this passage in a 1978 essay for a retrospective exhibition of Berman's work, the poet Robert Duncan seized on the word *context* as crucial to an understanding not only of Berman's collage and assemblage art but of a range of aesthetic and social practices that coalesced in California during the fifties and sixties:

> The question of "context" in the affair goes beyond the usual matter of context in such trials, for Berman's very art is the art of context. From the first, the intent of *Semina* was not a choice of poems and art works to exercise the editor's discrimination and aesthetic judgment, but the fashioning of a context. The collage itself, which had been seen by Dadaists and by Surrealists as a mode of attack upon the real or upon established relations, . . . had, after all, projected in the attack the context of what we recognize as Dada and the Surreal. Now, in our conscious alliance with the critical breakthru of Dada and Surrealism as in our alliance with the Romantic Movement at large, we began

FIGURE 1. Cameron, Untitled *("peyote vision")*, ink drawing, c. 1957. Cameron Parsons Foundation.

to see ourselves as fashioning unnamed contexts, contexts of a new life way in the making, a secret mission. (*SP* 198)

As Duncan notes, aesthetic breakthroughs can go beyond offering new techniques to opening up entirely new ways of perceiving and conducting life, as happened with Dada and surrealism: the adjectives "Dada" and "surreal" now describe attitudes, activities, and perceptions—*contexts*—that extend far outside the realm of art per se. Inspired by Dada, surrealism, and romanticism and by a shared sense of rebellion against the mores of postwar American culture, the poets and artists who participated in the context that Berman helped establish did not set forth to launch a movement; rather, they fashioned "unnamed contexts," both in their collage-based art works and in their social relations, which had the "secret mission" of proposing "a new life way." In the playful, erotic, transgressive, communal, collagist approach to making art that arose at this time, there is an untold story—a story about an undiscerned yet eventful and influential turn in post-World War II American poetry and the visual arts toward a contextual practice.[2]

A contextual practice initiates an art devoted to contexts, building works not around a central idea, theme, or symbol but by plucking and arranging images, materials, language, or even people from the surrounding milieu, "fashioning . . . contexts of a new life way in the making." Of necessity a vernacular procedure tied to the everyday and the overlooked, contextual practice works by uncovering new energies and images through juxtaposing found materials or by directing aesthetic attention to an existing but previously ignored context. With its juxtapositional bent, contextual practice applies the most far-reaching formal innovation in the arts of the twentieth century—the principle of collage—in striking and unforeseen ways to the conduct of life. In this way, contextual practice combines the structural principle of collage with a transformative aesthetics that can be designated an "erotic poetics." With poets and artists at its forefront, the period from 1945 to 1970 saw an urgent return to the body; the body and sexuality were invoked as central carriers of culture, infusing eroticism not only into works of art but also into anarchist politics, post-Freudian psychology, and emergent forms of ecstatic mysticism. Contextual practice disclosed an erotic poetics of burgeoning force that had a profound effect on the social life of the time and that continues to haunt contemporary art and culture.

In order to understand how contextual practice appeared and why its impact has not been acknowledged fully, it is helpful to consider its historical background. Beginning with romanticism in the eighteenth century, a paradox governs the history of artistic innovation: the more autonomous art becomes, the more it subsumes cultural functions that belong to other realms, such as religion, philosophy, psychology, and politics. By this I mean not that art takes its subject matter from these other realms (which it has always done) but that by virtue of a newfound autonomy it substitutes itself for cultural practices whose legitimacy it draws into question, spawning strange amalgams such as art-as-religion, art-as-philosophy, art-as-psychology, and art-as-politics.[3] In the first half of the twentieth century, as this trend accelerated on every side, innovative work in the arts was animated particularly by the marriage of aesthetics and epistemology, which resulted in a reconception of the medium of art through a questioning of its essence, its limits, and what can be known within it. Modernists often envisioned an art that would occupy an equivalent place in modern culture with that of science—that most autonomous and subsuming of cultural practices—in which artistic ways of knowing, both objective and subjective, would approach in complexity and sophistication scientific ways of knowing. Just as modern science upset many of the categories providing stable forms of knowledge for the society at large and reconfigured the categories in new and forceful ways, the arts upset and reconfigured the generic categories that comprise the frameworks for how things can be known in art.

In the course of generic innovation, the arts invented the new hybrid frame or meta-genre of collage. Although genres in various arts had been broken and reframed as new hybrids starting in the nineteenth century, the first work of art that bore the designation "collage" (*Still-Life with Chair Caning*) appeared in 1912, when Picasso glued to a canvas a piece of oilcloth on which a chair-caning pattern was printed. He then painted a cubist chair around the "imitation" seat, thus throwing into question the whole notion of art as an imitation of life. A discarded commodity, the oilcloth already resided within the contemporary world; pasting it into a canvas to "represent" chair caning—that is, transferring into his art an element from life that already had a representational purpose—Picasso parodied the Western belief that art imitates life. By suggesting new relationships between representation and understanding and between art and life, the developing meta-genre of collage fed on the breakdown and interpenetration of genres. In skeletal form, collage can be defined as combining two actions: the selection of objects from the real world for incorporation into an artwork, and the juxtaposition of objects in unexpected—that is, nonlinear, irrational, or antihierarchical—ways.[4] For theorists such as Theodor Adorno, David Antin, Marjorie Perloff, and Gregory Ulmer, collage became, in the words of Ulmer, "the single most revolutionary formal innovation in artistic representation to occur in [the twentieth] century" (Hoffman 384).[5] Following Picasso's breakthrough, it played an especially central role in the epistemologically adventurous movements of cubism, Dada, and surrealism.

After the devastation of World War II and the revelation that "enlightened" science had invented the means for the unimaginable brutality of the Holocaust and Hiroshima, many in the arts participated in a sweeping revulsion against instrumental thinking and began to substitute an emerging existential impulse for the epistemological one. As their trust in dominant ideas, ideologies, faiths, methodologies, and institutions seemed to reach a nadir, the urgent question for these artists changed from how to invent advanced methods for probing the basis of knowledge to how the modern methods and forms recently discovered might suggest new ways to make sense of and to conduct individual and social life. During what W. H. Auden called in 1947 the "Age of Anxiety," the response of some influential poets, such as Robert Lowell, Sylvia Plath, and John Berryman, and certain painters, such as Jackson Pollock, Franz Kline, and Willem DeKooning, was to dramatize the struggles of a psychologically wounded individual against an oppressive social reality.[6] Among a number of less celebrated artists and poets, a contextual practice grew up that enabled the expression of social critique both through art works and through aesthetically motivated lifestyles. As Robert Duncan remarked, these countercultural artists looked to the anarchism, antirealism, and eroticism of the Dada and surrealist movements and to the formal inventiveness of collage for inspiration. Contextual practice intensified earlier efforts at aesthetic provocation and generic mixture by bringing an erotic poetics much more forcefully into the conduct of daily life. When their aesthetic practices devolved from primarily epistemological to existential concerns, poets and artists in California and New York in particular embraced sexual and drug experimentation, anarchist communalism, political protest, and research in occultism, archeology, anthropology, and phenomenology—all as part of the "work" of art.

During the postwar period, avant-garde poetry made an extraordinarily generative contribution to the arts and to the larger culture. The label that describes this poetry comes from the title of Donald Allen's groundbreaking 1960 anthology, *The New American Poetry*. Allen took it upon himself to name particular movements within the New American Poetry, dividing the cutting-edge poets of the time heuristically into four porous groups: the Black Mountain School, the San Francisco Renaissance, the Beat Generation, and the New York School. With William Carlos Williams as their most apparent common denominator, these poets valorized the body, the vernacular, and the everyday, using open verse forms that stress spontaneity and the gathering of disparate materials addressed to a particular context. The erotic poetics of the New American poets also marks a rebirth of Whitmanian virtues of informality, openness, vulnerability, nakedness, ecstasy, and camaraderie. The present study draws its poetic exemplars primarily from the ranks of the New American poets, focusing especially on Robert Duncan (1919–1988) and Robert Creeley (1926–2005). The other two central figures that round out a presentation of the contours of contextual practice are Wallace Berman (1926–1976) and the folk music anthologist, filmmaker, and painter Harry Smith (1923–1991). A number of other poets play a significant role herein—Charles Reznikoff (a member of the earlier generation of Objectivists, but newly active during the postwar period), Allen Ginsberg, Jack Spicer, David Meltzer, and Denise Levertov—as do Jess (Collins) and other California artists and filmmakers and the radical psychoanalytical thinker Norman O. Brown. Although contextual practice is a significant component of artistic currents that have been treated in detail, such as the Beat Movement, Pop Art, Fluxus, and the performance art movement under the aegis of John Cage, this study will concentrate on figures who were not central to these movements, figures who by their very eccentricity and marginality can help bring an unrecognized artistic practice into the sharpest focus. And it will make a case not often mooted regarding the arts of the twentieth century in general: that poetry and poetics are at the heart of the contextual turn.

With Duncan, Creeley, Berman, and Smith as primary figures, an account of contextual practice can be given that makes clear its relevance to a wide range of artists and art forms during the postwar era, while also bringing to light new elements in and among these four figures. Until now, the majority of critical attention Creeley and Duncan have received is as members of the Black Mountain movement in the arts. This has obscured Creeley's role as a theorist of the art of context and Duncan's placement at the epicenter of the erotic arts of assemblage in California. Smith and Berman have managed nearly to escape extended critical discussion until quite recently. Signs that this neglect is waning can be seen in the scholarly symposium "Harry Smith: The Avant-

Garde in the American Vernacular," hosted by the Getty Research Institute in 2001, and in the Santa Monica Museum's landmark exhibition *Semina Culture: Wallace Berman and His Circle* (Duncan and McKenna), which traveled the United States from 2005 to 2007.[7] In many of the chapters, Duncan plays a central or contributory role, emerging as the most committed, accomplished, and influential practitioner of an erotic contextual art. By choosing Duncan, Creeley, Berman, and Smith as primary subjects rather than, say, Charles Olson, Frank O'Hara, Joseph Cornell, and John Cage, I mean not to ignore the contextual practice of the latter four artists but to offer an account that centers on figures who at once force us to rethink critical orthodoxies about the period and who produce work that cannot be readily understood without recourse to a notion of contextual practice.

The Chapters

The first chapter, "Forging a Contextual Practice: Assemblage and Erotic Poetics," introduces the two major aspects of contextual practice. The first half of the chapter concentrates on the groundbreaking 1961 exhibition *The Art of Assemblage*, organized by the Museum of Modern Art, which joined the new collage art created after World War II with its prewar European precursors. Designating the new art "assemblage," the curator, William Seitz, argues that the term more accurately describes the postwar innovations that extend collage into three dimensions, and beyond that into installations and happenings. Throughout the catalog, he takes pains to demonstrate the significant role poetry plays in the art of assemblage. In particular, he labels the contextual quality of assemblage—its use of objects with associations or as metaphors—as "poetic" in order to signal the contribution of poetry to a visual art that moves beyond formalism. The second half of the chapter focuses on erotic poetics, discussing Norman O. Brown's counterculture classic, *Love's Body* (1965), an aphoristic work of visionary psychoanalysis informed by the poetry of his good friend Robert Duncan. Duncan, in turn, critiques *Love's Body* as itself an unacknowledged work of prose poetry, disclosing thereby many of the premises of the erotic poetics he shares with Brown. Within Brown's aphorisms and Duncan's poetry and poetics, psychoanalysis mingles with liberatory anarchism and the sexual mysticism of Tantra and the hermetic. This blend of the sexual, the political, and the mystical represents a précis of the erotic directions taken by contextual practice.

The second chapter, "The Contextual Art of Robert Creeley's Interviews," reads Creeley's interviews both as works of contextual art and as expositions of its theory. One of the most erotically and theoretically engaged contextual practitioners, Creeley forged a poetry of intimacy that constantly probes the writer's relationship to impinging contexts of every sort: the body, other people, social and political conditions, aesthetic concerns, dreams and memories, drugs, words and numbers, and the media used for inscription. In his book of conversations, *Contexts of Poetry* (1973), he presents interviews conducted with him by others as documents of contextual practice, making *Contexts of Poetry* probably the first book of interviews included by a writer within his or her own oeuvre. The chapter examines Creeley's interviews from three angles: by looking at the innovative relationship to context in his poetry and poetics, by rehearsing his model of conversation as an existential encounter, and by analyzing his invocation of artistic aphorisms as a form of what the philosopher Pierre Hadot calls "spiritual exercises." As part of the larger project of chronicling the rise of contextual practice, the chapter also discusses the emergence of the interview genre in the postwar period. Creeley's interviews demonstrate how talk about art bleeds into talk as art. In fact, much of the New American poetry can be characterized as a precipitation of verse out of conversation or as epistolary poetry.

The third chapter, "Assemblage as Archeology and History: Harry Smith's *Anthology of American Folk Music* and Charles Reznikoff's *Testimony*," follows on the concerns of the first two chapters with a further discussion of how collage informs contextual practice. From a theoretical perspective, the art historian and philosopher Donald Kuspit demonstrates how the open-ended qualities of postwar assemblage make it like an archeological excavation into the present world. Harry Smith, an enigmatic artist, filmmaker, musicologist, and anthropologist, practiced assemblage as a form of archeology, excavating for occult patterns in the present moment and in the arts of many times and places, seeking solutions to the "problem of rhythm in relation to thought." An influential and assiduous contextual practitioner, Smith incessantly created artworks and acted roles in daily life, making him a proto-performance artist as well. The chapter concludes with an extended comparison of Smith's epoch-making musical assemblage *The Anthology of American Folk Music* (1952) (drawn from 78s recorded in the late twenties and early thirties) to Charles Reznikoff's two-volume *Testimony: The United States* (1885–1915), extracted from law books covering trials during the same tumultuous turn-of-the-century period in which the folk songs of Smith's anthology were com-posed. These two works recount an unorthodox history of the United States, told from the perspective of the underclass and structured as assemblage on a grand scale.

The discussion of Smith in the fourth chapter, "Visionary Assemblage: Harry Smith and the Poetry of Allen Ginsberg, Robert Duncan, and Jack Spicer," con-structs a continuum of visionary poetics based on a comparison of his work to that of three poets whom he knew personally. He was closest to Ginsberg, and in fact the indigent Smith lived for extended periods of time in Ginsberg's New York City apartment. In the poem "Journal Night Thoughts" (1961), Ginsberg records an evening of drug visions in the company of Smith. The poem thus affords a vehicle for comparing and contrasting their stances toward the erotic, especially toward tantric mysticism. Duncan, who like Smith hailed from a Theosophical background that incorporates Tantrism, evinced an abiding in-terest in the occult and a penchant for metaphysical collage. A fundamentally syncretic thinker, Duncan coined the term "Grand Collage" to describe his own work and that of the mystically inclined poets, artists, filmmakers, and composers who surrounded him. Through a consideration of Duncan's poem "The Architecture, *Passages* 9" (1964), the chapter highlights elements common to his work and that of Smith: use of assemblage as a method, engagement in occult speculation, pursuit of shamanistic states, fascination with dream land-scapes, and conversion of the artist's room into a cave of alchemical transmuta-tion. With the third poet, Jack Spicer, Smith collected records in Oakland in the late forties that informed both *The Anthology of American Folk Music* and Spicer's "Most Educational Folk-Song Program West of the Pecos" on KPFA, the fledgling public radio station. Like Smith, Spicer theorized and practiced a contextual art of dictation and divination, in which mind-altering substances keep the artist's ego at bay and help open the way for what is "outside" to enter the composition.

One of the pioneers of West Coast assemblage art, Wallace Berman was a highly influential catalyst for the art and culture of postwar California. The fifth chapter, "Surrealism and Kabbalah in Semina Culture: Wallace Berman Cultivates the Erotic in California Poetry and Art," investigates the erotic poetics of the poets and artists who congregated around *Semina*, the journal he produced from 1955 to 1964. Through *Semina* (which consists of collages, poems, and photographs on loose-leaf cards, stuffed into decorated envelopes and mailed to friends), Berman acted as midwife at the communal birth of a contextual practice. The best-known poets involved in *Semina* were Duncan, David Meltzer, Michael McClure, John Wieners, Philip Lamantia, Bob Kaufman, and Jack Hirschman; artists included Bruce Conner, Jess, George Herms, Jay DeFeo, Joan Brown, Cameron, Dennis Hopper, and Berman himself. Although the Semina cohort imitated to some extent the group ethos of surrealism, they were attracted less to doctrinaire surrealists than to heretics such as Jean Cocteau and Antonin Artaud. Emulating Artaud's peyote sessions with the Tarahumara Indians, many of the Semina figures took peyote in the fifties and contributed to *Semina 5*, an issue devoted to Mexico. Another erotic element in the mix of Semina culture was Kabbalah, which formed the basis for Berman's art incorporating Hebrew letters and for the poetry of Meltzer and Hirschman. Duncan introduced many poets to Kabbalah; his volume of poems *Letters* (1958) brings kabbalistic readings forcefully into the poetry of the period. Joining surrealism with Kabbalah, Semina culture was rooted in contextual practice, which often included mail art and other works created as conversation. The catalog *Semina Culture: Wallace Berman and His Circle* demonstrates the ascendance of contextual practice through works of collage and assemblage created by artists, poets, photographers, filmmakers, and former child film stars—works with a palpable eroticism fed by drug use, sexual display, mysticism, and anarchism.

A lifelong champion of mysticism, anarchism, and sexual display (but not of drugs), Duncan reached a point of crisis in his erotic poetics during the Vietnam War, which mimicked the crisis felt by the nation. The sixth chapter, "Before Caesar's Gate, Robert Duncan Comes to Grief: The Vietnam War and the 'Unengendered Child,'" investigates Duncan's erotic collage poetry of the Vietnam War period, as found in the second edition of *Caesar's Gate* (1972) and in poems from the late sixties and early seventies in *Ground Work: Before the War* (1984). This was a phase of Duncan's work dominated by unappeasable grief, which was occasioned by the war, by the demise of his friendship with Denise Levertov sparked by their disagreement over the relation of poetry to protest, and by his recognition that as a homosexual poet he was in mourning over never having had a son. Duncan explores the grounds of his grief about war and about being "sonless" by identifying with gay predecessors Walt Whitman and Federico García Lorca, both of whom suffered this same complex of emotions during their own experiences of war.

The painful dissolution of Duncan's friendship with Levertov after their close identification for two decades was part of a psychic disturbance he called an "anima rebellion," which reached its most virulent form in his condemnation of Levertov as an avatar of the ferocious Hindu goddess Kali in "Santa Cruz Propositions" (1970). My seventh chapter, "In Robert Duncan's 'Anima Rebellion,' Denise Levertov Meets the Goddess Kali," explores how the erotic charge that Kali carries for Duncan shows up in his figuring of death as a realm of sexual frustration in *Caesar's Gate* (and in collages by Jess that accompany the text) and recurs in the early poems of *Ground Work* that invoke a terrifying mother figure. Also present in his most famous poem, "My Mother Would Be a Falconress," this figure of the predatory mother represents the only mythological image in Duncan's work not submitted to a thoroughgoing hermeneutical inquiry. Arising ultimately from the loss of his mother at birth, the "anima rebellion" represents a grief he finds too deep to face directly, and it forces a breakdown in his own erotic poetics at the end of the period treated in this study.

The conclusion, "Jerome Rothenberg's 'Symposium of the Whole,'" explores Rothenberg's anthology of ethnopoetics, *Technicians of the Sacred: A Range of Poetries from Africa, America, Asia, & Oceania* (1968), in which he takes Harry Smith's *Anthology of American Folk Music* and Donald Allen's *New American Poetry* as exemplars of an anthology composed as assemblage. Rothenberg's conception of the erotic poetics lurking within the art of assemblage is also deeply informed by Duncan's poetry and poetics. Citing Duncan's phrase "a symposium of the whole" as a talisman for his enterprise, Rothenberg creates a Grand Collage of "primitive" and archaic poetries from around the world, which he juxtaposes with avant-garde poetry and performance art. *Technicians* can be seen as a culminating work of contextual art and as a transition into the related cultural and artistic movements of the seventies and eighties, such as multiculturalism, ethnopoetics, conceptual art, minimal art, performance art, and investigations of the relationship between orality and literacy.

FORGING A CONTEXTUAL PRACTICE

Assemblage and Erotic Poetics

The Art of Assemblage

This chapter looks at the two major components of contextual practice—assemblage technique and erotic engagement—and at how both were given impetus by avant-garde poetry. The standard history of postwar culture holds that the leading art forms were those that made a strong case for the artistic maturity of the United States: jazz, film, and abstract expressionism. There is no question that the improvisatory and vernacular aesthetics of these defining American contributions exerted a powerful national and international influence, and all three nurtured in various ways the emergence of a contextual practice. The standard account overlooks, however, the roles of poetry and poetics as effective spurs toward development of a contextual art that turned against American triumphalism and toward emergence of a counterculture: for the visual arts and film, poetry provided a crucial impetus toward development of assemblage, which was a timely advance in the art of collage; likewise, poetry had a profound effect on some of the most radical intellectual thought of the postwar period. This chapter examines two representative documents in which poetry points the way toward a new contextual practice: the catalog for the watershed exhibition *The Art of Assemblage*, which originated at the Museum of Modern Art in 1961, and Norman O. Brown's highly influential *Love's Body* (1965), a book in dialogue with Robert Duncan's poetry and poetics and one of the key assemblage texts of the sixties counterculture.

Alert to a postwar departure in the art of collage, the Museum of Modern Art mounted a groundbreaking show in 1961, *The Art of Assemblage*, consisting of 252 works of collage and assemblage by 141 artists. To document a lineage for the new work, the exhibit included major figures from earlier in the century, such as Pablo Picasso, Marcel Duchamp, Carlo Carrá, Juan Gris, Kurt Schwitters, Jean Arp, Hannah Höch, Francis Picabia, Max Ernst, Man Ray, and Méret Oppenheim. More importantly, though, it introduced the work of assemblage emerging among artists in the United States, notably Joseph Cornell, Bruce Conner, Robert Rauschenberg, John Chamberlain, George Herms, Robert Indiana, Jess, Jasper Johns, Edward Kienholz, Marisol, Robert Motherwell, Louise Nevelson, and David Smith. The catalog was written by associate curator William Seitz, who had recently joined the museum staff after teaching for seven years at Princeton University. Author of a dissertation that was the first major study of abstract expressionism, Seitz turned to assemblage as the next significant artistic force. In the catalog, he alleges that the postwar arts have asked collage to take on a much greater burden than an artistic form might have been capable of shouldering in the past. To signal this new role, he elevates the term *assemblage* to represent not only a technique in the arts but also "a complex of attitudes and ideas" (10). Earlier in the twentieth century, attitudes and ideas were most fully embodied in new artistic movements, such as cubism, futurism, Dadaism, and surrealism, rather than in the techniques invented within these movements: collage, assemblage, montage, photomontage, frottage, *parole in libertà*, sound poetry, *musique concrète*, and new forms of performance. In the fifties and sixties, though, the technique of assemblage can be found across a span of artistic movements, taking on the burden of the entire complex of aesthetic and cultural activities that I am calling contextual practice.

Throughout the catalog, Seitz contends that assemblage unites poetry and the visual arts and that it would not exist without cooperation between them. Speaking historically, he notes that the movements of futurism, Dada, and surrealism all began life in poetic techniques and manifestos. He also emphasizes the early connection between poetry and art by drawing attention to the specifically visual poetics of French poets Stéphane Mallarmé ("*Un Coup de dés*") and Guillaume Apollinaire (*Calligrammes*) and of Italian poet F. T. Marinetti, whose typographical collages function equally as literary and visual artworks. Beyond visual poetry, he finds a juxtapositional aesthetic characteristic of collage in the texts of Eliot, Joyce, Pound, cummings, Moore, and

Ionesco and in the music of Webern, Satie, Varèse, and Cage. In this sense, the unique cooperation between poetry and visual art at the heart of collage informs some of the most daring and emblematic of modernist works. After World War II, he suggests, poetic qualities become even more pronounced in the contextual practice of assemblage.

Seitz theorizes that assemblage boasts two poetic features that have not been foregrounded in earlier works of collage: associational density and temporality. Initially, as Clement Greenberg contends, collage was primarily a formal discovery that aided the drive toward abstraction and constructivism; when Picasso and Braque pasted paper or cloth onto a painting, drawing attention thereby to the "literal flatness" of the canvas (Greenberg 71), they reached "a major turning point in the evolution of Cubism" as an art on the way to abstraction (Greenberg 67). Assemblage, by virtue of its disjunctive planes and textures, can be said to resemble the formalist trends of abstract painting and constructivist sculpture, but Seitz maintains that "it diverges sharply from these traditions . . . because its raw elements are association-ally 'charged,' preformed, and often precisely identifiable (nails, photographs, old letters, weathered wood, automobile parts, leaves, doll's eyes, stones, or whatever)" (25). Postwar assemblage often moves beyond purely formal concerns to stage interactions among the clusters of associations accruing to the mundane objects it employs. These interactions partake of the whole range of rhetorical devices developed by poetry, such as metaphor, analogy, and irony. Complementing this associational and rhetorical density, the temporal traces borne by objects within an assemblage also take it beyond formalism: "When paper is soiled or lacerated, when cloth is worn, stained, or torn, when wood is split, weathered, or patterned with peeling coats of paint, when metal is bent or rusted, they gain connotations which unmarked materials lack" (Seitz 84). In this sense, the materials of assemblage become like words, whose temporality, or "materiality," derives from their usage over centuries, during which they acquire layers of connotations on their own and in relation to other words. Overall, assemblage involves a poetics by virtue of its objects, which bear traces of time and associations to prior functions, and by virtue of the rhetorical interchange it sets up between these objects.

Looking to specify more precisely the cooperation between visual art and poetry, Seitz formulates three levels of signification in assemblage: "that of tangible materials, that of vision, at which colors and other formal qualities alter each other and blend like tastes or scents, and finally that of 'literary' meanings" (83). This formulation bears a remarkable resemblance to Ezra Pound's influential division of poetry into three main elements: *melopoeia* (the musical quality of words), *phanopoeia* (poetic images), and *logopoeia* ("the dance of the intellect among words"). In speaking of "'literary' meanings," Seitz reaches for a poetic concept such as logopoeia, which "employs words not only for their direct meaning, but . . . takes count [*sic*] . . . of habits of usage, of the context we *expect* to find with the word, . . . and of ironical play" (Pound, *Essays* 25). In assemblage something like logopoeia occurs: "Because overtones and associations as well as physical materials are placed in juxtaposition, it could almost be said that a constellation of meanings can exist independently of the colors, textures, and forms which are its carriers" (Seitz 83). Although Pound states that the "aesthetic content" of logopoeia "cannot possibly be contained in plastic or in music" (25), Seitz locates the innovation of postwar assemblage precisely in its adaptation of logopoeia to the visual arts, its foregrounding of the lively play of meanings that accrue through the contexts associated with the already existing objects brought together in the artwork:

> Even taken in isolation, the possible meanings of objects and fragments are infinitely rich, whereas . . . professional art materials such as paint, plastic, stone, bronze, etc., are formless and, in the Platonic sense, are pure essences of redness, hardness, or ductility. Found materials are works already in progress: prepared for the artist by the outside world, previously formed, textured, colored, and even sometimes entirely prefabricated into accidental "works of art." . . . As element is set beside element, the many qualities and auras of isolated fragments are compounded, fused, or contradicted so that . . . physical matter becomes poetry. (85–86)

With the distinction in mind between painting (with its pristine materials awaiting the hand of the expressive artist) and assemblage (whose works are made of objects bearing their own associations and history), it becomes clear that assemblage marks a distinct departure from the abstract expressionist aesthetic that arose in the forties, for which Greenberg was the most vocal champion. One major contributor to this shift from formalism to contextualism was the rediscovery of Dada. Although Picasso, Braque, and Gris hold pride of place in the overall genealogy of collage, we must look to Dada, and especially to Kurt Schwitters and Marcel Duchamp, for the origins of much that is distinctive about the assemblage movement after 1945.[1] Having aspired to overthrow the hierarchy of Western values during and after World War I, Dada inspired new experiments in the interpenetration of art and life undertaken by assemblage artists after World War II. Turning away in disgust from instrumental logic, Dada elevated irrationality and chance: "it accorded to unsureness, accident, confusion, disunity, and discontinuity a share of the attention formerly reserved for . . . their moral opposites, and released a constellation of physical and intellectual energies through which an artist could (and still can) operate in a way that, at least in the West, was previously impossible." Loosening the stranglehold of logic, classification, and morality, Dada set in motion the pursuit of "a nonrational metaphysic of oppositions," in which unmotivated chance would take its place alongside intended actions. Dada's overturning of values and explosive release of creative energies was a major advance in what can be seen as a Dionysian "revaluation of all values," instigated near the end of the previous century by Friedrich Nietzsche. Taking on the terms of Dada within their own lives and work, postwar artists and writers arrived at a position analogous to that not only of Nietzsche but also of Asian philosophies such as Daoism and Zen Buddhism, which are intent on confounding common sense and balancing polar opposites (Seitz).

One of the most important consequences for contextual practice of the opening afforded by Dada's purposelessness was to encourage poets and artists to retreat from intentionality and egotism. Accepting randomness and dissociation as preconditions, the contextual artist enters the work of art in a new ontological and ethical position, surrendering control and intention and becoming as much a discoverer or spectator as a creator: "Like a beachcomber, a collector, or a scavenger wandering among ruins, the assembler discovers order as well as materials by accident" (Seitz 38). Another analogy for this way of working would be archeology, which we will explore further in Chapter Three. Applied both to materials and to form, the principle of digging or spontaneous discovery is an aesthetic hallmark of contextual practice. Charles Olson's "composition by field" (and his image of the poet as "archeologist of morning") and Jack Kerouac's "spontaneous bop prosody" were equally influential methodologies among the New American poets; likewise, Cage's schemes of chance composition and indeterminate performance made a huge impact on the visual and performing arts.[2] Like Schwitters, who built his collages and his *Merzbau* collage architecture from the detritus of the city, most practitioners of assemblage went "beachcombing" in an urban environment, which not only offered materials for construction but could be perceived as a work of art in itself. The urban environment "is truly a collage landscape: an unplanned assemblage of animated gasoline displays, screaming billboards, hundred-mile-an-hour automobiles jammed bumper to bumper, graveyards of twisted and rusting scrap, lots strewn with bed springs and cracked toilet bowls" (Seitz 76). This notion of the urban scene as assemblage also informs Allen Ginsberg's "Sunflower Sutra" (1955), from which this strophe is taken:

> and Hells of the Eastern rivers, bridges clanking Joes Greasy Sandwiches,
> > dead baby carriages, black treadless tires forgotten and unretreaded,
> > the poem of the riverbank, condoms & pots, steel knives, nothing
> > stainless, only the dank muck and the razor-sharp artifacts passing
> > into the past—

> (*CPAG* 146)

Speaking of this poem, Thomas Crow notes, "Ginsberg's endless clusters of substantives . . . offered a direct analogue to the accumulations of objects and found materials in assemblage art" (*Sixties* 29).

The neo-Dada recognition that the urban environment can be perceived as an assemblage gave birth in the late fifties to the happenings presented by Allan Kaprow, Jim Dine, and Claes Oldenburg and to the events hosted by the Fluxus Group. In an essay titled "The Legacy of Jackson Pollock" (1958), Kaprow invoked the authority of Pollock to sanction the huge aesthetic leap taken by these artists beyond abstract expressionism:

> Pollock, as I see him, left us at the point where we must become preoccupied with and even dazzled by the space and objects of our everyday life, either our bodies, clothes, rooms, or, if need be, the vastness of Forty-second Street. Not satisfied with the suggestion through paint of our other senses, we shall utilize the specific substances of sight, sound, movements, people, odors, touch. Objects of every sort are materials for the new art: paint, chairs, electric and neon lights, smoke, water, old socks, a dog, movies, a thousand other things that will be discovered by the present generation of artists. (Kaprow 7–9)

In the late fifties and early sixties, poets and artists in New York and California were at the forefront of this alchemical conversion of everyday life into artistic material and were pushing their contextual practice into other arts. In New York, those making a crossover included Jackson Mac Low; the New York School poets such as Frank O'Hara, John Ashbery, Barbara Guest, and James Schuyler; Joseph Cornell; John Cage; and Pop-artists-to-be such as Robert

Rauschenberg, Jim Dine, Claes Oldenburg, Larry Rivers, and Jasper Johns. In California, there was a similar ferment among Beat poets Allen Ginsberg, Jack Kerouac, Gary Snyder, Joanne Kyger, and Philip Whalen; San Francisco Renaissance poets such as Robert Duncan, Robin Blaser, Jack Spicer, and Michael McClure; and junk artists such as George Herms, Wallace Berman, Bruce Conner, Jess, Helen Adam, Edward Kienholz, and Joan Brown. The assemblage aesthetic spread from poets and visual artists to theater and dance: in New York, this occurred in happenings and Fluxus events, the Living Theater, Judson Dance Theater, and the Artists' Theater; in California, it could be found in the plays of Robert Duncan and Helen Adam, poetry readings at the King Ubu Gallery and the Six Gallery, and in Anna Halprin's Dancers' Workshop and Rachel Rosenthal's Instant Theater. The poetic qualities of the assemblage aesthetic also made a profound impact on independent filmmakers, such as Cornell, Maya Deren, Robert Frank, Jonas Mekas, Conner, Larry Jordan, Stan Brakhage, Rudy Burckhardt, Kenneth Anger, James Broughton, and Harry Smith—and on composers, such as Cage, Lou Harrison, Harry Partch, La Monte Young, and Pauline Oliveros.

A visual artist located at the intersection of art, poetry, film, and performance in San Francisco, Jess (1923–2004) is a vital illustration of the poetic possibilities of assemblage. His deep investment in poetry followed most directly from the intimate intertwining of his work with that of Duncan, his marriage partner. Jess not only read, wrote, translated, and listened to poetry, he also used collaged language (often as puns) within his artwork, appended poems to paintings, illustrated and made covers for poetry books and magazines, and created linguistically rich collage books—such as his volumes of cut-ups of *Dick Tracy* comics (called *Tricky Cad*) and *O!*, a book of his collages and poems. Beginning in the early fifties, Jess embarked upon four series of works that engaged in the poetic transformations inherent to contextual practice: "Paste-Ups," or collages; "Assemblies," or assemblages; "Translations," "richly impastoed paintings transformed from black-and-white book illustrations or old photographs"; and "Salvages," "reconstituted paintings from the artist's past or those found in second-hand stores and thrift shops" (Auping 15). Like other assemblage artists, Jess's contextual practice involves intensive scavenging, which he figures as a form of salvation: "all of my work—'Paste-Ups,' 'Assemblies,' 'Translations'—comes from salvaging. I salvage loved images that for some reason have been discarded and I come across them. I've, at times, found wonderful things on the street, just thrown away. If you find something that you really respond to that someone else has thrown away, that's a kind of mini-salvation" (Auping 26).

In one of his "Assemblies," *A Letterbox from Hellgate* (Fig. 2), from 1961, the year of *The Art of Assemblage*, Jess brings together salvaged materials analogous to those in Ginsberg's "Sunflower Sutra."[3] Thomas Evans describes the *Letterbox* as "comprised of a Dictaphone casing, a bookend, a carved-wood tray, an oyster shell, pliers, hinges, clock springs, screws, clips, jewelry, a saltshaker depicting a bear sitting on top of a honey comb, hanging crystals, a hypodermic needle loaded with a dead locust, a pot-metal elephant head wearing dark glasses, and more" (Schaffner 89–90). The basic shape of the object resembles a bust, with the Dictaphone casing functioning as a head and the phallic ladder of hinges appearing to be a tongue. Since the Dictaphone and the "tongue" refer to speech, as does the open mouth of the elephant in

FIGURE 2. Jess, *A Letterbox for Hellgate*, 1961. Assemblage, height: 25 in. © 2009 The Jess Collins Trust. Used by permission. Collection: Odyssia Skouras Quadrani. Photo: Ben Blackwell.

which the shell is poised, Jess's calling the piece *A Letterbox* makes it seem like a device for turning speech into letters, as a stenographer would do when she typed the words captured in the Dictaphone. Many of Jess's works are language machines that translate objects or images from one medium to another. The most intriguing extension of this principle of linguistic metamorphosis occurs in the series of "Translations." Jess considers the "Translations" acts of salvage because, he says, "all of the images I've used for that series I've found in old books, magazines, postcards, or photos that were close to the end of their life sitting and rotting in a used bookstore, and they have spoken up out of the matrix of images that surround them" (Auping 26). When he "translated" the small black-and-white images into full-scale color paintings, he copied the visual information meticulously but also emphasized extreme painterly values by using wildly divergent, often pastel colors and by building up globs of oil paint into an exaggerated impasto that approaches the status of bas-relief. There is a tension between photorealist imagery and excessive painterly indulgence, which combines with subject matter that is sentimental or scientific and accompanied by poetic citations; these features join to create an intricately queer contextual practice that is at once campy and mystical—for, as Jess reminds Michael Auping, "The term *translation* has hidden into it 'being translated into the empyrean, into heaven'" (27). From the realm of poetry, Jess borrows the notion of a translation that is extremely literal and yet, because of the poetic labor involved in rendering a poem in a different language, becomes a work within the oeuvre of the translator. For Jess, salvation and translation form guiding principles for an art that eschews originality and bases itself on the selection and manipulation of found materials.[4]

Love's Body as Poetry and Poetics

As I have begun to suggest, collage after World War II went through a series of transformations within the arts, with poetry and visual art taking the lead. Although some visual artists, among them Romare Bearden, Ray Johnson, and John Evans, held firmly to the discipline of gluing objects to a two-dimensional surface, most artists involved with collage crossed over into creating or inhabiting three-dimensional spaces. Many continued to migrate from assembling hybrid objects to creating installations and staging happenings. In the *Art of Assemblage* exhibition, for instance, Cornell installed fourteen of his enigmatic and haunting boxes in a theatrically darkened room. Working both inside and outside museum spaces, the Fluxus group carefully broke down distinctions among art, ritual, and daily life. Likewise, poets extended the work of assemblage in a variety of directions: the "composition by field" advocated by the Black Mountain group, the Dada- and surrealist-influenced poetry of the New York School, the chance poetry of Cage and Jackson Mac Low, and the combination of junk art and mysticism in the Beats and other California poets. In the wider intellectual world, contextual practice spawned intercultural juxtapositions, in which manifold cultural strands were intertwined in new, nonlinear ways. During this period, for example, Herbert Marcuse's *Eros and Civilization* (1955), Norman O. Brown's *Life Against Death* (1959), and Marshall McLuhan's *Gutenberg Galaxy* (1962) brought together poetry and scholarship in a similar union to that of poetry and found objects in the art of assemblage. The scholars too believed that the new arts held the key to a crucial regeneration of culture.

As the title of Marcuse's work suggests, this time period also saw an eruption of the erotic into American culture that joined with assemblage in forming a contextual practice. Through avenues such as the influence of Freud and the pill on sexual mores; anarchist communalism; drugs; adaptations of surrealist desire; bebop, rhythm and blues, and rock 'n' roll; and explorations of embodied mysticism and rituals from around the world, practitioners in all of the arts found an erotic inspiration that gave assemblage its electric charge. By engaging with erotic energies at the gateway between art and life, poets and artists created new forms that were adopted by the sixties counterculture, and thus contextual practice helped propel a wave of eroticism to the farthest reaches of society. To a large extent, the arts in California and New York City were the vortices that set in motion the counterculture. Sally Banes asserts that in Greenwich Village in 1963, "numerous small, overlapping, sometimes rival networks of artists were forming the multifaceted base of an alternative culture of the late 1960s, . . . forging new notions of art in their lives and in their works, and—through their art—new notions of community, of democracy, of work and play, of the body, of women's roles, of nature and technology, of the outsider, and of the absolute" (2). Two historians, Rebecca Solnit and Richard Cándida Smith, make the same claims for California in the fifties and early sixties, when artists, poets, and filmmakers in Los Angeles and the San Francisco Bay Area were forging not only new forms of assemblage but also new communities and new lifestyles: "The California artists were among the first Americans to explore alternative lifestyles and spirituality in ways that would become widespread in the 1960s" (Solnit x).

To continue introducing contextual practice, I would like to refine Wil-liam Seitz's insight that assemblage is based on poetics by looking at the specifically erotic element in that poetics. The remainder of this chapter treats the interaction of two of the most eloquent spokesmen for a postwar erotic poetics, Norman O. Brown and Robert Duncan, both of whom draw together poetry and psychoanalysis.[5] Brown radicalized Freud's concept of "polymorphous perversity," expanding its reach from a description of in-fantile sexuality to becoming the goal of an erotically embodied politics and mysticism. Duncan, a similarly passionate disciple of Freud, was an explo-sively libidinous poet, who insisted on the centrality of sexuality, anarchism, and mysticism to the cultural assemblage he called "Grand Collage," which he considered "a poetry of all poetries" (*BB* vii). Although Duncan and Brown spent decades elaborating an erotic poetics, its contours can be seen in a brief look at Brown's aphoristic assemblage *Love's Body* (1966), and at Duncan's interpretation of it as a work of poetry and poetics.

The two met in 1959 when Brown was a visiting classics professor at the University of California at Berkeley. Their extensive correspondence testifies to a warm friendship, sustained for Duncan by Brown's provocative interpre-tations of Greek mythology—in *Hermes the Thief* (1947) and in his translation, with lengthy introduction, of Hesiod's *Theogony* (1953)—and by his advocacy of a radical psychoanalysis, as promulgated first in *Life Against Death: The Psychoanalytic Meaning of History*, published the year they met. Brown, in turn, was enthralled with Duncan's poetry and poetics and was indebted to Duncan for introducing him to the works of the "classical" Imagist poet H.D., whom Duncan cherished as a model for poetic investigations in mythology and psychoanalysis.[6] Brown read with admiration Duncan's latest book of poetry, *Letters* (1958), and tried to arrange for the publication by Wesleyan University Press of his next book, *The Opening of the Field*.[7] The friendship blossomed when on visits to the East Coast Duncan stayed with Brown and his wife in Middletown, Connecticut, where Brown taught at Wesleyan Uni-versity, and it was still strong enough a decade after they met for Brown to invite Duncan to teach a course for the graduate program in the history of consciousness he was directing at the University of California at Santa Cruz.

Love's Body, Brown's most influential book, was written between 1958 and 1965. Known as much for its aphoristic style as for its enlisting of psycho-analysis in a prophecy of political, social, psychological, and spiritual trans-formation, *Love's Body* epitomizes the erotic poetics of contextual practice and had a profound impact on the emerging counterculture of the time. In a defiant, iconoclastic tone, Brown announces his intention "to construct an erotic sense of reality" (81) that will overturn the routinized, oppressive reality principle of Western culture. Trumpeting the constitutive role of the erotic at every level of human life, Brown builds on psychoanalytical insights into society and religion in Freud's *Moses and Monotheism* and garners support for his perspective from psychoanalytical theorists such as Melanie Klein, Sándor Ferenczi, Otto Fenichel, and Géza Róheim. This theoretical orientation runs counter to Plato's canonical principle that ideal forms constitute the true reality and to the subsequent Platonic strain within Western philosophy and Christianity. Specifically, Brown reverses the process of erotic sublimation in Plato's *Symposium*, opting for an erotic mysticism that grounds its symbolism in sexuality instead of seeking transcendence: "Not an ascent from body to spirit, but the descent of spirit into body: incarnation not sublimation" (222).[8]

Joining what has been called the "Freudian Left," whose early members included Wilhelm Reich and Marcuse, Brown advocates a mystical eroticism that he aligns with the gnostic or hermetic tradition in Western culture (embodied particularly for Brown in William Blake and Jacob Boehme) and with the tantric tradition of Eastern culture.[9] In passages like the following, Brown explicitly unites the Freudian Left with Tantra:

> Knowledge is carnal knowledge. A subterranean passage between mind and body underlies all analogy; no word is metaphysical without its first being physical; and the body that is the measure of all things is sexual. All metaphors are sexual; a penis in every convex object and a vagina in every concave one.
>
> Symbolism is polymorphous perversity. Orthodox psychoanalysis warns against the resexualization of thought and speech; orthodox psychoanalysis bows down before the reality-principle. The reality-principle is based on desexualization; in symbolic consciousness thought and speech become resexualized. . . . Nothing wrong, except the refusal to play: when our eyes are opened to the symbolic meaning, our only refuge is loss of shame, polymorphous perversity, pansexualism; penises everywhere. As in Tantric Yoga, in which any sexual act may become a form of mystic meditation, and any mystic state may be interpreted sexually. (249–50)

Aligning Freudian insights into the Id with tantric mysticism, Brown draws attention to the importance of the poetic use of language, which he calls analogy or symbolism. The erotic reading that finds the sexual body symbolized in every utterance, "the resexualization of thought and speech," is a form of what I am calling erotic poetics. Erotic poetics, like tantric yoga, engages in a constant conversion between the sexual and the realms of the psychological, the social, the political, and the spiritual. A powerful strain in the re-animation of culture after World War II, erotic poetics is at the core of the counterculture that emerged in the fifties and sixties, just as analogous forays in erotic poetics form the basis of the tantric and occult countercultures in many other times and places.

When it appeared in 1966, *Love's Body* was both vilified and championed. Brown's friend Marcuse, for example, reacted ambivalently toward it. In an early review that faults Brown for turning his back on active political struggle, Marcuse applauds him for insights into the transformative nature of poetry. Marcuse quotes two passages—the last sentence of the book, "Everything is only a metaphor; there is only poetry," and a passage from an earlier section, "Turning and turning in the animal belly, the mineral belly, the belly of time. To find the way out: the poem"—saying of the latter passage: "This is one of Brown's most advanced formulations: a vision of the truth. But poetry is made in history and makes history; and the poem which is 'the way out' will be (if ever) written and sung and heard here on our earth." Marcuse avers that in *Love's Body* "Brown had such a poem in mind, and he started to write it," but argues that the "poem" went astray when he turned to Christianity for his symbolism of "sacrifice, death, transubstantiation" (Marcuse, *Negations* 238–39). In his "Reply to Herbert Marcuse," Brown acknowledges that his notion of revolution is fundamentally poetic. To accomplish a revolution, "The thing to be abolished is literalism; the worship of false images; idolatry." Brown contends that the problem with capitalism is that it disallows the poetic and fetishizes the literal, and he agrees that it takes a poet to perceive this: "Allen Ginsberg saw it just the way it is: Moloch. A false idol fed with real victims. This is no joke." Responding to Marcuse's charge that he has succumbed to the same old religious mystification, Brown makes a Feuerbachian claim: "The real atheism is to become divine. In a dialectical view, atheism becomes theurgy, god-making; demystification becomes the discovery of a new mystery." This avowal of the potency of mystery at the heart of demystification dovetails with Brown's diatribe against literalism: "Literalism is idolatry of words," he insists; "the alternative to idolatry is mystery," which he aligns with poetry (Marcuse, *Negations* 244).

To illustrate his contention that the world, when viewed from the standpoint of erotic poetics, is something much more mysterious than "a collection of commodities," Brown cites in his "Reply" a passage of prose poetry from Robert Duncan's *Letters: Poems 1953–1956* (1958), one that he had previously cited near the end of *Love's Body* (258): "When silence blooms in the house, all the paraphernalia of our existence shed the twitterings of value and reappear as heraldic devices" (Marcuse, *Negations* 245).[10] Like assemblage, poetry has the courage to view the objects of the world not as instruments or commodities but as symbolic participants in an exchange of energy—an exchange between the world and the human and between the body and the spirit. To describe this exchange, Brown turns to Charles Olson's theory of projectivism and to another poem from Duncan's *Letters*:

> To reconcile body and spirit would be to recover the breath-soul which is the life-soul instead of the ghost-soul or shadow; breath-consciousness instead of brain-consciousness; body-consciousness instead of head-consciousness. The word made flesh is a living word, not a scripture but a breathing. A line that comes from the breath, from the heart by way of the breath. Aphorism as utterance: a short breath, drawn in pain. Winged words, birds released from the sentence, doves of the spirit. (*Love's Body* 231)

In "A line that comes from the breath, from the heart by way of the breath," Brown summarizes two of Olson's assertions about prosody in his influential essay "Projective Verse" (1950): Brown combines the first, "the line comes (I swear it) from the breath, from the breathing of the man who writes, at the moment that he writes" (Allen 389), with Olson's observation that a poem is propelled by "the HEART, by way of the BREATH, to the LINE" (390). The last sentence of Brown's paragraph is a paraphrase of "XIX: Passages of a Sentence," a prose poem in Duncan's *Letters*. In the poem, birds are flying through a sentence, creating a wind with their wings that is "a beating of the air in passage or a word" (*Letters* 33). Words become both wings and the wind that lifts them—which is another way of figuring the interdependence of body and spirit. The citations from Duncan's poetry are particularly crucial to *Love's Body*: Clayton Eshleman reports that, in a 1990 conversation with Brown, "He told me that his discovery of the poetry of Robert Duncan had made the writing of *Love's Body* possible." Eshleman pressed him by pointing to William Blake's persistent presence in Brown's apocalyptic eruptions. "No, it was Duncan, he insisted, then saying: And

I couldn't figure out how to get more of him into the book" (Eshleman, "Headpiece" 171).[11]

In a series of notes from 1970–71 entitled "Ground Work," Duncan reflects on his relationship with Brown during the time he was teaching at the University of California at Santa Cruz (fall quarter 1970). He is especially concerned with the 1966 *Love's Body*, which he views not just as a defense of poetry, as Marcuse had, but as itself a work of poetry. Duncan argues that Brown's earlier books, *Hermes the Thief* and *Life Against Death*, with their respective Marxist and Freudian notions of revolution, do not strain ultimately toward "a new sociology or a new psychology" but toward "myth." By making myth primary, Brown steps beyond the bounds of academic argument and into the realm of poetry, for "expound as he made every effort to do, justify as he might, the ways of myth to the serious and academically accepted matters of society and psyche, myth remain [*sic*] a matter of poetry[11] ("Ground" 5). In *Love's Body*, poetry stealthily takes over even more ground. Although Brown insists emphatically that literalism kills and that everything is metaphorical, he does not recognize, Duncan asserts, that both revolution and sexuality are metaphors for poetry, which is itself the art of metaphor: "The treachery of *Love's Body* toward the realms of social and psychic interpretation which it manipulates is that it leads on to a victory of poetry as the prime reality over all other intellectual grounds" (6)—even the sexual. Duncan points out that Brown's seemingly radical statement, "The unspoken meaning is always sexual," actually hides another, truly unspoken meaning, for in *Love's Body*, as in much critical analysis since the introduction of Freud into the academy, the sexual is that which *must* be spoken of: "In Brown's post-Freudian persuasion only the sexual is ultimately respectable as content" (7). "What is it," Duncan asks, "that is truly unspeakable?"

> As a poet I find myself attackt [*sic*] for my being ultimately concerned with the experience of poetry and language. We may have begun to accept that sex is not a mere instrument but a primary ground of experience, but it is still rank heresy to take language, the pleasure and functions of words in their operations as such, as being the ground of primary information. . . .
>
> With what animus men would reject the suggestion that the poem presents itself as event and as person, and, where it refers to a deeper and/or further reality, refers to a metapoetry, not to a metaphysics or a metapsychology. (7–8)

What Brown has released in *Love's Body*, Duncan contends, is the primary eroticism of poetry—of a realm as fully at odds with Freud's reality principle as is the "polymorphous perversity" of the totally erogenous body Brown hopes to restore. This eroticism of language and creativity cannot be confined to instrumental or practical considerations, even "apocalyptic" ones such as social revolution or sexual liberation, for its fullest expression comes in a self-reflexivity that Duncan calls "metapoetry." This metapoetry has much in common with the cult of love because both pursuits involve an erotic turning inward that increases the power of the activity by concentrating on its own properties rather than on the outside world:

> Just as Love going deeper into the matter of love, being in love with being in love, altho this is what makes men lovers, is viewd as a disorder of feeling by men who are not lovers, so Poetry going deeper into the nature of poetry is, not only in literature departments but in certain schools of poetry and among certain critics and leaders of the art, attackt as a disorder of art. (6; spellings in original)

Although Brown does not recognize that *Love's Body* has turned resolutely toward a poetry that seeks to realize and understand its own nature, Marcuse had sensed it and, though applauding poetry as a vision of truth, had rejected its self-involvement as an end in itself. Siding ultimately with the reality principle, Marcuse admonishes Brown: "But poetry is made in history and makes history" (Marcuse, *Negations* 238). Duncan lays bare the unacknowledged grounds of this conflict between Brown and Marcuse:

> Nobby [Norman O. Brown's nickname], professing, even to himself, to be a scholar and teacher, begins to find himself out to be a poet—it is still, today, a guilty secret. His "colleagues" begin to suspect his work leads only to itself and not to proper grounds of learning. All their mistrust of Poetry is aroused. If he could only convince them that something as *real* as sexuality or psychoanalysis was the reference point of his perspectives, that he was not just making perspectives leading to perspectives. (9)

For Marcuse, author of *Eros and Civilization: A Philosophical Inquiry into Freud*, the scandal of *Love's Body* is that it turns away from politics in favor of poetry and Christianity. From his own perspective, Brown courts scandal by urging a reinhabitation of the body—accomplished by denying repression, speaking unspeakable desires, and proclaiming an end to history in the apocalyptic present. Duncan argues that *Love's Body* becomes scandalous when it opts for the imaginal reality of poetry, which is more revolutionary than politics and more erotic than the Freudian vision of every convexity a penis and every concavity a vagina, and which is as spiritual as the scriptural and mystical authors Brown cites. According to Duncan, Brown "does not seek to free us from bondage, from the depths of a sexual trouble or brooding—he no more comes to harrow Hell than did Dante in his Comedy—but to free *from us*, in that very Hell, that poem. It is to convert us to the purposes of a poetry, to make us his readers not his lovers . . ." (9)—readers who can recognize "*Love's Body* as a prose poem" (10). In offering what amounts to a poetics of eroticism in *Love's Body*, Brown discovers an erotic poetics, a prose poetry that invokes "perspectives leading to perspectives" through the symbolic transfer of energies from the sexual to the political to the cosmic and back again.[12]

Although the last words by Brown in *Love's Body* are "Everything is only a metaphor; there is only poetry," the final words of the book, from Lama Anagarika Govinda's *Foundations of Tibetan Mysticism*, describe the state of an "Enlightened One" who has erased "the discrepancy between mind and body": "every word and every gesture, and even his silence, communicate the overwhelming reality of the *Dharma*." For Brown, overcoming the "antinomy between mind and body, word and deed, speech and silence" is the mystical goal of *Love's Body* and of poetry in general (266). With its elaborate description of chakras ("wheels" of energy located within the body), whose activation by the fundamentally erotic kundalini (the "coiled" serpent power) leads to enlightenment, the tantric system expounded by Govinda offers Brown an arresting sexual symbolism for depicting mystical ecstasy, one that arises from a tradition profoundly foreign to the Freudian Left upon which he has relied extensively in *Love's Body*. Brown's marriage of Freud with Tantra in the last chapters of the book is striking because it illustrates a direction taken by many in the arts after World War II. Facing what they perceived as the utter bankruptcy of Western culture after the devastation of the depression and the war, many avant-garde artists composed an assemblage out of philosophies, practices, or traditions in which "the discrepancy between mind and body" had been overcome. The directions explored include the psychologies of Freud, Jung, and Reich; the Dionysian "gay science" of Nietzsche, the phenomenology of Maurice Merleau-Ponty and Martin Heidegger, and the process philosophy of Alfred North Whitehead; the efficacy of drugs; romanticism in all of the arts; the "primitive" religions of North and South America, Africa, Asia, Australia, and Oceania, as represented by ethnography; the gnostic strain of Christianity (from its Hellenistic beginnings to Medieval

and Renaissance alchemy and occultism to Boehme and Blake) and of Judaism (Kabbalah and Hasidism); and the tantric strain within Asian religions,
which can be found in traditions of Hinduism (such as Shaiva and Shakta
sects), Buddhism (Tibetan Vajrayana and Japanese Zen), Jainism, Ismaili
Islam, and Daoism.

Fundamentally, all of these directions can be labeled "erotic" in the sense
that Georges Bataille gives to the term in *Erotism*, where he contends that
there are "three types of eroticism": "physical, emotional, and religious" (15).
Religious studies scholar Jeffrey Kripal enlarges Bataille's definition, making
it the basis for his provocative assessment of the tantric and gnostic currents
in world religions:

> Drawing on a wide comparative sweep of sources—from Plato's philosophical
> reflections in the *Symposium* on eros as a contemplative technique, through
> India's philosophy of Being as *ananda* or orgasmic "bliss," the *ch'i* of Chinese
> Daoist sexual yoga, and the tantric Buddhist notion of orgasm as a form of
> subtle reason, to Wilhelm Reich's cosmic orgone, Georges Bataille's *erotisme*,
> and the Lacanian and feminist *jouissance*—what I have named the erotic is an
> explicitly dialectical category that embraces all those advances made through
> the analytical categories of sexuality and gender . . . but also reaches out to the
> nonordinary states of intense mystical rapture, religious revelation, charis-
> matic energy, and literary and philosophical creativity. (*Gift* 172–73)

This expansive view of the erotic as a dialectical category—"another energetic
category more open to some of the more fantastic and imaginative potentials
of human creativity and sexual experience" (172)—accords well with Brown's
and Duncan's understandings of the erotic as a source of creativity and a
transformative energy for the arts and culture in the postwar period.

In this sense, "context" cannot be seen as a purely neutral term, for the
contextual turn of poets, artists, and filmmakers during the fifties and sixties was charged with eroticism. Seeking to dissolve the defensive rigidity and
self-enclosure of postwar American society, contextual practice entailed an
opening out to otherness. It demanded of its practitioners not mastery but
situatedness and a noncontrolling, Id-affirming vulnerability that seems all
the riskier in a sociopolitical climate that values restraint, containment, rationality, and self-protection. The pioneering aesthetic and personal vulnerability of such poets as Robert Creeley, Duncan, and Ginsberg and artists such
as Wallace Berman, Harry Smith, Jess, and George Herms provides a model

for an *arte povera* that finds erotic and mystical sustenance in the objects of the surrounding world. In contextual practice, objects that are salvaged from urban decay serve as conduits for shamanic forays and erotic encounters. During a time that consolidated and policed sociopolitical boundaries under the banner of "Americanism," these artists exposed themselves to "invasion" by images that were "out of bounds"—images from the unconscious, mythology, mysticism, and the vast anthropological record, images whose force invaded and undermined the jingoistic, macho, market-oriented, security-minded temper of the times. Contextual practice involves assembling materials from disregarded locations near at hand and from the most distant sites in time and space, creating a Grand Collage whose purpose is not consolidation and mastery but anarchism, cross-fertilization, and ecstasy.

2

THE CONTEXTUAL ART OF
ROBERT CREELEY'S INTERVIEWS

Content Is Never More Than
an Extension of Context

One of the first ways in which contextual practice broke out into the larger culture was in prose depictions of the lives of artists. The newly intimate relationship between art and life can be gauged by the avidity with which the actions and insights of contemporary artists were consumed by the public in the form of interviews, profiles, and lifestyle novels. Some of the most influential presentations occurred first in fictional accounts, notably Kerouac's *On the Road* (1956) and *The Dharma Bums* (1958) and J. D. Salinger's *Franny and Zooey* (published initially in the *New Yorker*, 1955 and 1957). These were followed by *New Yorker* profiles, such as those of Marcel Duchamp, Jean Tinguely, John Cage, Robert Rauschenberg, and Merce Cunningham, written by Calvin Tomkins (1962–1964), and Jane Kramer's profile of Allen Ginsberg (1968). At the same time, the long-running series of interviews with writers in the *Paris Review* began with George Plimpton speaking to E. M. Forster in 1952; it included, by the midsixties, interviews with ancestors and adherents of an erotic poetics of assemblage such as William Carlos Williams, Marianne Moore, Aldous Huxley, Ezra Pound, Blaise Cendrars, Jean Cocteau, Louis-Ferdinand Céline, Henry Miller, William Burroughs, Norman Mailer, Allen Ginsberg, and Edward Albee.[1] The fiction, journalism, and interviews revealed not only the aesthetic, political, and religious views of their subjects but also opened a window into a new contextual practice that, regardless of its long preparation in earlier eras of American and European culture, looked remarkably fresh and starkly oppositional in the "containment culture" of the United States in the fifties and sixties.[2]

The interview in particular emerged in the postwar period as a key form encouraging identification of a large audience with the individuality of the subject interviewed. Learning to mimic the beliefs, motives, self-scrutiny, and self-aggrandizement of interviewees led readers to a growing sense of the self as a project under construction, an artwork in its own right. In the introduction to a volume of *Paris Review* interviews, Alfred Kazin reveals the historical legacy that the interview as a form bestows on this contemporary version of *bildung*: "The classic interview, which Boswell and Eckermann practiced in order to write their respective books on Johnson and Goethe, is . . . a form of Wisdom Literature. . . . The classic interview with a Great Man probably had its origins in religious discipleship, and the purest example of it is still Plato's Dialogues. What the interviewer really asks is: How Are We To Live?" (Kazin vii). Although artists and writers in the fifties and sixties may not have achieved the monumental stature of a Johnson, a Goethe, or a Whitman (whose classic interview was with Edward Carpenter), their interviewers recognized that the question of how to live was newly urgent in the cold war context. Responding to the continuing breakdown of authoritative institutions for offering advice, interviews took over what Walter Benjamin felt was the primary duty of the old-fashioned storyteller: providing counsel.

In addition to exposing new ways of living, interviews also served to justify new forms of art. Because American culture is relatively new and has unmoored itself from the grounding provided by the European, African, or Asian cultures carried over ambivalently by its immigrants, the arts have not merited a traditional place of honor within it and artists have felt a need to defend the value of their work more vociferously than artists in more traditional cultures.[3] Notwithstanding their stated purpose of investigating issues of craft, form, or influence, interviews with American practitioners in the arts invariably evoke ethical or metaphysical arguments for the defense of aesthetic principles. Ultimately, the interviews wind up combining aesthetics, ethics, and metaphysics into portraits of an artistic way of life. In the postwar era, these interviews contributed substantially to the reception and expansion of the arts by demonstrating artistic thinking and the existential implications of artistic work. Especially for younger people, the interviews, reviews, and essays by artists, writers, filmmakers, dancers, dramatists, and musicians provided an alternative education outside that offered by schools and colleges. Demonstrating new artistic modes of thought, the interviews offered models for realigning values and reconceiving artistic, political, ethical, and spiritual goals.

Interviews that take place face-to-face in a specific setting often have salient contextual attributes. The more skillful interviewers describe the context carefully and resist the temptation to edit out the interviewee's responses to it, which can be very revealing. In this sense, interviews play directly into a contextual practice in which aesthetic acts galvanize contexts in new ways, while contexts provide materials and an arena for making art. Among artists of this time, Robert Creeley maintained an unremitting focus on contexts, which is why the title of his collection of early interviews, *Contexts of Poetry* (1973), signals so much about his poetic orientation. Like the notion of "ground" in the gestalt model of perception, context tends to be ignored in traditional aesthetics as a subsidiary factor that might or might not impinge upon the "figure" of the work of art. For Creeley, however, context emerges as inseparable from an interactive erotic poetics, not only providing its ground but also entering into its unfolding activity. By examining the concept of context as Creeley develops it in his interviews, particularly those with Ginsberg, William Spanos, and Linda Wagner, we can begin to see how he makes the interview a vital aesthetic encounter, which helps in turn to account for his centrality as a theorist for the arts at midcentury and his exemplary status for a vast number of poets, artists, musicians, friends, students, and readers.

As Creeley understands it, context refers to individual people present, to social and political conditions, to aesthetic positions taken by his forebears and cohort, to dreams and memories, to words and numbers, and to the physical media used for inscription.[4] In the interview from which the volume takes its name, "Contexts of Poetry," he describes how media such as the typewriter, the paper (its size and properties), and the ambient music (radio or phonograph) provide the physical, sensory context for what was at that time a carefully staged, solitary writing practice. Creeley devotes the interview, which was actually a conversation with Ginsberg at the 1963 Vancouver Poetry Conference, to specifying exactly which media he uses and the effect each has on his writing. Expressing surprise at the restrictions Creeley places on the conditions for composition, Ginsberg recounts writing a breakthrough poem on a train between Kyoto and Tokyo ("The Change—*Kyoto-Tokyo Express*"

[*CPAG* 332–38]) and asks Creeley, "[W]hat happens to you if you suddenly realize something—do you have to—arrange your paper? What do you do then—you lose it!" Creeley replies, "You're right! . . . the limit of my ability to write . . . is that I have to secure a physical context in which I can 'work.' It not only has to be qualified by having paper and the rest of the paraphernalia, but it has to have equally a social qualification" (*Contexts* 38). In the course of this conversation, the physical situation of composition acts like a metaphor for the entire issue of contexts. By making himself aware of how his dispositions toward media and space determine the content of what he writes, Creeley takes a huge step beyond his early maxim "Form is never more than an extension of content" and begins to make his way toward a mature aesthetic practice in which "Content is never more than an extension of context."[5]

In the most general sense, the context is a charged environment of contingent factors, making demands upon the artist and soliciting a response. The response becomes artful by virtue of heeding the actual conditions that obtain within the context:

> I'm trying to describe a state in which one primarily feels what is happening as a fit balance. If you do things like ski or swim or drive, for example, you know that sense of feeling when the car is operating smoothly, when the balance of the steering and the movement of the car is coinciding with an intention of your own and is following with a sense of grace, an appropriateness. Everything is, in effect, falling into place. You're not intentionally putting it there, but you're recognizing the feeling of its occurring there. (*Contexts* 35)

From Creeley's midcentury perspective, art is primarily a commitment to context, a continual "equilibration" (to use Duncan's term), in which the artist intends not to reach a predetermined outcome but to interact gracefully with new conditions as they unpredictably arise. Instead of investigating the idea of America, as William Carlos Williams sought to do in "To Elsie," Creeley contends that the only way after World War II "to witness and adjust," "to drive the car" (Litz 219), is to relinquish the modernist quest for aesthetic closure and throw oneself willingly into the uncontrollable existential present, with its many contextual frames.

In the interview, he takes pains to clarify terms for the awareness needed for graceful interaction with a context: "I'm awfully bewildered," he admits, by a conceptual muddle involving "confusions between certain terms—the states of consciousness—e.g. the difference between recognition, understanding, realization, knowing" (35). Although these four terms refer to roughly equivalent mental processes, it's significant that "recognition" and "realization" recur in Creeley's essays and interviews. If looked at closely, these two notions reveal several facets of his poetics: an intention to remain open to what appears in a context; a desire to participate with and measure himself in relation to a context; and an ability to make that interaction with context apparent in a work of art. In contrast to recognition and realization, "understanding" and "knowing" refer more directly to the epistemological orientation of modernism. Emerging beyond the modernist horizon, Creeley seeks to enter into the context as a situation to which one belongs; it is neither a wholly subjective perspective nor an objective reality open to scientific scrutiny at a distance. By making this shift, Creeley joins Charles Olson, whose rejection of the sufficiency of either subjective states or scientific/technological knowledge can be seen in the aphorism he translated from Heraclitus: "Man is estranged from that with which he is most familiar" (Olson, *Special View* 14). Olson protests a separation of human beings from their contexts, in which a purely "inner" world distorts human reality as much as a purely "outer" one. Creeley loved to quote this aphorism, hearing it as a call for an art responsive to all of its contexts, an art that returns human beings to the intimacy of direct involvement with one another, the world, and themselves.

This reorientation informs in turn the entire gamut of New American poets—Black Mountain, Beat, New York School, San Francisco Renaissance, and so forth—for whom poetry can be seen as a mode of interacting with context through language. The vernacular vibrancy of the speaking voice that unites Creeley with poets as disparate as Ginsberg, Frank O'Hara, Bob Kaufman, and Spicer is just one way to directly address contexts; like Creeley, many of the poets engage context through phenomenological conjecture as well.[6] In his single-minded focus on a contextual art that questions all received understandings, Creeley moves beyond accepted definitions of poetry: "I cannot define a poem. It's a curious state of mind to have arrived at. I cannot tell you what I think a poem is. I think that has to do with the fact that all the terms of consciousness are, at the moment, undergoing tremendous terms of change" (36). At the time of the interview, in 1963, Creeley looks out at the national context of the Civil Rights Movement ("Now this reality, which has become *the* dominant reality in the States today, is the Negro reality, it is not the white reality, it's the Negro reality" 36–37) and at the international movement to end colonialism ("a whole shift of controls and communication terms that are actually centered in Africa and Asia") and avers, "my point is that the very premise on which consciousness operates is undergoing modifications that none of us, I think, are at the moment capable of defining. We can only recognize them" (37). Because the social, political, and economic context is shifting, the poem must shift as well, maintaining an alert stance toward a new reality and a willingness to engage it in conversation. Far from being an exercise in navel gazing, contextual practice as Creeley understands it demands a tensile awareness that ties the artist to present reality in every conceivable direction.

Conversation and Collaboration

During his lifetime, one of Creeley's most extraordinary contextual practices was his conversation. He was a marathon talker, passionate about testing ideas, news, poetry, and people within an interlocutory situation. The striking vividness of his moment-to-moment living included an emphatic verbal connection to the people and places in whose company he found himself. Like Creeley, many of the New American poets were uncommonly prodigious talkers, committed to exploring the interanimation of art and life through conversation. Poets such as Creeley, Olson, Duncan, Ginsberg, O'Hara, and Spicer banked everything on the efficacy of talk, applying poetic principles to the demands of daily life and current events. To converse with any of these figures was to enter a charged milieu, where aesthetic insights and assumptions were probed for what they might contribute to the question of how to be in the world, both individually and collectively. The poem often precipitated directly out of the dialogic solution, epitomizing the poet's loquacity in memorable phrases, rhythms, and images. For this reason, interviews and other recorded conversations with these poets carry more than an autobiographical or testimonial value, offering a window into the ongoing conversational exchange from which the poetry emerges. This exchange also included letters, as a glance at the poems designated "Letters" throughout Olson's *Maximus Poems* or the epistolary poems in Duncan's *Letters* will confirm.[7] Identified early as an intensely solitary, even solipsistic poet, Creeley nonetheless thrived on conversation and sought tirelessly the kind of "attunement" with others that David Antin advocates in his talk poem "tuning." Antin typifies the New American poets' devotion to exploring a context through talking, calling his unrehearsed discourse before an audience a "talk poem." His philosophical notion of tuning as a context-dependent mode of understanding requires the same constant adjustment that Creeley calls for in his depiction of writing as akin to driving.[8]

One way Creeley demonstrated his investment in a conversational art of continual adjustment was through extensive collaboration with artists and musicians. In music, his main interlocutor was jazz bassist Steve Swallow, but with visual artists he worked on a huge variety of projects, which included books, prints, broadsides, posters, sculptures, and installations. Over the course of fifty-five years, he joined in at least forty-three projects with the artists (some more than once) René Laubiès, Dan Rice, Fielding Dawson, John Altoon, R. B. Kitaj, Bobbie Louise Hawkins, Robert Indiana, William Katz, Arthur Okamura, Elsa Dorfman, Joe Brainard, Marisol, Jim Dine, Tom Clark, John Chamberlain, Robert Therrien, Martha Visser't Hooft, Duane Michals, Karl Klingbiel, Francesco Clemente, James Surls, Cletus Johnson, Susan Rothenberg, Sol LeWitt, Alex Katz, Max Gimblett, John Millei, Donald Sultan, Georg Baselitz, and Archie Rand. Artists loved to work with him because what they made between them became truly a collaboration, rather than a matter of one "illustrating" the other's creation. Archie Rand describes his partnership with Creeley in appreciative terms echoed by many others: "A collaborative medium goes so against the heroic isolated macho image of what an artist is in American culture. There's a time when you just have to have the generosity to merge. Collaborative work with a poet is an exhilarating democracy" (Cappellazzo and Licata 27). Often, as in the case of *Drawn & Quartered* (Fig. 3), Creeley's book with Rand, the poet's dialogue with the artist took the generous form of responding in writing to images sent him.

Artists were impressed by Creeley's ability to look carefully at what they were doing and speak back to their concerns in terms that made sense to them. Clemente, for instance, who worked with Creeley on several projects, testifies to the "gratifying experience" of being "understood" aesthetically by Creeley:

> Part of my fascination with these particular collaborations is how every time he [Creeley] seems to perceive what the form of the work is. He invents his own corresponding form that somehow has the same structure [as the paintings]. . . . I think that is the most gratifying experience that any painter or poet can have—to be understood . . . it's very hard for somebody else to talk about what you're making and make sense. When a poet does that it really does make sense and it's an extraordinary feeling. You know that you're not crazy and you're not alone. (Cappellazzo and Licata 26)

FIGURE 3. Robert Creeley and Archie Rand, from *Drawn & Quartered*. New York, Granary Books, 2001.

In many of Creeley's collaborations, he and the artist worked toward "a mutually agreed-upon goal," for which Creeley attempted to "echo the artist's concerns, interests, obsessions." This allowed Creeley to stand aloof from his preoccupations but to find something compelling in the artist's work that would open up, paradoxically, a new avenue within his own concerns (Yau 48). One of the most demanding and gratifying forms that Creeley undertook, collaboration is conversation at its most responsive.

And sometimes for Creeley, at its most erotic. One of his most explicitly erotic poetic sequences can be found in *His Idea* (1973), a project in partnership with the photographer Elsa Dorfman. *His Idea* was actually a four-way collaboration, since it was initially the idea of a man who commissioned Dorfman to photograph him making love with his wife. After Dorfman mounted an exhibition of the photographs, she asked Creeley to write poetry for a book version, which was published with seven photographs and nineteen poems. As is the case in most of Creeley's collaborations, the poems more often engage the artworks in conversation than comment on them as visual objects. In one two-page spread, for instance, a photograph of the couple wrapped tight in coitus faces this poem (Fig. 4):

So sweet
the body
so expected.

Who comes,
comes
on time.

(*CPRC* 530)

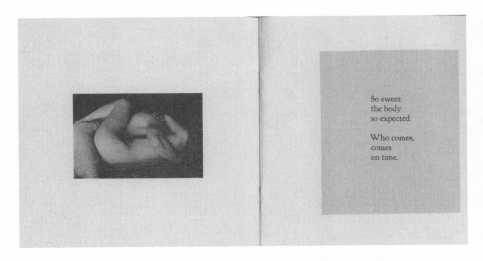

FIGURE 4. Robert Creeley and Elsa Dorfman, from *His Idea*. Toronto, Coach House Press, 1973.

Rather than describe the intertwined limbs visible in the photograph, the poem concentrates on temporal issues pertinent to sexual experience in marriage: expectation and the timing of orgasm. Creeley evokes a long-term relationship, in which the pleasures of love making have become expected and there is no anxiety about whether or when orgasm is achieved. Making love still brings intense pleasure, but the pleasure comes not from the excitement of joining with a new partner but from the conversation, only part of which is verbal, that sustains long-term intimacy. Erotic conversation is both the poem's subject and the subject matter of the collaboration between Creeley and Dorfman. In notes to the exhibition of the photographs, Dorfman commented on her discomfort and her curiosity during the photo session, in what was for her a novel situation of watching other people have sex (Cappellazzo and Licata 24–25). Creeley, who was one of the great erotic poets of the twentieth century, offers Dorfman a poem meant to calm anxiety, reminding her that the intimacy she witnessed and captured in her camera was, from the perspective of the subjects, merely one episode in a long conversation between two thinking bodies.

Within the realm of the interview the conversation is likely to be of much shorter duration, with meaningful collaboration not guaranteed. Interviews can, though, have an open-ended, unforeseen quality. For Creeley, an interviewer can go so far as to provoke an existential anxiety, causing him at times to see the interview as a stark confrontation of a kind not usually acknowledged in mundane discussion—and quite different from reciprocal conversation with an artist. In the preface to *Tales out of School: Selected Interviews*, he begins with the curious claim that the interviews "are a nearly anthropological evidence . . . that there was indeed a person as 'myself' somewhere consistent with a world now well past but still as inexplicable as when it first all began." It is not altogether clear grammatically whether the word "inexplicable" refers to "myself" or "a world"—a purposeful ambiguity because for Creeley the sense of self and the apprehension of a world are co-creative. In this sense, the interviews document his attempt to navigate by conversation an identity within an unbounded context. He goes on to assert that such interchanges allow him to reach a primordial sense of identity-in-motion that he might not have arrived at by other means: "The questions and answers . . . will prove beyond the shadow of a fictive doubt that an 'I' was 'there,' and that 'he' made persistently evident all the usual rhetorical apparatus and determination necessary to keep afloat the boatlike 'self' one presumes to be the point of one's existence" (vii).[9]

Offering an existential conception of the interview, Creeley makes use of an image that Olson borrowed from Egyptian hieroglyphics—of the self as a boat—in order to contend that the self comes into being through its ability to navigate a context. This navigation offers not only the promise of new connections between ideas and events but also the risk that one's beliefs or sense of self will prove inadequate to the dialogical context of an interview.

That risk is evident in the 1977 *boundary 2* interview with William Spanos that Creeley chose to reprint in *Tales out of School*. The interview had already achieved notoriety for two reasons: Spanos transcribed it using a modified version of Antin's talk poem notation, leaving a corresponding space for every pause in speech and marking every verbal emphasis with italics; and it is governed by Spanos's intention to translate the terms of Creeley's poetry and poetics into Heideggerean literary theory. As Spanos lectures Creeley on how to frame his concerns in the proper phenomenological vocabulary, we hear the poet responding, "Right," "Yeah," and "I hear," able only to interject words of consent. Because of Creeley's remarkable willingness to enter new contexts, he doesn't appear irritated but seems to appreciate learning a new vocabulary and testing his own existential ideas against those of Spanos. Near the end of the interview, for example, Creeley arrives, with the eager participation of his interlocutor, at a new definition of "occasion," one of the key terms in his poetics and one that also fascinates Spanos:

> "It came to pass" is the sense I feel in the word "occasion." "It was this way."
> "What was the occasion for your doing that?" . . . It's not only the circum-
> stances, what was around[—]the context, let's say. What was in hand, what
> was seemingly the case. . . . "Then as I remember there were two cars here and
> somebody was standing there." But the occasion is what factually, as you say,
> *falls*, what comes to pass. And that's to me the only substantial authority in
> the whole event is what happened. So I love that sense I used to fear, writing
> occasional poems, until I probably got much more relaxed about what after all
> an occasion might be. (*Tales* 181)

As another term for the notion of context, "occasion" inflects it toward an awareness of time and space and what happens within them. The word *falls* refers to the etymology of occasion, which both speakers have been playing with during the interview, and it emphasizes "what happened," which Creeley calls "the only substantial authority in the whole event." At this juncture in the conversation, Creeley advances a nuanced definition of "occasional" poetry that encompasses ideas of context, adjacency, facticity, fallenness (or *thrownness*, in Heideggerean terms), and happening.

By rising to the occasion of a difficult interview like that with Spanos, Creeley harvests new conceptualizations of his central beliefs. On the other hand, it is less clear that Spanos takes away from the encounter new apprehensions about his theoretical position, since he seems to ignore the challenge that Creeley and other New American poets issue to those who wish to converse with them: to put one's own beliefs at risk and try out new ways of perceiving and making sense of the world. Admittedly, this demand has led at times to a kind of cultish imitation by followers of the poets that can abrogate true conversation, but the invitation to reimagine the world and one's place in it through the agency of poetry also can provoke dynamic dialogue and startling insights. When the reader or interviewer does not wish to enter very far into the context defined by the poet's carefully adumbrated stance, though, resistance arises, as can be seen in an interview with the critic Linda Wagner. In the course of a cordial discussion, a mutual resistance accrues when Wagner ignores terms the poet uses to describe his work and asks him to frame it using hackneyed categories that Creeley seeks to undermine by refusing to stand outside the act of composition.

The resistance builds up during a discussion of Creeley's taxonomy of the terms *poetry* and *prose*. In response to a question about the difference between the two, he offers this distinction:

> Poetry seems to be written momently—that is, it occupies a moment of time. There is, curiously, no time [i.e., no passage of time] in writing a poem. I seem to be given to work in some intense moment of whatever possibility, and if I manage to gain the articulation necessary *in* that moment, then happily there is the poem. Whereas in prose there's a coming and going. Much more of a gathering process that's evident in the writing. In fact I think I began prose because it gave me a more extended opportunity to think in something—to think around and about and in terms of something which was on my mind. (*Contexts* 105)

This existential division between poetry as the act of a moment and prose as a gathering of thought over time matters to Creeley, for he spends three-and-a-half pages elaborating on and restating it, emphasizing that each mode has its own requirements and virtues. In response, Wagner asks, "Of the two modes, which do you prefer?" Creeley replies, "Well, again, I don't prefer either. I'm led to use either as I can" (108). This interchange is puzzling because the thrust of the description of his writing process has been that it does not rely on volition or preference or setting out with a specific goal in mind. Instead, he places himself in a vulnerable position where the subject matter and his feelings about it can be discovered in the act of composition. Creeley understands writing as taking place within a gift economy, in which he is "given" the opportunity to write and respects that opportunity by paying attention to the terms of the experience that arise within it. Rather than speaking of goals or preferences or intentions, he uses the term *recognition* to signal the active but nonvolitional awareness that occurs during the act of writing.

Wagner chooses to ignore Creeley's insistence on alert passivity and asks him, "You plan to do more prose, I assume, as well as poetry?" "Yes," he answers, "I do plan to do more prose. I must say, though, that as soon as I *plan* to do more prose, I do absolutely nothing" (110). To illustrate how fruitless he finds planning, he tells an anecdote about committing to write another novel after completing *The Island* (1963). He proposed a topic and received an advance from his publisher and then found himself stymied. "But as soon as I plan to do it," he laments, "I've all but stopped it." He became so "hysterical" about the situation that he offered to return the advance. Probing the reason for his inability to write on demand, Creeley notes, "As soon as it becomes programmed in any way, in the sense that it isn't momently recognized, it's a very, very problematic context in which to try anything" (110–11). We can infer from this statement that not all contexts are conducive to writing; Creeley finds inimical a context that projects acts of recognition into the future and thus forecloses the present. When Wagner hears this anecdote, she does not respond to Creeley's evident anxiety about planning. Instead, she asks, "Have you any plans for writing criticism?" and then follows up that question with another: "Does the pursuit of prose of whatever kind make you any less a poet?" (111). At this point, an exasperated Creeley begins to dispute her terms: "Well, I'm not 'pursuing' prose. I'm not after it" (112). He then explains, "I would rather be a 'writer' than a 'poet' or a 'novelist.' So that then I would use whatever mode was relevant to the things given me to write, as *they* determined it, not me." A page later, he is still trying to make her understand: "But you see, I'm not interested in being a poet or a novelist as something that has a stable content" (113). This refusal to ascribe "a stable content" to being a writer resembles the statement he made in "Contexts of Poetry": "I cannot define a poem."

By abjuring definition in favor of context, Creeley joins the eponymous hero of Ed Dorn's *Gunslinger*, who condemns "definition" as a form of reification that ignores context by giving priority to the blunt instrument of general categories. In the poem, the Gunslinger draws his gun with lightning speed and "describes" an antagonist as "a plain, unassorted white citizen" (28), thus depriving him of life by confining him within a sociological definition. Like Dorn and Creeley, Bob Dylan, another master of the interview form, also rejects the trimming of live thoughts and actions to fit conventional definitions. Dylan too views "definition" as society's attempt to restrain the wayward individual and suck the marrow from his or her unruly life. He leaps agilely during interviews in order to parry attempts to define him and his music, remarking at one point, "Greed and lust I understand, but I can't understand the values of definition and confinement. Definition destroys" (xii). In certain interviews, Creeley struggles like Dylan to avoid being trapped in conceptual containers, chafing against designs to secure his agreement with common assumptions about the definition and purpose of art. In such an interview situation, artists like Dylan and Creeley display a far greater appetite for uncertainty than do their interlocutors. The artists insist on uncertainty as a necessary precondition for a contextual practice, preferring the risk of engagement within a present context to an intentional fulfilling of categorical expectations.

Creeley recognized Dylan as a comrade-in-arms, as he confesses in the poetic sequence, "In London": "Wish I was Bob Dylan— / he's got a subtle mind" (*CPRC* 463). When asked by an interviewer about his plans for the future, Dylan responds very similarly to the way Creeley does to Wagner: "I try not to make any plans. Every time I go and make plans, nothing really seems to work. I've given up on most of that stuff" (58). Resisting casting his life or work within mental frameworks that ignore context, Dylan combats impertinent questions during interviews much more vociferously than does Creeley. In the documentary film of his 1965 concert tour of England, *Dont Look Back* (1967), Dylan excoriates a reporter from *Time* magazine for writing in a journalistic mode that boils down to a manipulation of commonly accepted categories. From the outset of their conversation, Dylan expresses bitter disdain for *Time*: "If I want to find out anything, I'm not going to read *Time* magazine . . . because they've got too much to lose by printing the truth. . . . They'd just go off the stands in a day if they printed really the truth." When the reporter asks defensively, "What is really the truth?" Dylan replies, "Really the truth is just a plain picture . . . let's say, of a tramp vomiting, man, into the sewer, you know. And next door to the picture, you know, Mr. Rockefeller—or Mr. C. W. Jones on the subway going to work. You know, any kind of picture. Just make some sort of collage of pictures. Which they don't do. There's no *ideas* in *Time* magazine, there's just these facts" (Pennebaker).

Dylan objects to *Time* because its "facts" fit preestablished journalistic categories, whose ultimate purpose is to re-enforce the status quo and prevent people from thinking for themselves. He proposes a different representation of reality, a collage, in which context is honored by the juxtaposition of scenes occurring simultaneously. Insisting that politicians and businessmen occupy the same urban context as social misfits, artists like Dylan and Creeley look for forms that make this context visible and that invite an existential reaction. Dylan claims that the juxtaposition he offers is not meant to elicit a stock political response but to awaken us to the context in which we live and to our ability to confront it actively. He reminds the reporter, "Each of us really knows nothing, but we all think we know things," and then challenges him to make decisions in light of the fact that we will all die and the world will go on without us: "You do your job in the face of that, and how seriously you take yourself you decide for yourself. OK? And I'll decide for myself" (Pennebaker).

Aphorisms

Dylan utters this challenge to the reporter using an existentialist vocabulary, with echoes back to the ancient Stoics and Epicureans. This mixture of philosophical stances can be found also in a selection of essays by the eminent French historian of philosophy Pierre Hadot, which have been translated into English with the appealing title *Philosophy as a Way of Life*. Hadot's essays on ancient and modern philosophy can help tease out some of what is at stake in postwar contextual practice, where the blend of aesthetics, ethics, and metaphysics produces something like "Art as a Way of Life." Among the New American poets, Charles Olson returned explicitly to some of the ancient philosophers whom Hadot discusses, and many of the other poets joined Olson in looking back behind, or else outside of, the entire Christian Era in order to invoke in their poetry a more capacious sense of what it means to be human in the postwar context. As Creeley explains in an introduction to his interview with Spanos, "Because of the Second World War, because that was what followed the Great

Depression, it was hard to believe in the world's general good faith or that the good guys would finally win" (*Tales* 122). Hadot contends that such times of crisis call for a nonprofessional philosophy, which offers not logical propositions but what he calls "spiritual exercises" that aim to change completely how we see things and how we live. Take, for instance, the advice of Horace to "seize the day and put no trust in tomorrow." About this maxim Hadot remarks,

> Horace's *carpe diem* is by no means, as is often believed, the advice of a sensualist playboy; on the contrary, it is an invitation to conversion. We are invited to become aware of the vanity of our immensely vain desires, at the same time as of the imminence of death, the uniqueness of life, and the uniqueness of the present instant. From this perspective, each instant appears as a marvelous gift which fills its recipient with gratitude. (224)

As Hadot explains, rapt attention to the present in an Epicurean philosophy such as that of Horace results in gratitude and astonishment—gratitude for each precious moment and astonishment at what occurs within it. Hadot quotes Lucretius regarding the astonishing quality of the present: "'If the whole world were to appear to mortals now, for the first time; if it was suddenly and unexpectedly exposed to their view; what could one think of more marvelous than these things, and which mankind would less have dared to believe?'"[10] "In the last analysis," Hadot claims, "the secret of Epicurean joy and serenity is the experience of infinite pleasure provided by the consciousness of existence, even if it be only for a moment" (225). This resolute focus on awareness of the present moment appears over and over in the writings of Robert Creeley. He underlines this when he describes for Spanos the experience of writing:

> It doesn't get you anywhere, does it? It isn't as though one is going anywhere in the nature of thought but one's frankly again discovering where one is, what the specific possibilities of the instrument seem to be. It's that inherent content of the art, it seems to me, that's far more significant than what the art gets to. . . . Bill, it's almost as if one is trying to propose and, hopefully, understand if it's still possible to be human in your mind. (*Tales* 134)

As an aid to "discovering where one is," Creeley practices in his writing what Hadot calls "spiritual exercises" that help to maintain scrupulous attention on the present, weaning himself from the urge to be elsewhere or otherwise. According to Hadot, spiritual exercises don't belong to a particular religion or belief system, but rather are devices for reorienting one's being toward the present, promoting a heightened perception, an expanded awareness, a sense of amazement, and a connection to other people and to the cosmos. Hadot claims this as the goal of the ancient pagan philosophies and of all the later ones based on them. It can also be seen as the goal of tantric philosophies within such religions as Hinduism, Buddhism, Daoism, and Islam.

Hadot posits that the image of the "sage" was used in ancient philosophy to symbolize the qualities a philosopher hoped to attain. The sage lives entirely in the present moment, without regret for the past or anticipation of the future. By marshalling his or her entire consciousness in the present—what Marcus Aurelius calls "delimiting the present" (227)—the sage enjoys a remarkably vivid life, for alertness in the present is a vertical expansion within the horizontal stream of time. In the interview with Spanos, Creeley tells of meeting such a sage figure in Southern Mexico, a Mayan of the Lacondan tribe, portraying the encounter as one of his several attempts to plumb a primary sense of the human. He was introduced by "an old time kind of adventurer self-styled anthropologist," who said:

> "How would you like to meet a Mayan?" I said, "Terrific!" . . . "He's the first person ever to come out of his particular situation, ever. The first human being of that particular cluster ever to go beyond its stated boundaries and to move out of its area of habitation into this world." And I said, "That would be an honor indeed if in my American sense it wouldn't bother him." . . . And so he said, "He's in the next room, I'll ask him to come out." So momently here was this man, another human being, standing there and in no sense "primitive" in the sense that his teeth were filed, the sometime imagination of the primitive caveman, just another extraordinary human being. I did again the American thing of putting out my hand. And he looked at it and then, and I was very relieved, he took it. What was extraordinary about this man was that *all* the senses were absolutely alert all over the body in the same way you'd experience the situation of a so-called wild animal as opposed to a domestic animal. I mean the sensory system was absolutely alert, not worried but he was entirely there. I've never met a human being who was so completely *where* he was, not that he knew where he was or was determined to stay there, but he was absolutely alive in the moment of each instant. (*Tales* 152–53)

Creeley recognizes that in the person of this Indian he was introduced to a sage, who embodied the poet's own fervent aspiration to focus attention exclusively on the present moment: "I mean, there was no abstraction in him. It was fantastic. I thought, 'You can do it.' I mean you can arrive at a consciousness that's present as opposed to one that's thinking about what happened last week or what is going to happen tomorrow as an imposition on the present instant" (153).

Hadot demonstrates that the texts of ancient philosophers that have come down to us consist not of the logical arguments we try to make of them but of spiritual exercises whose purpose is to make possible the unabstracted state of awareness that Creeley senses in the Lacondan. To engage in a spiritual exercise involves applying a philosophical aphorism over and over again, so that it becomes a habit of thought that focuses an increasing awareness in the present context. In his interviews and critical writings, Creeley gives direct evidence of such spiritual exercises, repeatedly employing aphorisms taken particularly from the works of writers and artists he admires. In the interview with Spanos, for instance, Creeley presents five aphorisms as touchstones for his thinking: the aphorism from Heraclitus that Olson quotes, "Man is estranged from that with which he is most familiar" (*Tales* 125); Olson's own statement that "We do what we know before we know what we do" (131); Duncan's definition of "responsibility" as "the ability to respond" (137); Olson's Epicurean verses, "He left him naked, / the man said, and / nakedness / is what one means // that all start up / to the eye and soul / as though it had never / happened before" (139); and a more Stoic Olsonian aphorism, "Limits are what any of us are inside of" (170). In the preface to *Contexts of Poetry*, Creeley reports that the repeating of such aphorisms constitutes a spiritual exercise with a profound effect on his life and writing: "What is interesting," he says, "is that which one *does* say, over and over, without being really aware of it. For better or for worse, these insistences must be the measure of one's acts" (n.p.). Although Creeley may not set out explicitly to undertake spiritual exercises, he realizes that his reiteration of aphorisms and catch phrases does constitute a way to measure the seriousness of his life and work.

For Creeley, the repetition of spiritual exercises becomes something like a genre. After *For Love* (1962), his writing made a radical shift—which still, four decades later, has not been adequately described—involving a change of focus that was like a change of genre. Beginning with *The Island* (1963) and *Words* (1967), the writing leaves behind the vicissitudes of the lyric *I* and takes on the character of an exquisite series of spiritual exercises aimed at focusing awareness on the present context. Creeley announces this new orientation in the preface to *Words*, which begins, "Things continue, but my sense is that I have, at best, simply taken place with that fact. I see no progress in time or any other such situation. So it is that what I feel, in the world, is the one thing I know myself to be, for that instant. I will never know myself otherwise" (*CPRC* 261). This statement reads like a Stoic credo, born from what Hadot calls a conversion experience. It posits Creeley squarely in the present moment with no sense of separation from the context in which he finds himself, no identity outside that awareness: "So it is that what I feel, in the world, is the one thing I know myself to be, for that instant. I will never know myself otherwise."

Reading between the lines of *Contexts of Poetry* and recalling later explanations by Creeley, I think that his actual conversion experience can be located in the conversation with Ginsberg at the Vancouver Poetry Conference. Near the end of the conversation, after enumerating for Ginsberg and the students present the strict conditions he required for writing (a secluded room, a typewriter, 8-1/2" x 11" paper, etc.), Creeley remarks, "I'm not satisfied with the habits of limit that I've created for myself, because not only have I given myself a million excuses for doing nothing nine-tenths of the time, but I've created a context in which only—I realize now—only certain kinds of feeling can come" (*Contexts* 40). That realization of self-imposed limits and his further conversation with Ginsberg launched Creeley into a completely new disposition toward writing. In a 1968 postscript to the 1963 dialogue, he notes that not long after it, "I began to try deliberately to break out of the habits described." This involved a route of gradually deeper engagement with the context of writing. First, he used drugs and "wrote in different states of so-called consciousness, e.g. when high" (41) and he also set aside his typewriter for a pen or pencil. These exercises began to free him to respond to the exigencies of the moment rather than to seek aesthetic closure: he learned "the possibility of *scribbling*, of writing for the immediacy of the pleasure and without having to pay attention to some final code of significance." Giving up the typewriter altogether, he started using notebooks and began to see that the size of the notebook page could determine the scope of what he wrote. In addition, he noticed how the notebooks themselves became a context full of writing: they "accumulated the writing, and they made no decisions about it—it was all there, in whatever state it occurred" (42).

At the end of the postscript, Creeley pledges allegiance to the poetics of the New American Poetry, in which the poem no longer aspires to be a self-enclosed object nor art a cloistered activity. With the gratitude of a convert, he says, "It would be impossible to thank Allen Ginsberg enough for what he was somehow able to reassure me of—or to thank those other friends whose way of writing was of like order: Robert Duncan, Charles Olson, Denise Levertov, and the many others, who were wise, like they say, long before myself" (43). In his own eyes, Creeley has finally joined the company that was his all along, a fellowship of which he was a member but whose existential commitments he had not felt able to match. And he maintained an unfailing allegiance to a continuous conversation with his "company" until the end of his life. A year before he died, I heard him give a poetry reading at the University of Chicago and was struck by its haunted quality; he invoked in his remarks the spirits of his poetic cohort and even seemed to "channel" them in some of his recent poetry. As the only one still living, he felt solely responsible for sustaining the poetry of Olson, Duncan, Ginsberg, Levertov, and Dorn alongside (or even inside) his own. There was, though, an air of desperation, as if he were stretching to keep helium-filled balloons tethered to the earth, holding open a conversation when all of the other speakers were gone.

It was no coincidence that Creeley's initial acknowledgment of his conversion to a more existential way of writing and the conversation that provoked it would appear in a book of his interviews. In 1973, Creeley may have been the first poet to publish such a book as one of his own works, and over the course of his life he may well have given more interviews than any other American poet. As an artistic endeavor, the interview genre offers Creeley an opportunity to extend the contexts of his poetry in two ways: by engaging an interlocutor in conversation and by presenting that conversation to a reading audience. From the perspective of the interviewer, Creeley's heroic commitment to an art of the present moment made him a magnet. Paradoxically, this man of exquisite self-consciousness and insistent self-effacement was always *out there* in dialogue with others. The result is that Creeley's interviews have taken a place as one of the indispensable theoretical statements of an art of context; arguably more than any other writer, Creeley raised the genre of the interview to the status of an essential context for poetry. Through reliance on the tape recorder, his interviews also enact one of the hallmark paradoxes of contextual practice: context can never be wholly present. This is true both in the sense that the context to which the artist responds is no longer available to the work's later audience and also in the sense that assemblage artists deliberately seek to create a new context by selecting materials from the most disparate sources, leaving in plain view the fact of their having been "torn" from elsewhere. Likewise, when regarding interviews like Creeley's as works of contextual art, we mustn't overlook the fact that the mediation of the tape recorder produces a technological effect of immediacy, creating a new genre through rendering a context both present (at the time of recording) and absent (to a later listener or reader).[11] As a medium that carried presence from a distance, the tape recorder joined film, television, and radio as powerful fixtures of the vernacular landscape of the time. Recognizing that new media are popular but ideologically freighted, contextual artists endeavored to break the ideological set and reframe media, often in the hopes of erotic, political, and mystical liberation.

ASSEMBLAGE AS ARCHEOLOGY
AND HISTORY

Harry Smith's *Anthology of American Folk Music*
and Charles Reznikoff's *Testimony*

"A Metaphor of Universal Becoming"

In the postwar arts, contextual practice resituates the relationship between art and life. At the beginning of the century, collage started out in the hands of the cubists as a radical new form able to incorporate unimagined objects into the picture plane. Futurism, Dada, and surrealism expanded the reach of collage by drawing from many more facets of the material world and by extending into temporal realms through drama, film, and hybrid exhibitions. These avant-garde movements in the first half of the century stressed the liberatory potential of art and intimated new modes of living that would take their cues from the uncanny, oneiric, ironic, or magical juxtapositions found in works of collage. Postwar artists developed the hints of a contextual approach to life into happenings, installations, Earth Art, performance art, and a variety of social experiments. Impeding a smooth development, though, from avant-garde collage to postwar contextual practice was the cataclysmic interlude of World War II. The wholesale razing of buildings, landscapes, and lives effected a cultural razing that undermined, more extensively than had earlier avant-garde movements, the value of the well-made, beautiful object—an outcome that Adorno's famous admonition against "poetry after Auschwitz" makes explicit.[1] From a cultural ground zero blasted out by the war arose a desire to evoke in new terms an intimacy among objects, human beings, and the activity of art. In a broken and fragmented world, contextual

practice took the risk of reimagining a cultural life with brokenness and frag-
mentation as givens.

This new contextual practice was characterized by an erosion of formalism and a celebration of informality. William Seitz signals this postwar difference by making assemblage the master term for his exhibition and by defining
it by virtue of vernacular materials and the "entirely new relationship between
work and spectator" (81) it creates. Moving away from the rigorously formalist
approach to collage championed by Clement Greenberg, Seitz draws attention to the cornucopia of vernacular materials incorporated in assemblage,
listing with the title of each work in his catalog its component substances. Edward Kienholz's *Jane Doe* (1959), for instance, is composed of "Wooden sewing
chest with fur-rimmed drawers containing painted wooden objects, rubber
dolls, and sandpaper; side cabinets, one velvet-lined, head and neck of female
mannequin, skirt of white bridal dress, oil paint" (160); and George Herms's
The Poet (1960) binds a "rusted klaxon" and a "stack of pages tied with string"
to a "wood table-base" (159). This wild proliferation of materials suggests "the
limitless diversity that relates assembled art to the world." Seitz also claims
that an art assembled from everyday materials achieves a greater intimacy
than the framed canvas, whether abstract or representational. Speaking of
Jane Doe and *The Poet*, works of gritty social critique by California artists, he
remarks that as objects, "however arresting, strange, or poetic may be their
effect, [they] resemble furniture more than they do sculpture; they fit more
naturally in a living room than they do in a museum" (81).

In "Collage: The Organizing Principle of Art in the Age of the Relativity of
Art" (1983), the art critic and philosopher Donald Kuspit discusses how postwar contextual practice signals a profound reorientation of the relationship
between art and life. Like Seitz, Kuspit sees a new artistic practice that represents a third way for art that is "no longer either representational (an imitation of nature issuing in an illusion of life) or abstract (a formal construction
issuing in a style)" (Hoffman 44). Rather than striving for a lifelike illusion
or an abstract style, collage acknowledges the shattered conditions of its "Age
of Relativity" by valuing fragments and incompleteness, eschewing claims to
self-sufficient being by throwing in its lot with the vagaries of becoming:

> The incongruous effect of the collage is based on its incompleteness, on the
> sense of perpetual becoming that animates it. It is always coming into being;
> it has never "been," as one can say of the more familiar, "absolute" type of

art. It is always insistent yet porous, never resistant and substantive. . . . What counts is that it remains incompletely constituted, for all the fragments that constitute it. There is always something more that can be added to or taken away from its constitution, as if by some restless will. (43)

Through its porousness and incompleteness, contextual art "is a metaphor of universal becoming" and thus as much an approach to conducting life as a form of art. Although this art of becoming eschews integration, it has a kind of integrity that comes from refusing to be enticed by preexisting categories and beliefs and from insisting on remaining open-ended. By declining to make determinate choices and opting for open-ended becoming, "Collage, for the first time in art, makes uncertainty a method of creation, apparent indeterminacy a procedure" (43). Uncertainty and indeterminacy not only introduce chance into the act of composition, they also drag along traces of the contexts from which objects have been wrenched. There are two levels of traces: those from whole objects fractured to produce fragments, and those from the entirely different objects in a specific setting that might have been chosen to enter the work. At either level, what has been rejected from the work remains associated with it as a "defining contour or fringe." Contextual practice "is very much about these dark fringes, these absences, as well as about the positive presence of . . . fragments. The informal fringe and the formal assertion of substance exist side by side in the collage, subtly mingling to generate its energy" (43). In contextual art, "material fragments . . . exist in a certain raw state" and they resist "synthesis into a conventionally unified art object," thus retaining a quality of worldliness that keeps the art closely allied with reality. Because the materials of assemblage do not objectify completely as art, they speak to the hither side of art "as clues to the nature of being-in-the-world." Rather than claiming the classical self-sufficiency of art, the fragments gathered by contextual practice declare themselves as worldly objects, as "artifacts found in a particular excavation at a particular site in the world." Digging into the present, assemblage disrupts complacent assumptions and reveals new ways of understanding how human beings are situated in the world: "The collage becomes simply a way of panning for the golden meanings of the world, an archeological investigation into a present (if hidden) truth" (51). Contextual practice offers more than we usually expect from an art form; it promises to reconstitute notions of meaning, of aesthetics, and of their interdependence by excavating "at a particular site in the world."

"The Problem of Rhythm in
Relation to Thought"

The phrase "an archeological investigation into a present (if hidden) truth" could describe much of the collage, montage, and assemblage art produced by the enigmatic painter, filmmaker, musicologist, and anthropologist Harry Smith (1923–1991). Nearly everything he made—from hand-painted, collaged, or superimposed films to paintings that graph musical performances to innovative ethnographic collections to the monumental *Anthology of American Folk Music* (1952)—is composed not in a narrative sequence but by juxtaposition of materials that draw their contextual fringes along with them. Smith grew up in the Pacific Northwest in a family devoted to the occult, and his early studies were in anthropology and linguistics. He moved to the San Francisco Bay Area in the midforties, where he painted on canvas, on walls, and directly onto film, often attempting to correlate visual rhythms to bebop jazz. In the early fifties he moved to New York City and remained there for most of the rest of his life. A polymath, Smith practiced simultaneously in a large number of fields—painting, filmmaking, ethnographic collecting (including his vast collection of sound recordings), and occultism—and was always looking for correlations among them. He is best known as an influential visionary filmmaker and for his brilliant selection and arrangement of "race," "hillbilly," and religious music in *The Anthology of American Folk Music,* which was in many ways responsible for launching the Folk Music Revival and also became a founding document, a veritable constitution, of rock 'n' roll.[2] The first concerted attempt to assess all the facets of Smith's career and place him within the cultural history of the second half of the twentieth century occurred at a 2001 symposium at the Getty Museum in Los Angeles, titled "Harry Smith: The Avant-Garde in the American Vernacular."[3]

To begin exploring his contextual practice and its relations to that of other American poets and artists, it might be helpful to envision the sorts of internal quandaries that would drive such a person to an existential commitment to an art of assemblage. For instance, imagine asking yourself, in all seriousness, What does it take to make life appear meaningful moment by moment? Say you're not content with just getting by day-to-day or with entering into the splashy events projected by the news media as a constantly consuming narrative. Or what if you engage in years of study in order to master one or more fields of knowledge but find that no intellectual discipline provides a strong enough purchase on how things happen that you would want to remain within its embrace? Or what if, with even more desperation, you find that no religion or philosophy or science or esoteric system seems capable of tagging all the reality hurtling at you from every direction? Then you might, like Harry Smith, try to forge your own skeleton key to unlock how things make sense. Smith believed this key was not conceptual but involved tuning into an underlying rhythm discernible in the way things happen. Focusing his attention on momentary conjunctions rather than on fixed ideas, he began to view life as a constantly evolving assemblage composition. Most of us look at reality on the alert for familiar patterns, ignoring as meaningless anything that doesn't settle into a recognizable construct, but Smith looked at every event, every coincidence of objects, as obeying or maybe creating a certain rhythm; from this perspective nothing that occurs can be discarded or ignored because it all participates in the ongoing composition of meaning. This is why, as many people remarked in near-reverential tones, Smith was never bored: "no matter where he was and whatever space he found himself he made it gigantic. . . . He always found the treasures of the world absolutely under his feet. Heard things and saw things and tasted things that nobody ever had before. If you were with Harry you could discover something new every moment and it was in complete disguise" (Harvey Bialy, *AM* 197).

Smith was always making art. Because his art practice relied on his understanding of how meaning happens, he was constantly engaged in it, forever building collections—bringing things into startling new relationships—and by so doing making explicit his notion that reality is composed of meaningful, if unanticipated, conjunctions. As one of his students put it, "Harry was always into the process. The one thing that he said to me that I particularly remember was the most important thing about reality is the relationship of objects. And he said that what makes everything real is the fact that things are ordered in the present status. In other words, things are set beside themselves and that is what makes reality. Reality is made up of just the placement of objects" (Henry Jones, *AM* 209). Smith not only collected things, he placed them in suggestive contexts that would allow them to call attention to themselves by virtue of what was around them, thus turning a collection into a work of art. Many people have noted that *The Anthology of American Folk Music* is a very peculiar kind of collection, ordered not by any simple method of classification but as an assemblage in which songs call out to one another along multiple axes of meaning. Smith acknowledges employing this mode of composition: "The whole *Anthology* was a collage. I thought of it as an art object" (*Self* 81).

To have practiced standard classification in keeping with the disciplines of folklore or ethnomusicology would have meant acceding to a preestablished order, rather than engaging in the active pursuit of meaningful patterns—the foremost concern of his every waking (and probably dreaming) hour.

In viewing composition as a boundless process, in which nothing that occurs is exterior to the artistic activity, Smith made a contextual practice from the avant-garde collage enterprise spearheaded by people such as Gertrude Stein, Hans Arp, and Marcel Duchamp. In "Composition as Explanation," for instance, Stein gives an early formulation of what will become the central idea behind contextual composition: "The composition is the thing seen by every one living in the living they are doing, they are the composing of the composition that at the time they are living is the composition of the time in which they are living" (516). Like Kuspit, Stein stipulates the crucial importance of becoming for an art of assemblage. If the artist recognizes reality as an ongoing assemblage, then she can signal that recognition by employing a method that foregrounds the compositional activity occurring constantly in the modern world. Across the gamut of his endeavors, Smith's contextual practice involves a number of processes that conduce to an understanding of and participation in "the composition of the time in which [he is] living." These processes include perspicacious collecting, diligent study, striking insight into hitherto unnoticed relationships, and finally surrender to the arbitrariness of the moment. One of Smith's students describes this methodology as an intertwining of purpose and chance: "he would just concentrate and study and work and go haywire, drive himself crazy, getting everything in exactly the right order and then he would just give it a kick and say 'that's it.' But he knew when he kicked it that he'd chosen the right moment and however it fell was going to be right" (Henry Jones, *AM* 210).

Like Duchamp, whose accidentally cracked *The Bride Stripped Bare by Her Bachelors, Even (The Large Glass)* (1915–1923) he keenly admired, Smith had a Dadaist's trust that the carefully prepared work of art achieves final realization only through a chance operation.[4] But unlike Duchamp's acolyte John Cage, whose compositional methods of chance and indeterminacy reflected a philosophical commitment to letting be, Smith joined the great bebop improvisers in insisting that an inherent rhythm to the way things happen can be found, although it can be apprehended only by the most rigorous, vigilant attention. In notes to *The Kiowa Peyote Meeting*, issued by Folkways in 1973, Smith lauds an ascetic rigor he finds in the singers and contends that their philosophical asceticism affords them an appreciation of the rhythmic nature of life: "I particularly hope that examples of the Kiowa approach to things will give an insight into how one people has dealt with the problem of rhythm in relation to thought" (*AM* 164). The desire to relate rhythm and thought has been around in Western philosophy at least since Pythagoras combined mathematics, music, and asceticism, and it reached its zenith in the works of Plato.

Smith himself invoked the Platonic tradition by reproducing on the *Anthology's* three LP covers the image of the divine monochord—in which the Ptolemaic universe is related mathematically to musical intervals—from a treatise by the Renaissance Neoplatonist Robert Fludd (Fig. 5).[5] It should

FIGURE 5. Cover, Harry Smith's *Anthology of American Folk Music.* Johann Theodor de Bry (Franco-Flemish, 1561–1623), *The Divine Monochord.* Smithsonian Folkways.

not be surprising, then, that in 1962 Smith calls upon Plato's example to explain how high his hopes had been for the *Anthology*: "I felt social changes would result from it. I'd been reading from Plato's *Republic*. He's jabbering on about music, how you have to be careful about changing the music because it might upset or destroy the government. Everybody gets out of step" (*Self* 83)—which was exactly the anarchic result Smith was hoping for. He affirms this statement when accepting the Chairman's Merit Award from the National Academy of Recording Arts and Sciences in 1991: "I'm glad to say that my dreams came true—that I saw America changed through music" (Sanders 30). Allen Ginsberg makes a similar argument for the efficacy of new forms of poetry in a 1961 essay that draws from the same Platonic figure: "When the Mode of the Music Changes, the Walls of the City Shake" (*Prose* 247–54). In a note furnishing context to the essay, he explains that his goal was to defend "libertarian-anarchist-sexualized" (253) poetry and prose and that the title comes "out of Plato out of Pythagoras—continuation of gnostic—secret and politically suppressed—liberty of consciousness and art—old bohemian—tradition" (254).

The relationship between rhythm and thought stands at the heart of Smith's conception of the universe. As the poet and biochemist Harvey Bialy testifies, Smith "had the uncanny ability to understand the basic connections between things that were seemingly completely disparate and the forces and dynamics and magnetic interactions and terrestrial activities and geomagnetic polarizations . . . that made culture, that made music, that made art, that made all of the things that are timeless in human culture" (*AM* 196). For Bialy, the ability to capture the relationship between rhythm and thought and to envisage the ways this relationship structures the artifacts of human culture made Smith "an extraordinary being that comes along maybe once in a hundred years or in a thousand years. Harry is a genius on the order of Da Vinci" (*AM* 197). Despite this ringing endorsement, Smith's achievement is not easy to evaluate. Although claims such as Bialy's are common from Smith's intimates, the same people (and others) offer testimony that paints Smith as a self-absorbed crackpot, an angry drunk, or a charlatan.

It is difficult for those of us who never met him to evaluate Smith because his creativity and philosophical principles seem to have been most dramatically on view in the context-dependent performances he staged for individuals or small groups of people—shows that might be visual (his films and paintings and collections) but might also be aural (his records and tapes that spanned a huge variety of sound worlds) or strictly verbal (as transcriptions of his interviews make apparent). The interviews collected in *Think of the Self Speaking* (1999) give a glimpse of his performative persona, which, in marked contrast to the philosophical earnestness of Robert Creeley, is a blending of the pedantic scholar, the raconteur, the trickster, and the madman. One way to measure the public effect of Smith's work without first-hand experience of the man is to note the cultural developments for which he was an inspiration or early participant: the folk music revival and the subsequent rise of rock 'n' roll; central aspects of visionary filmmaking; the concert light show; facets of modern alchemical magic; and creative and intuitive impulses in countless individuals.[6]

One of the most nuanced attempts to gauge Smith and his achievement can be found in the introduction to *Think of the Self Speaking*, in which Ginsberg tells Hal Willner about his long and eventful friendship with Smith, striking a balance between admiration for his work and exasperation at his personal habits. In the midst of recounting an evening at Smith's apartment, during which he was plied with marijuana and then shown a number of Smith's early films, Ginsberg comments appreciatively on the subtly interpenetrating rhythms in those works:

> What he had done was set . . . certain ones of them, short ones, to [Thelonius Monk's] *Misterioso*. . . . I saw that his point was that the actual frames moved in relation to the music—he had been calculating the frames to the Monk music. In addition, he had a theory that the time of movement would be a crosscurrent of . . . certain kinds of brain waves, the average heartbeat pattern, certain biological rhythms . . . , and he was animating his collages and setting the time according to archetypal body rhythms. His references to this were certain drumming patterns of the Australian Aborigines [and] Zulu music. (*Self* 3)[7]

Smith's recognition that African music and visual patterns rely on common rhythms has been confirmed in the many books of Robert Farris Thompson on the African arts and their influence on the Western hemisphere. In *Flash of the Spirit*, for instance, Thompson characterizes Mande cloth (Mali), made of narrow bands of striped patterns, as "rhythmized textiles." He speaks of the "narrow-strip textile, enlivened by rich and vivid suspensions of the expected placement of the weft-blocks," as achieving a visual design meant "to be scanned metrically." Specifically, the cloth displays a "visual resonance with the famed off-beat phrasing of melodic accents in African and Afro-American music" (207). Smith took this "visual resonance" further in some of his early abstract paintings, in which he matched Dizzy Gillespie's music with brush strokes, note by note (Foye 19–20; see Fig. 6).

FIGURE 6. Harry Smith, *Manteca* (ca. 1948); painting of "Manteca," Dizzy Gillespie Orchestra, ca. 1947. Courtesy of Harry Smith Archives.

FIGURE 7. Brian Graham, "Harry Smith cooks at Allen Ginsberg's apartment," 1986.
© Brian Graham.

Notwithstanding his awe at the technical range and rhythmic subtlety of
Smith's radical genius, Ginsberg found entering Smith's apartment a frightening prospect: "He had no source [of income] but he was a genius, like the
painter Albert Pinkham Ryder. I got to be scared of going up there because
he'd get me tremblingly high on grass and show me these amazing movies.
I'd be totally awed and intimidated by the universality of his genius in music
and painting. . . . But he'd always hit me up for money, if he could capture
me, get me up there and hypnotize me with his films" (Self 4; see Fig. 7).
Although he generously gave substantial support, both financial and otherwise, to Smith over the years, Ginsberg makes palpable the pressure Smith
placed on the people in his life. In the largest sense, this might be called
a pressure for acknowledgment; Smith wanted his talent acknowledged so
that he would be given enough money to fund his ambitious projects (and,
just incidentally, to stay alive); he wanted his solutions to the "problem of
rhythm in relation to thought" acknowledged as signal innovations in modern art and scholarship; and he wanted people he knew to acknowledge the
creative possibilities inherent moment-by-moment in their own lives. The
pressure for acknowledgment made Smith a difficult person to be around,

and yet such demands and the discomfort they provoked arose directly from conversational encounters between Smith and others—a form of contextual practice akin to the conversational art of Creeley and many of the other New American poets.

Assemblage as History

Smith's existential commitments and search for insight into the interplay of rhythm and thought can be found not only in his immediate encounters with individuals but also in the capacious form of *The Anthology of American Folk Music.* To consider the *Anthology* as a whole is to imagine an entire history of the United States in the form of an assemblage. One way to ascertain the ambitions of a such an assemblage history would be to compare it to another: the Objectivist poet Charles Reznikoff's two-volume *Testimony: The United States (1885–1915): Recitative* (1934, 1965, 1968, 1978–79), a poetic rendering of courtroom testimony taken at the end of the nineteenth and beginning of the twentieth centuries and redacted by Reznikoff (1894–1976) mainly during the sixties.[8] These two *sui generis* works are similar in that they present buried American histories, made up of the assembled voices of people who have no ready access to public discourse. By virtue of their rescue by Reznikoff and Smith, these voices find a way into the national conversation, disclosing facets of the culture usually absent from official histories.

Reznikoff and Smith work to remove subjective reactions from their compositions in favor of a striking presentational immediacy, offering poems and songs whose style and content are characterized by a shocking rawness at odds with "common" and even "advanced" norms of aesthetic taste.[9] Although both artists cultivate rawness as a deliberate effect, their works do not, on closer inspection, claim to be unmediated; both foreground incisively the social and economic contexts, the "defining contour or fringe," to quote Kuspit, from which they extract the material for their large-scale assemblages. In Reznikoff's case, the conventions of the judicial system, the constraints of the economic position of the speakers, and the exigencies of courtroom reporting and law book editing all mediate the testimony. The songs Smith selects are mediated by the recording techniques of the thirties (including the usual three-minute time constraint per side for a 78 rpm disc), by the real and imagined tastes of the audiences the recordings sought to attract, and by the scarcity of the discs when Smith began collecting them in the forties. By highlighting both rawness and mediation, Reznikoff and Smith generate a kind of cognitive friction that urges readers and auditors to reflect on the relationship among three primary modes of legitimation: authenticity, authority, and authorship.

To construct their assemblages, Reznikoff and Smith engage in acts of salvage such as those of Jess and the intuitive architect of junk art, Simon (Sabato) Rodia (1879–1965), rescuing materials long buried within neglected media.[10] In Rodia's case, his *Watts Towers* (1921–1954; see Fig. 8) are built of "steel rods, wire screening and concrete, broken dishes and colored glass, pieces of green Seven-Up, blue milk of magnesia, and other bottles, fragments of mirror, shells, and a variety of stones" (Seitz 77). An Italian-born

FIGURE 8. Simon Rodia, *The Watts Towers* (1921–1954). Library of Congress, Prints & Photographs Division, photograph by Carol M. Highsmith [LC-HS503–445].

tile setter, Rodia constructed his three hundred-foot towers single-handedly over the course of thirty-three years. Thomas Crow contends that "Rodia's daring self-reliance and democratic aspiration" provided a prominent example for California junk artists of the fifties and sixties, who "were regularly drawn to the cheap disposability of collage and assemblage (much work in the period was never meant to be permanent)" (Crow, *Sixties* 25).[11] In a 1959 poem, "Nel Mezzo del Cammin di Nostra Vita" (*RB* 21–24), Robert Duncan celebrates the *Watts Towers* as an example of a democratic, anarchic art that promises to open metaphysical space for individual creators, rather than glorifying church or state. Citing the first line of Dante's *Commedia* as the title of his poem, Duncan effectively compares Rodia's vernacular towers to the three towering canticles of Dante's vernacular poem. Duncan also would have noticed a numerological correspondence; just as each of Dante's three canticles has thirty-three cantos, so the three towers were erected in the course of thirty-three years.[12] The poem applauds Rodia's transmutation of the detritus of urban life into an enduring artistic structure:

> the great mitred structure rising
>   out of squalid suburbs where the
> mind is beaten back to the traffic, ground
>   down to the drugstore, the mean regular houses
> straggling out of downtown sections
>   of imagination defeated. "They're
> taller than the Church," he told us
>   proudly.
>
>   Art, dedicated to itself!
>
>   (22)[13]

Like the *Watts Towers*, *Testimony* is a monument made of bright, discarded materials by a "little guy" (to adopt a populist expression), an assemblage rising from a proletarian base to overtop fictions of nationhood. A lawyer who chose to do "piece work" rather than pursue a career in law, Reznikoff earned a meager living writing definitions for a legal encyclopedia; when he finished with entries for the letter "Z," he began over again with entries for "A." In his free time, he sought out the testimony of individual witnesses buried among legal opinions in the regional law books for the period 1885–1915, recasting this legal detritus into tightly compressed verse narratives that highlight climactic incidents in the lives of lower-class Americans. The terse, shocking narratives are colored by violence, malice, and brute stupidity, and they shed light particularly on instances of industrial negligence, racism, and child victimization. Having experimented earlier in his career with verse narratives of proletarian lives and with casting legal testimony in poetic prose, Reznikoff began publishing *Testimony* in its present form in the sixties; eventually, the full work appeared after his death in two volumes, totaling 530 pages.[14] The many short poems, organized first by region and then under ironic, quasi-sociological headings, such as "SOCIAL LIFE," "DOMESTIC LIFE," "BOYS AND GIRLS," "MACHINE AGE," "PROPERTY," and "NEGROES," create an historical assemblage of the United States at the turn of the twentieth century. Reznikoff captures traces of a crucial period of turmoil and transition through the testimony of individuals whose speech bears witness to the inhuman underside of the nation.

In the *Anthology of American Folk Music*, Smith presents a small portion of the "race," hillbilly, and religious recordings from the twenties and thirties that he had collected on the West Coast in the forties, often rescuing rare pressings from heaps of 78s destined to be melted down for shellac during the war. Like Reznikoff, he gravitated toward materials that escaped the eyes of professional scholars and institutions—things that, when presented in the right context, would convey entire modes of life. In the *Anthology*, Smith resuscitates the recorded work of Southern rural musicians, such as Clarence Ashley, Uncle Dave Macon, Mississippi John Hurt, Dock Boggs, and Blind Lemon Jefferson, documenting every aspect of the performances, providing mock headlines that condense the contents of each song, and organizing them under the general headings of "Ballads," "Social Music," and "Songs"—a nonprofessional taxonomy that works like the general headings in *Testimony* not to classify the songs but to hold open a contextual space for interaction. As Smith points out in his notes, many of these songs relate incidents that go back into the nineteenth century. In fact, these incidents parallel the events that Reznikoff versifies; it's as though the terrible accidents and acts of aggression to which Reznikoff's speakers testify have been turned into anguished and haunting songs by the singers in Smith's anthology. Or, to take the hint offered by Reznikoff's subtitling *Testimony* as *Recitative*, it's as though the compositions of Reznikoff and Smith belong to a single assemblage opera of American history, in which Reznikoff's poetry forms the recitative and the songs in the anthology act as arias, duets, and trios. The opera is presided over by forces of contingency and fate—or perhaps, chance and violence—tragic, irrational powers that work against the redemptive narratives that Americans like to tell about themselves. The uncompromising quality to both works deflates hopes and illusions; at the same time, many people find these ingeniously composed assemblages surprisingly exhilarating for the sympathy they evoke for lives running counter to the channels of social institutions.

Testimony and the *Anthology* braid together three "progressive" eras of American history: the end of the nineteenth century and beginning of the twentieth, the late twenties and early thirties, and the sixties. These were eras of social upheaval, in which serious challenges were mounted against the excesses of capitalism on behalf of a leftist coalition of unions, civil rights groups, and advocates for the poor. The middle era, spanning the Great Depression, was an especially crucial time in the formation of these two works.[15] During the late twenties, Reznikoff began combing the regional volumes of the West Publishing Company's federal and state court reports for the years 1885–1915, and he published his first reworkings in 1932 under the ironic title "My Country 'Tis of Thee." The time period from 1925 to 1933, from which Smith draws the material for his *Anthology*, was the heyday of the recording of regional artists by major record labels, which sought to exploit a revivalist impulse by capturing singers who would already sound "old-fashioned" to their regional audiences (Cantwell 190). When the songs in Smith's *Anthology* and the poems in Reznikoff's *Testimony* were heard and seen again by new audiences in the sixties, they had acquired an aura of double authenticity; they spoke not only from the heroic moment of the leftist thirties, but they drew their subject matter from an earlier, more mysterious era that had confronted other primary traumas and ruptures in American culture—slavery, industrialization, westward expansion, and mass immigration.

In the sixties, many of the singers in the *Anthology of American Folk Music* and all of the Objectivist poets, of whom Reznikoff was one, were rediscovered and lionized as touchstones of authenticity by the baby boom generation, to whom they seemed oracular voices speaking from beyond the grave. Although their voices had mostly fallen silent in the forties and fifties, the singers and poets were still very much alive. As the singers began touring nationally and internationally and recording again, and as the poets began giving readings and interviews and publishing once again, this perceived quality of authenticity lent them a prophetic mantle. *Testimony* and the *Anthology* remain quite canny, though, about the fact that the aura of authenticity is imparted, paradoxically, by the grace of mechanical reproduction. Without the court reporters and the West Publishing Company, the voices heard in Reznikoff's *Testimony* would be lost. In addition, as Michael Davidson points out, the rules of the legal system determined for Reznikoff's poem both what can be said and how it is said, and the organization of the West series provides the geographical categories that structure the entire poem (*Ghostlier* 151–53). The recording of the singers whom Smith gathered in the *Anthology* transmuted a mundane and unremarkable social practice that was part of the background of life in the South into the high romance of the radio, the phonograph, and the movies. As Greil Marcus notes, "Many copies of these records were bought by people without phonographs. They bought the discs as talismans of their own existence; they could hold these objects in their hands and feel their own lives dramatized. In such an act, people discovered the modern world: the thrill of mechanical reproduction" (*Republic* 121). The voices of a Dock Boggs or a Blind Lemon Jefferson sounded "old" to ears in the sixties because of abrasive, nasal, or guttural vocal styles and because of the primitive recording techniques that can be heard on the *Anthology*.[16] For a generation raised on television, there were two archaic qualities that made these songs sound as if they were intoned from beyond the grave: first, the singing styles, modal melodies, and verses whose imagery appeared to be drawn from the unconscious depths of American culture; and second, the technology, outmoded by several removes, that thus conveyed a sense of unbridgeable distance. In this way, both the voices and the soundscapes operate as *objets trouvés* for the assemblage that Smith composes.[17]

Not only do these works of assemblage history call into question the category of authenticity by focusing attention on the opposing poles of rawness and mediation, they also play havoc with commonsense notions of authority and authorship. With regard to authority, each of these works implicitly challenges professional and disciplinary norms. Smith confounds folklorists by both ascribing to and undermining their conventions. With remarkable thoroughness, he adopts every feature of musicological methodology, noting for each song its title (including the Child number for the ballads), singers, instrumentation, date of recording, and original issue number, and supplying a précis of all known historical facts about its content; he also gives for each song a discography of the performers and a bibliography and then compiles for the project as a whole an exhaustive index of artists, titles, subjects, and instruments. Working against this professional decorum, though, is a contextual practice that operates at two levels: that of the "handbook" that accompanies the discs and that of the arrangement of the songs. Visually, the mysterious handbook (Fig. 9) has a bumptious, pastiche quality that makes it hard to decide whether it is a magical synthesis or a joke. Robert Cantwell summarizes well the visual domains from which Smith draws in order to create his assemblage:

> Photostatically reproduced, strongly reminiscent of the organs of transient or marginal political coalitions . . . , the handbook is at once a catalogue, like the republished antique Sears-Roebuck catalogues, a discography, a manual, a scrapbook, a sort of stamp or coupon book, a sort of official document, like a passport, as well as a tabloid newspaper: a bricolage of printed ephemera that like junk sculpture incorporates many alien forms, each set off in its own character against all the others and against the whole. (194)

As assemblagist and editor, providing not only an introduction to the collection but also a comic headline summary for each song, Smith undermines the authority of musicological and folklorist conventions by taking on some of the functions of an author. This role is especially evident in the way he orders the songs by number rather than by any known method of classification. Eschewing generic, subregional, and especially racial classifications (which were ubiquitous not only when the recordings were made but also when Smith edited his anthology), his juxtaposition of the songs proceeds by an occult, serial logic based on stylistic features or subject matter. For example, Smith's headline summaries of songs 19–24 (Fig. 10) hint at thematic connections among "Stackalee," by Frank Hutchison; "White House Blues," by Charlie Poole and the North Carolina Ramblers; "Frankie," by Mississippi John Hurt; "When That Great Ship Went Down," by William and Versey Smith; "Engine One-Forty-Three," by the Carter Family; and "Kassie Jones," by Furry Lewis:

> 19) THEFT OF STETSON HAT CAUSES DEADLY DISPUTE, VICTIM IDEN-TIFIES SELF AS FAMILY MAN; 20) McKINLEY SWEARS, MOURNS, DIES, ROOSEVELT GETS WHITE HOUSE AND SILVER CUP; 21) ALBERT DIES PREFERRING ALICE FRY, BUT JUDGE FINDS FRANKIE CHARMING AT LATTER'S TRIAL; 22) MANUFACTURERS [sic] PROUD DREAM DE-STROYED AT SHIPWRECK, SEGREGATED POOR DIE FIRST; 23) GEOR-GIE RUNS INTO ROCK AFTER MOTHER'S WARNING, DIES WITH THE ENGINE HE LOVES; 24) CRACK ENGINEER JONES IN FATAL COLLI-SION, KNEW ALICE FRY, WIFE RECALLS SYMBOLIC DREAM, LATER CONSOLES CHILDREN.

FIGURE 9. Cover to *Handbook* for Harry Smith's *Anthology of American Folk Music*, 1952. Smithsonian Folkways.

Out of the murders, assassinations, and wrecks portrayed in these songs, Smith highlights themes of class warfare, obsessive affection, family grief, and the mysterious temptress Alice Fry. By summarizing the contents of the songs as headlines or telegrams, Smith foregrounds thematic continuities, tying the disparate lyrics into a sustained assemblage that chronicles a broad swath of American history as seen from the bottom up. In *Invisible Republic: Bob Dylan's Basement Tapes*, Greil Marcus shows how Dylan has mined repeatedly

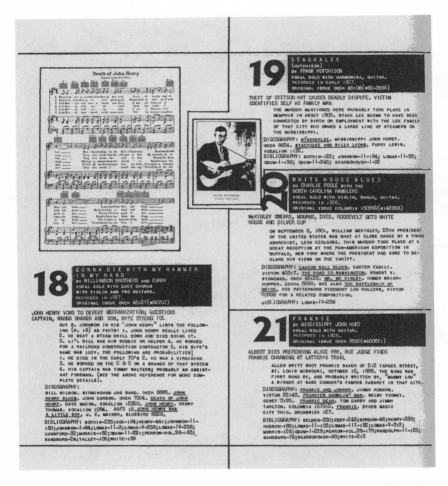

FIGURE 10. Page from *Handbook*, Harry Smith's *Anthology of American Folk Music*, 1952. Smithsonian Folkways.

the American history chronicled in Smith's *Anthology*. Another practitioner of highly mediated historiography in the early sixties, Andy Warhol, uses his *Disasters* series of photo-silkscreens to chronicle executions, suicides, auto and plane wrecks, and the iconic figures, such as Marilyn Monroe and Jacqueline Kennedy, whose public confrontations with death turned them instantly into legendary characters.[18]

If Smith imparts an authorial stamp to the *Anthology* by framing and ordering the songs in his own way and undermining through his summaries of song contents the professional norms he invokes in his careful annotations, Reznikoff does something similar in his redaction of courtroom testimony. Like Smith, Reznikoff was at home in the world of scholarship. In fact, history was a lifelong preoccupation, which Reznikoff pursued in verse, fiction, and actual historiography, and its conventions set the norms that *Testimony* implicitly challenges. In flaunting these norms, Reznikoff joins William Carlos Williams, whose highly partisan history *In the American Grain* appeared in 1925. Like Williams, Reznikoff endeavors in *Testimony* to let the language of the subjects speak for itself. He differs, though, by choosing unknown subjects who tell of experiences both commonplace and extreme, rather than ventriloquizing, as Williams does, famous actors in history. And unlike Williams, Reznikoff does not appoint heroes and villains, for he remains leery of ideologies buried in historical narratives—whether the schoolbook narratives of American exceptionalism and triumphalism or the personal forms of coherence given to history by poets such as Pound, Zukofsky, and Olson in their epic collages. *Testimony* undermines notions such as progress or decline just as it undermines ideologies of all stripes. It displays social strife as often unmotivated (and unbearable) and then implicitly challenges the reader to make sense of it and do something about it. To bring home this challenge, Reznikoff has subtle ways of involving the reader, as in this short poem from the "MACHINE AGE" section of the 1891–1900 division of the book:

> The storm came up suddenly
> and lightning
> struck a telephone pole, splitting it
> and sending electricity along the wires.
> A quarter of a mile away
> a doctor was sitting in his house
> quietly reading a book under his telephone—
> and was found in his chair
> dead, his hair on fire
> and red lines along his neck, chest and side. (II.129)

We know the approximate historical date of the incident recounted in this poem, and we find it among a series of poems that detail industrial accidents, but it seems to speak of something more ominous than mere accident. The uncanny reach of modern technology into an individual life that the poem exhibits echoes Henry Adams's prediction of an unlimited power becoming available to an individual, made when Adams stood face-to-face with an electric dynamo at the Paris Exposition of 1900. Here and throughout *Testimony*, Reznikoff investigates how social and technological forces overwhelm the capacity of people to respond to them. As Bruce Holsapple explains, in *Testimony* "violence from natural causes has transformed into violence from social causes. We are now threatened from inside" (142). In the poem above, the doctor stands in for the reader, intimating that the reader of *Testimony* is implicated in and will be affected by what he or she reads. In the modern age, we are all reading a book beneath a telephone and we are all susceptible to having our lives disfigured by the experience. Like Smith's *Anthology*, Reznikoff's *Testimony* depicts scenes of violence and unaccountable fate with little hope for amelioration—and offers such scenes as the basis for a true history of the United States. Drawing his phrasing exclusively from courtroom testimony, Reznikoff focuses on the terrible incident and how the witness relates it (note the detail in this poem of the "red lines along his neck, chest and side"), leaving aside the verdict, the sentence, or the damages awarded. The court plays a role in this history not for its guarantee of "justice" but because it brings to light things that otherwise would remain hidden. Likewise, the flat tone of the narrative corresponds to the factual orientation of courtroom testimony. The voice of the poet seems to vanish.

In an early review of Reznikoff's novel *By the Waters of Manhattan* (1930), Lionel Trilling praises Reznikoff's restrained, factual style as "remarkable and original in American literature" (371) and compares it to "the dry, casual prose-tempo of the Icelandic sagas" (372). Trilling's comparison brings us back to questions of authority and authorship in *Testimony* and the *Anthology*. As with the songs in the *Anthology*, there is a folk quality to Reznikoff's project that earns Trilling's admiration. This folk quality accounts for the "casual" tone to both works, and it also imparts a sense of anonymity. Although they leave editorial footprints, Smith and Reznikoff try hard to disappear into their artworks, ceding authority to the voices they select and arrange. Their contextual practices, though, keep the material fresh and allow it to startle and eventually to haunt an audience. Geoff Ward discusses Smith's handling of his material and the *Anthology*'s relation to its audience in terms that could apply equally to *Testimony*:

> The work does not seek to control its materials, but to collage them in the
> most provocative and questioning ways for the audience to turn over, and so
> half-create, and so take out into a world that can never now be quite the same

again. The work . . . restores an element of creativity to consumption by hand-
ing over such complex historical materials. Smith was quite clear that his work
was a counter-cultural and political statement: "I felt social changes would
result from it." (143)

As previously noted, Smith's assessment of the effect of the *Anthology*
proved remarkably accurate. Reznikoff's *Testimony* has yet to become directly implicated in social change, but a hint of its power can be found in
the fact that for the 1999 Venice Biennale, the artist Ann Hamilton covered
huge walls with passages from it. Speaking of her installation, Hamilton says,
"I'm thinking that I am the American representative, and it's the eve of the
millennium. . . . I want to bring to the surface the questions we should be
asking" (Dobrzynski 1, 30). By offering histories in the open-ended form
of assemblage, Reznikoff and Smith succeed in creating works that remain
challenging and provoke questions many years after composition. The fateful images, the raw presentation, the artful ways of incorporating the reader
or listener all contribute to a form of American history that negates safe assumptions or assumptions of safety, bringing "to the surface the questions
we should be asking."

VISIONARY ASSEMBLAGE

Harry Smith and the Poetry of Allen Ginsberg,

Robert Duncan, and Jack Spicer

"To Have the Serpent Intertwined in Their Eyeballs"

This chapter compares Smith to three poets who were his contemporaries and whom he knew personally: Allen Ginsberg, Robert Duncan, and Jack Spicer. By comparing and contrasting Smith with poets who occupy positions on a visionary continuum running from the unashamedly personal art of Ginsberg to the avowedly impersonal art of Spicer, we can begin to appreciate the range of his contextual practice. The first poet to consider is Ginsberg. In contrast to Smith and Reznikoff, who share a commitment to creating historical assemblages that absent the voice of the author, Ginsberg finds the Poundian model of personal intervention in history tremendously attractive. The collage composition of major poems such as "Howl," "Kaddish," "The Change: *Kyoto-Tokyo Express*," "Wichita Vortex Sutra," and "Plutonian Ode" differs from *Testimony* and the *Anthology* in that a personal voice stakes its ground in the social and political assemblage. Unlike Smith and Reznikoff, who lived in New York City at the same time but were unaware of each other, Smith and Ginsberg were friends for more than thirty years, made works of art for each other, and were reunited in the 1995 exhibition at the Whitney Museum of Art *Beat Culture and the New America: 1950–1965* (Phillips). At certain periods, Smith lived with Ginsberg for months at a time, causing the poet so many headaches that he was greatly relieved to secure Smith a sinecure in his last years as shaman-in-residence at the Naropa Institute in Boulder, Colorado (*Self*).

Given that Smith and Ginsberg inhabited substantially the same world, it is remarkable how much they diverge aesthetically while practicing a contextual art. Similar to Creeley in employing a rhetoric of emotional nakedness, Ginsberg issues an urgent plea in his politicocosmic poetry for compassion and mutual recognition of our desiring loneliness. Although Smith's art, like Ginsberg's, arises from a maverick sensibility planted in direct opposition to an entire range of social institutions, his disdain for personality can be found not only in the absence of biographical references in his art but also in the lies he tells about himself, in the tricks he plays so assiduously to hold others at a distance, and in his utter disregard for his own physical and emotional well-being. In their contextual practices, Smith and Ginsberg erase distinctions between life and art in radically different ways. Ginsberg's practice can be summed up in his aphorism "First thought, best thought," which advocates a spontaneous, wildly associative, and unrevised poetry that inherits the surrealist doctrine of automatic writing and accompanies Jack Kerouac's "spontaneous bop prosody."[1] By contrast, Smith asserts that, since the universe already operates on the principle of spontaneous juxtaposition, his job is to study in great detail the conjunctions that take place in reality and submit the patterns he finds there to laborious compositional techniques. Ginsberg and Smith maintain what might be thought of as an inverse or complementary relationship with regard to the respect each accords to the personality as a source for aesthetic exploration. Their respective employment of drugs is a notorious example of this complementarity: where Ginsberg took them to explore and transcend personal demons and invite cosmic revelations, Smith ingested substances to construct a working environment for deliberately calibrated explorations of objects and forces at play in the world.

Ginsberg recalls meeting Smith in 1960 at the Five Spot in New York, where Smith was notating rhythms while Thelonius Monk played (*Self* 2). They became friends, Ginsberg, says, because "we had a common interest in Tibetan Buddhist imagery and in drugs" (3). Ginsberg's 1961 poem "Journal Night Thoughts" (*CPAG* 275–79), in which Smith plays an important part, gives a vivid window into their common interests at this time. Illustrative of Ginsberg's stream-of-consciousness assemblage technique, the poem reveals how drugs not only evoked mystical experiences but also drew him toward his own psychological fixations. It narrates an evening devoted to marijuana that

Ginsberg spent in Smith's unnerving company; during the night, the poet recalls a variety of earlier drug sessions and muses upon the outrageous images that make up Smith's vast repertoire of cultural oddities. Nearly four years after writing the poem, Ginsberg added a commentary along the right margin, identifying Smith as his visitor and specifying the drugs whose effects he recalls during the poem: yagé (ayahuasca), psilocybin, LSD, nitrous oxide, and mescaline. The drugs signify entire contexts that Ginsberg draws into his practice; as Marcus Boon argues, different kinds of drugs affect writing in diverse ways. Boon devotes individual chapters of *The Road of Excess* to the relations of literature to five classes of drugs—narcotics, anesthetics, cannabis, stimulants, and psychedelics—all of which Ginsberg used at one time or another, with varying effects on his erotic poetics.

The poem begins with Ginsberg already intoxicated and staring into Smith's hypnotic gaze, which registers so strongly as a "pressure" that it propels hallucinations that hover around the transfixing eye into which the poet peers:

In bed on my green purple pink
    yellow orange bolivian blanket,
the clock tick, my back against the wall
—staring into black circled eyes magician
    man's bearded glance & story
the kitchen spun in a wheel of vertigo,
the eye in the center of the moving
      mandala—the
      eye in the hand
      the eye in the asshole
      serpent eating or
      vomiting its tail
—the blank air a solid wall revolving
    around my retina.

(275)

As the citations in the last chapter from *Think of the Self Speaking* attest, Ginsberg finds Smith both fascinating and scary. Here, the "magician / man's bearded glance" magnetizes Ginsberg's attention, converting Smith's literal eye into a tantric series of mystical eyes that break forth from a mandala, a powerful hand-gesture (*mudra*), and the base of the spine. Coiled at the spine's base resides a serpent (kundalini), dormant but ready to awaken and move up through the spiritual centers (chakras) of the body. These matters constitute part of the shared lore of "Tibetan Buddhist imagery and drugs" that fascinated Ginsberg and Smith, both of whom pursued a lifelong interest in Tantra, the esoteric mystical tradition that runs as a counterculture throughout South and East Asia. The erotic energy cultivated by the tantric adept is figured as a serpent that rises up the spine through six major centers of consciousness (which Ginsberg represents as "eyes") and then achieves spiritual union at the seventh, the crown of the head. Whether in Hindu, Buddhist, or Daoist forms, Tantra employs a series of highly ritualized aids: the sacred meditational diagram (mandala or *yantra*), the divine name chanted or silently repeated (mantra), the bodily posture or gesture (*asana* or mudra), the vocalized scripture or devotional song, and the transgressive acts of ingestion and intercourse (the "five M's").[2] These techniques form part of a vast, alchemical system for uniting the individual with cosmic reality by progressively raising erotic energy from the sexual act into mystical ecstasy. Ginsberg and Smith were two of the pioneering instigators of a tantric counterculture that erupted into the West during the postwar period. Through the means of drugs, textual research, travel to South Asia, and delving into a number of Western mystical movements within the long hermetic tradition, artists such as Ginsberg and Smith began to create an erotic poetics whose tenets spread out seductively into the culture at large.[3]

Another area of investigation for postwar researchers in this tantric or gnostic tradition was the lore of indigenous religions around the world, as filtered through the writings of anthropologists and the exhibits of "primitive" art. In "Journal Night Thoughts," Ginsberg returns to Smith after a page and a half of remembered drug experiences, only to have Smith feed his vertigo on macabre stories about Natchez sun ceremonies and the Spiro Mounds, an eight-hundred-year-old Caddoan Mississippian site in Oklahoma with prominent serpent iconography. Smith sparks hallucinations by regaling the poet with what Ginsberg calls in his marginal commentary *"Smith's Anthropological Gossip"*:

> Natchez, he was saying with his head one side
> > of the center of the wheel
> > > of Vertigo—
> burned babies in the blaze of a fiery house
> > sending them back to the Sun—
> They drank a black elixir, and threw it up

> To have the serpent intertwined
>   in their eyeballs—
> One man was born with genitals all over
>   his body—there were 15,000,000
>   Indians in North America then—
>   The mushroom image in the Spiro Mound
>
>   (277)

Ginsberg illustrates "Journal Night Thoughts" with a drawing by Smith, "Southern Cult Composite: The Staten Island Massacre" (1984; Fig. 11), which incorporates motifs from the poem, such as hands with eyes in their palms and intertwined rattlesnakes. The content that seems especially to fascinate Ginsberg in Smith's bizarre stories is the phallic imagery: the serpent in the eyeballs, the genitals all over the body (fifteen million it seems, because of the way the line breaks), and the mushroom in the mound. This phallic imagery unites the physical genitals with transgressive social rituals and ecstatic mystical experiences.

These images lead up to one taken directly from Smith's animated collage film, *Heaven and Earth Magic*, a print of which Ginsberg had recently purchased because Smith was desperately short of funds (*Self* 4): "Here is the Homunculus wavering in the brain, / the aggregate of ignorant patterns / looking like Denny Dimwit / The genitals are larger than the head" (277; see Fig. 12). Notwithstanding the interest he shared with Ginsberg in the phallic qualities of the alchemical homunculus (the "little man," whose creation often involved the use of human sperm), Smith would never have considered him an "aggregate of ignorant patterns," for such occult patterns were exactly what Smith sought to know. Subsequent to noting the phallic apotheosis induced by Smith's anthropological gossip, Ginsberg returns in the poem to narrating apocalyptic drug scenes, accompanied by paranoid statements such as "I dreamt I had to destroy the human / universe to be Messiah" (278).[4] After a further string of remembered drug visions, Ginsberg falls back finally into the embrace of two of his lifelong erotic obsessions: mother and queer sex. Although he has tolerated a parade of bizarre visions that tested his mental equanimity, the glimpse of "my mother's skull not yet white" is the one threatening vision to which he shouts, "GO / BACK!" (279). Significantly, the poem's final scene follows immediately on this command: a compensatory depiction, in loving detail, of an episode of happy sex, in which, he reports, "I come in the ass of my beloved." After receiving like treatment, Ginsberg

FIGURE 11. Harry Smith, *Southern Cult Composite: The Staten Island Massacre*, 1984, ink, pencil, charcoal on paper, 20 x 15 in. Courtesy of Harry Smith Archives.

FIGURE 12. Harry Smith, Frame still from *Heaven and Earth Magic*, ca. 1957–1962, 66 min., 16 mm, black and white, sound. Courtesy of Harry Smith Archives.

returns to the image of "the eye in the asshole," calling it a mystical "third eye" (279); by doing so he transposes the *ajña cakra*, the clairvoyant third eye in the center of the forehead, downward, thus claiming a visionary power for his anal eroticism. Unlike Smith's forays into esoteric erotic lore, Ginsberg's mystical excursions circle back to his body, his personal experience, and his relationships with others. For Ginsberg, the erotic energy released by drugs and tantric mysticism must be brought back down into the bodily, psychological, interpersonal, and even political realms that Smith's visionary experiences generally skirt.

Grand Collage

Robert Duncan's lifelong exploration of the conjunction of the sexual and the mystical, informed by both hermetic and tantric traditions, makes him a central figure in the postwar creation of an erotic poetics. When Smith lived in Berkeley in the late forties, the Berkeley Poetry Renaissance, whose primary figures were Duncan, Jack Spicer, and Robin Blaser, was in full swing. During that time, Smith and Duncan traveled in a larger circle of filmmakers, poets, and painters in Berkeley and San Francisco, and there is evidence that by 1948 they had met.[5] In their mystical approaches to contextual practice, both figures regard the artist as participating in a larger reality that can be discerned but not controlled. Smith states, "My movies are made by God; I am just the medium for them" (*AM* 2). Duncan, who often described himself as a "derivative" poet, believes the mind is a collage that reflects the larger cultural assemblage: "[O]ur minds are made up of collages. Invented and can be perpetually invented; endlessly new and old juxtapositions re-informing us" ("Taste" 41).[6] By contrast, the two part company, as with Ginsberg and Smith, on the matter of personal psychology and individual experience, which Duncan explores assiduously with the aid of Freudian analysis but Smith approaches only by physiological means—for example, by using drugs for psychological derangement and by calibrating his films to biorhythms. Although they differ with respect to psychology, the most salient similarity between Smith and Duncan is that both were raised in theosophical families; this early training in magical thinking imparted a distinctive direction to their work.[7] The theosophical belief that there is a secret key to the universe hidden in the scriptures and arts of every society sets each of them on an inexorable quest to ascertain connections and correspondences among the images of the world's cultures.

In *The H.D. Book*, his inquiry into the sources of his own conception of poetry, Duncan considers the influence of theosophical notions on modern writers (especially H.D., Ezra Pound, and D. H. Lawrence) and on the domestic world of his family. He recalls as a child hearing voices whisper from another room:

> And in the inner chamber, the adults, talking on, wove for me in my childish overhearing, Egypt, a land of spells and secret knowledge, a background drift of things close to dreaming—spirit communications, reincarnation memories, clairvoyant journeys into a realm of astral phantasy where all times and places were seen in a new light, of Plato's illustrations of the nature of the soul's life, of most real Osiris and Isis, of lost Atlantis and Lemuria. (*H.D. Book* I.5 5)

This hypnagogic overhearing helped ignite an overheated imagination in the young Duncan, who developed the habit of looking for hidden connections among the multifarious phenomena before him. Later, this would enable him to assert that the founder of the Theosophical Society, Helena Petrovna

Blavatsky, evinced in the incredible hodge-podge of her writings an intuitive understanding of how the esoteric and the avant-garde might work together. "In the mess of astrology, alchemy, numerology, magic orders, neo-Platonic, kabbalistic and Vedic systems combined, confused, and explained, queered evolution and wishful geology, transposed heads" (9), Blavatsky discovered, Duncan claims, "the collagist's art" (10). The elements of collage he discerns in Blavatsky (who for her own part insisted that her works were revealed to her in the Astral Records) include a "charged fascination" with the material being composed, an obedience to unknown but compelling feelings, and a new respect for discarded phenomena: "*Isis Unveiled* and *The Secret Doctrine*, midden heaps that they are of unreasonable sources, are midden heaps where, beyond the dictates of reason, as in the collagist's art, from what has been disregarded or fallen into disregard, genres are mixed, exchanges are made, mutations begun from scraps and excerpts from different pictures . . . to form the figures of a new composition" (10). Taking on and eventually refining this compositional method, Duncan advances toward his mature poetics, which he comes to call Grand Collage, a kind of mystical art of assemblage, in which the poet sees hidden correspondences among disparate sources, claiming no originality for his art other than in the finding and arranging of the materials. More than a poetic method, Grand Collage offers Duncan an overarching principle of the imagination: "in this realm of men's languages," he states, Grand Collage proposes "a poetry of all poetries" (*BB* vii).

Duncan's Grand Collage creates a new context by drawing together highly charged artifacts from around the world, from which he seeks to construct the "poetry of all poetries." Like Blavatsky's books, but much more artfully and self-consciously, Duncan's poems are "midden heaps," in which "genres are mixed" and materials extracted not only from acknowledged masterpieces but from "disregarded" or "unreasonable sources," providing "the figures of a new composition," an assemblage that remains constantly in process. In the fifties and sixties, Duncan began two open-ended series of poems, *The Structure of Rime* and *Passages*, which wind through the books he published in the last thirty years of his life; these resolutely incomplete series participate in the essential nature of assemblage, which, to quote Kuspit again, "is based on its incompleteness, on the sense of perpetual becoming that animates it" (Hoffman 43). The ultimate subject of Duncan's "poetry of all poetries," as of the many varieties of Smith's assemblages, is humanity writ large—that is, a vision of the totality of human possibilities: "Mankind that does not come

to an end . . . has become for me the central theme—a Man of all men, mul-
tiphasic, beyond what we can know but central, as we are immediate realities
of Man, to what we are. This was the Adam in whom all the species have their
identity. In the traditions of the Jewish Kabbala this Adam falls apart into
the lives of all men—his identity hidden in our identities" (*FC* 115)—as if this
Adam were the true human being and each of us a tiny homunculus. Such an
erotic poetics, based on a notion of nested levels of reality, carries the implicit
conviction that *anything* human beings are capable of doing or thinking or
saying must be accounted for in the larger picture of what we are, which is
ultimately one species among many. Taking seriously this contextual view of
the Grand Collage of life forms, Duncan proposes the need for a "symposium
of the whole" (*SP* 98)[8]:

> If I seek to picture Man in his multiplicity for myself, and in that multiplic-
> ity to imagine a composition in which goods and evils belong to the order of
> things . . . , it is because I feel the world as creation and what is happening as
> a drama, the processes of the actual world as the deepest drama. The stars,
> the dark depths of space beyond, and the light streaming from the sun, speak
> to us; the earth, the waves and winds, the twittering of birds and the glances
> of animals, speak to us. The fall of a rock, the shifting of sands can be read
> and, in one way of reading, the story of the earth is revealed, in another way
> of reading, elusive apprehensions of our own inner fate or identity in process
> emerge. (*FC* 121–22)

Smith too seems to "feel the world as creation and what is happening as
a drama, the processes of the actual world as the deepest drama," and this
apprehension underlies, for instance, his superimposed films and his ambient audio recordings, in which he composes visual or auditory patterns in a
collage drama beyond individual volition. Notions of assemblage similar to
Duncan's also figure prominently in Smith's conversation, which often takes
the form of reading the world in order to find "elusive apprehensions of . . .
inner fate" and to watch an "identity in process emerge." This sort of contex-
tualist "reading" appears in interviews he gives, during which Smith bounds
from topic to topic without transition. He builds an "identity in process"
by repeated jump-cuts that confront his interlocutor like a series of dares,
as if to say, "I dare you to keep up with the leaps of my mind. I dare you to
pretend to have expert knowledge in the entire range of the topics I draw
together. I dare you to maintain your equanimity and not be confounded by

my outrageousness." Forming a clear picture of Smith and his achievement is so difficult because he conducts himself like Proteus or Taliesin, eluding the grasp of pursuers and interlocutors by constantly shifting shape, a trickster first and foremost. Even the self-deprecatory tone audible in recorded conversations with him sounds like a dodge, as though he were daring his audience *not* to recognize that he has a universal mind.

Smith's parry-and-thrust attitude joins a range of his stylistic attributes, which might be summed up as a blending of the vernacular and the cosmological. Many of the objects Smith collects—folk music, string figures from around the world, paper airplanes from New York City, Ukrainian painted eggs, Seminole patchwork patterns for women's dresses—are funky, downhome, or beneath professional notice, and his penchants for an extravagant cobbling together of rejected materials and for speaking like a teller of tall tales reflect those interests. On the other hand, Smith has a fastidious, meticulous, alchemical side, which accounts for his spending years engaged in cataloging and calibrating the elements of a project; this side of his style produces paintings and films that are symmetrical or otherwise geometrical, numerological, and diagrammatical. In Smith's practice the vernacular and the cosmological share a preference for use value over aesthetic value. Smith's art seeks not to excite critical admiration or to appeal to canons of taste but rather to be efficacious, to make something happen. In that sense, the work is purely iconic rather than expressive; it doesn't make a statement—whether in the form of artistic commentary or political commitment or personal revelation—but rather invites participation. Speaking of his Kiowa peyote recordings, for instance, Smith makes the point that his collecting is all done for iconic purposes:

> When I was in Oklahoma, I realized that it was possible to perform some kind of saturated study of something. It just happened that it was with recordings, although I went there to make films. . . . The Seminole project grew out of that, but I didn't record their music. Then the egg business grew out of the Seminole stuff. . . . The problems that I'd set myself on have to do with correlating music to some kind of a visual thing, into some kind of a diagram. It was much simpler to skip the music entirely and study diagrams that had already been made. . . . I'm sure that if you could collect sufficient patchwork quilts from the same people who made the records, like Uncle Dave Macon or Sara Carter's houses, you could figure out just about anything you can from

the music. Everything could be figured out regarding their judgment in relation to certain intellectual processes. (*Self* 85)

In his films, paintings, collections, and conversations, Smith ties iconic elements together to create previously unsuspected examples in the mode of Duncan's Grand Collage. In series such as the *Passages* poems, Duncan joins Smith not just by way of their mutual interest in assemblage but also through their research in hermetic philosophy and magic, their shamanistic pursuits, their fascination with American Indian lore, their metaphorizing of filmic projection, their depiction of dream landscapes, and their construction of the artist's room as a cave of alchemical creativity. By discussing a 1964 poem from Duncan's *Passages* sequence, "The Architecture, *Passages* 9" (*BB* 26–28), I can suggest how the preoccupations he shares with Smith are woven throughout the sequence. "The Architecture" registers elements of the Victorian house in San Francisco's Mission District that Duncan shared for many years with Jess. The poet acknowledges a long-standing engagement with architecture: "My father had been an architect and, until he died, when I was sixteen, I had been preparing to enter that world. Ideas of architecture still continue in my art today as a poet" (*FC* 112).[9]

The poem begins with a prose quotation from Gustav Stickley's *Craftsman Homes* (1909), a book of architectural plans: ". . . it must have recesses. There is a great charm in a room broken up in plan, where that slight feeling of mystery is given to it which arises when you cannot see the whole room from any one place . . . when there is always something around the corner" (26). For Duncan, the design of the house mirrors the design of the poem. They cannot be laid out in a rationalized, comprehensive fashion but, as an assemblage, must be approached piecemeal and from a variety of angles; both must maintain a sense of incipience, as though "there is always something around the corner." Smith likewise transformed each of the rooms he occupied during his life into a charged, mysterious space, in which the conjunction of objects signified incipient metaphorical relationships. The musician and photographer John Cohen describes one such space, Smith's room at the Chelsea Hotel in 1968:

A visit to his room is a somewhat mystifying experience, for what appears on first impression as orderly piles of books and objects is actually a storehouse for cross-disciplinary investigations of visual, anthropological, and musical phenomena. The closet is filled with women's dresses from the Florida

Seminole Indians. One corner of the room, marked with a "Keep Off" sign, is filled with Ukrainian Easter eggs; on the bureau are stacks of mounted string figures; behind the table is a movie camera alongside portfolios of his paintings and graphic work. In another corner is a clay model of an imaginary landscape which is re-created from a dream. On the walls hang empty frames from which the pictures have been ripped out. . . . Small file cabinets of index cards are distributed between stacks of research books. Each book becomes more exotic by its juxtaposition with other such books—Mayan codices beside Eskimo anthropology studies, under a collection of Peyote ceremonial paintings, et cetera, et cetera. (*Self* 66–67)

Duncan's poem "The Architecture" maps out how an artist's living space such as his own or Smith's instantiates the Grand Collage and becomes a charged locus for contextual practice. The house at 3267 20th Street (Fig. 13) was both a work of assemblage in its own right and a breeding ground for the interpenetrating poetic and visual oeuvres that Duncan and Jess created. In a retrospective catalog entitled *Jess: A Grand Collage 1951–1993*, Michael Auping asserts that "the association between Jess and Duncan is itself a collage that extends beyond Duncan's poetry or Jess's art to an interactive collage encompassing the house they inhabited, itself symbolic of the products of their combined imaginations" (39). The house not only held Duncan's extensive library and classical record collection and Jess's studio but was packed with works of art on every surface imaginable; Jess even made cut-outs in one wall to carry fragments of a stained glass window patterned with poppies that had been broken before they moved in. Many of the art pieces on display inside the house consisted of the assemblages ("Assemblies") and elaborate black-and-white collages ("Paste-Ups") that form two of the main series pursued by Jess for many years. The presence of these objects drew attention to the dizzyingly elaborate contextual art that obtained throughout the Victorian house with an Arts and Crafts interior. Describing Jess's working environment, Auping characterizes the house and studio as "a warehouse of surplus imagination and a dense accumulation of symbolic fragments that are continually being added to and collaged together as a constant reinvention of a self" (14–15).[10]

In "The Architecture," after the extract from Stickley, Duncan presents himself as looking out "from the window-shelter" (an important element of Stickley's Craftsman design) while listening to Bertolt Brecht and Kurt Weill's *Mahagonny*—the basis, coincidentally, of one of Smith's major cinematic projects. From his vantage point in the window seat, Duncan sees a series of symbolic objects with which Smith would have felt right at home:

from the bookcases   the glimmering titles arrayed   keys
Hesiod • Heraklitus • *The Secret Books of the Egyptian Gnostics . . .*

La Révélation d'Hermès Trismégiste
Plutarch's Morals: Theosophical Essays
Avicenna
The Zohar
The Aurora

(26–27)

FIGURE 13. Ben Blackwell, "3267 20th Street, house of Robert Duncan and Jess." Used by permission.

These "keys" make up a selection of esoteric texts from the theosophical tradition in which Duncan and Smith were raised. The texts—which he presents himself as "reading while the music playd / curld up among the ornamental cusions"—proffer correspondences between different levels of reality and thus model for Duncan the metaphorical connections he explores in his poetry. Similar hermetic "keys" are in the foreground of one of Jess's most striking portraits of Duncan, *The Enamord Mage: Translation #6* (1965), now in the de Young Museum in San Francisco (Fig. 14). Employing a multicolored but somewhat muddy palette and seemingly random areas of remarkably thick impasto, the painting "translates" a 1958 black-and-white photograph of Duncan seated at a desk. The shape of the poet's head in the upper left quadrant is balanced in the lower right quadrant by a block of eight books, consisting of *Thrice Greatest Hermes* (two volumes), *Pistis Sophia,* and the

FIGURE 14. Jess, *The Enamord Mage: Translation #6,* 1965, oil on canvas mounted on wood, 24–1/2 x 30 in. © 2009 The Jess Collins Trust. Used by permission. Collection: de Young Museum, San Francisco. Photo: Ben Blackwell.

Soncino Press edition of *The Zohar* in five volumes.[11] In the poem, Duncan intercuts the invocation of a theosophical reading scene with quotations from Stickley, thereby drawing attention to symbolic elements in Arts and Crafts architecture. By one passage he cites, for instance, Duncan hints at an occult significance to the staircase: "the staircase, instead of being hidden away in a small hall or treated as a necessary evil, made one of the most beautiful and prominent features of the room because it forms a link between the social part of the house and the upper regions" (27). If we take the phrase "upper regions" in a metaphysical sense, then the excerpt discloses an architecture in which a staircase becomes a Jacob's Ladder, a shamanic device for climbing out of the mundane realm and into the visionary.

Like Smith, who began making audio recordings of American Indian ceremonies as a teenager, Duncan had been fascinated by shamanism as early as the period 1939–1941, when he undertook an ambitious project in prose poetry that he called "Toward the Shaman."[12] Alluding in "The Architecture" to the visionary world of the Indians, he includes in the closing section two quotations from the ethnologist Truman Michelson's *The Owl Sacred Pack of the Fox Indians* (1921), which report conversations between Owl and his shamans regarding a medicine kit Owl gives to human beings. In the first, Owl says of the pack, "'You are to make it,' I told you in the past. I do not suppose you recognize me. 'Owl' is what I am calld. This is how I am'" (27).[13] At this point, Duncan's collage poem has an implied narrative: through his reading the poet has climbed the mystical stairs and had a shamanistic encounter with the Owl spirit. Not coincidentally, the owl was Duncan's chosen totem animal, emblematic of a disability that kept his two eyes from focusing on the same object, which earned him the epithet "owl-eyed." In the context of this poem, recognizing Owl constitutes self-recognition: "*I do not suppose you recognize me*," queries Owl. "Oh, yes I do!" we can imagine Duncan replying. After 1955, when he wrote the poem "An Owl Is an Only Bird of Poetry" (Allen 41–44), Duncan's house began to fill with owl images sent by friends, so that the owl became not only an uncannily strange presence but a most familiar one. The owl's paradoxical familiarity and strangeness symbolizes a tension maintained throughout the *Passages* series between the domestic and the visionary. Moreover, in "The Architecture," the act of reading stands on the threshold between these two realms as a necessary creative process for bridging them. The concluding section of the poem portrays the liminal process of reading as a form of projection both cinematic and psychological. "The Architecture" ends with an image of the printed page as a movie screen on which lamplight shines, seducing the poet into its narrative:

> Phantastes, At the Back of the North Wind,
>   The Princess and the Goblin,
>   The Princess and Curdie,   Lilith
>
> the lamplight   warm   upon the page where I ·
>   romance · in which lost, reading ·
>
> "   *You will often tell the story. If you do that you*
> *will be able to marry those you love. You will fear*
> *me. If I even see you, you will die.*"
>
> . . . "which belong to the inner and individual part of the family life."
>
>   (28)

In these final segments, Duncan draws together the domestic scene of the poet reading works by George MacDonald (the nineteenth-century fantasist), the shamanic vision of Owl, and the final clause of the sentence quoted from Stickley about the staircase as a link between the "social part" and the "upper regions." The juxtapositions make evident Duncan's profound attachment to the personal and the psychological, which differentiates him from Smith. In addition, by presenting the vision of Owl as a projection on the white screen of a page, Duncan equates the "romance" of reading—a domestic pleasure that occurs in a safe, cozy, enveloping space—with the romance of cinema. Like Smith, Duncan believes in the visionary potential of cinema, which accounts for his lasting friendships with underground filmmakers such as Stan Brakhage, Kenneth Anger, Larry Jordan, James Broughton, and Bruce Conner. As it does for these filmmakers, the domestic world becomes for Duncan the ground from which oneiric flights to higher realms take off. Although cinema's oneiric quality has been remarked on from its beginnings, one particular film, Hans Richter's *Dreams That Money Can Buy* (1947), makes the equation of dreams and cinema explicit, and it became in turn an inspiration to postwar avant-garde filmmakers. With dream sequences designed by Man Ray, Max Ernst, Marcel Duchamp, Fernand Léger, Alexander Calder, and Richter himself, the film brought art installations directly into cinema. Maintaining a central conceit of an analyst figure who sells dream visions to neurotic patients, the film encompasses the same interplay of cinema, dreams, and psychoanalysis that fascinated and provoked Duncan. In his working method, Smith too explores and exploits the oneiric quality of film: not only does he claim that for years during the composing of *Heaven and Earth Magic* he would waken himself after a few hours of sleep and transfer to film what had transpired in his dreams, but he also states that the most effective way to enter fully into his monumental film *Mahagonny* is to fall asleep while viewing it.[14]

Reflecting on his home with Jess as a place of permission that encourages a concatenation of the romance of oneiric reading, the shamanistic flight, and "the inner and individual part of the family life," Duncan affirms, "The household Jess and I made I have seen as a lone holding in an alien forest-world, as a campfire about which we gathered in an era of cold and night—a made-up thing in which participating we have had the medium of a life together" (Bertholf, "Concert" 80). For gay marriage partners making a home during the Cold War, the world outside held much that was bitter and benighted. Beyond the unmistakable dangers posed for these men by a hostile social reality, though, an encounter with extraordinary beings such as Owl or his shaman would be fraught with danger for anyone: "If I even see you," the shaman says, "you will die."[15] Against such a threat, Duncan relies upon the ballast of the domestic to ground his artistic flight. Ultimately, however, he knows that danger can never be banished from the psyche, for the encounter with thanatos is a central reality of the Freudian world that haunts Duncan's poetry: the danger that what you see may kill you must belong also to "the inner and individual part of the family life." For the most part, Smith eschewed "family life," giving the impression that, for all his burrowing like a pack rat into the apartments in which he resided, he possessed no sense of the domestic whatsoever. Lacking an interest in cultivating the protective warmth that Duncan figures as "a campfire about which we gathered in an era of cold and night," Smith left himself constantly exposed to winds from Outside.

"The Big Lie of the Personal"

A visionary practitioner of contextual art with a sensibility close to that of Harry Smith, Jack Spicer was a poet who despised the intrusion of the personal into art and who claimed to receive his poetry as dictation from "Outside."[16] Like Duncan, Spicer was born in California and was a central figure in the Berkeley Poetry Renaissance of the late forties and the San Francisco Renaissance of the fifties and sixties. In a career that spanned merely twenty years,

Spicer wrote the influential serial poems brought together as *The Collected Books of Jack Spicer* (1975) and developed an original theory of poetic composition. Within his poetic oeuvre, Spicer's obsession with American folk music runs as a leitmotif. Inveterate collectors, Spicer and Smith combed Bay Area record stores together, and in 1949 Smith appeared on Spicer's "Most Educational Folk-Song Program West of the Pecos," aired over the new Pacifica radio station, KPFA.[17] Like Smith, Spicer eagerly sought to alter the mental states of his friends, making them drunk ahead of appearing on his broadcast in hopes of inducing them to improvise bawdy verses for old folk songs over the air—thus illustrating his contention that an "authentic" folk song can be adapted to any context (Herndon 375). Kevin Killian, Spicer's biographer, points out that Spicer's penchant for folk song parody harks back to his days with Allan Sherman at Fairfax High School in Los Angeles. Sherman created the long-running television game show "I've Got a Secret" in the fifties, and in the sixties he released LPs of updated folk songs and parodies, beginning with *My Son the Folksinger* (1962) and culminating in the hit, "Hello Muddah, Hello Faddah (A Letter from Camp)" (Killian 1).

Rather than imitate Sherman's Jewish *shtick* by fashioning "ethnic" versions of popular folk songs, Spicer appropriates folk material into his poetry as a means of reaching his primary goal of effacing the poet's ego. Peter Gizzi points out that Spicer

> uses almost exclusively a populist, often folkloric, and widely accessible vocabulary and frames of reference: ghost stories, murder mysteries, baseball, Martians, romantic love, popular outlaw heroes like Billy the Kid and Joe Hill, and war stories. . . . And here Spicer's initial attraction to Lorca as a Virgil-esque poetic predecessor is clear: they share a fascination with the folkloric, not only as an "authentic" texture in their work but as a sophisticated model of intertextuality. (181)[18]

In this sense, Spicer joins Smith and Reznikoff in drawing seemingly "anonymous" folk elements into a sophisticated assemblage that creates a radical critique by causing the author's voice to dissolve into the act of composition. Like Duncan and Smith, Spicer counters notions of genius and originality by claiming that he is a conduit rather than a creator. He and Duncan conceive of intertextuality in slightly different ways, though; Duncan sees himself as a "derivative" poet occupying an interpersonal "field" of poetry, while Spicer believes that his poetry is a form of dictation from "Beyond." In a theory that

likely would satisfy Smith, Spicer conceives of the poet's primary job as pushing the personality aside to allow what is Outside to speak through.

In the course of four lectures he gave in Vancouver and Berkeley in 1965,
the year of his death, Spicer develops a set of analogies to illustrate a theory
of impersonal poetry to which he subscribes. He begins by recounting the
famous story of the genesis of W. B. Yeats's *A Vision*: as Spicer tells it, riding
on a train between San Bernardino and Los Angeles in 1918, Yeats found his
new wife falling into a trance and beginning to channel voices. Yeats "finally
decided he'd ask a question or two of the spooks as Georgie was in her trance.
And he asked a rather good question. He asked, 'What are you here for?' And
the spooks replied, 'We're here to give metaphors for your poetry'" (Gizzi
5). A second analogy that Spicer develops for an impersonal poetry involves
Jean Cocteau's film *Orphée* (1950), in which a modern poet, Orpheus, receives
and publishes under his own name poems dictated over the car radio by a
dead poet. Finally, to emphasize that the source of an authentic poem is completely from the Outside, Spicer characterizes his poetry as written by Mar-
tians. Using these three analogies for a poetics of dictation, Spicer advocates a
wholly impersonal visionary art, which contrasts strongly with the emotionally vulnerable art of Ginsberg. Cognizant of this difference, Ginsberg speaks
warily of their interaction:

> He was friendly toward me, but held a different vision of poetry. I think he
> had a thing that has nothing to do with Ego, messages come through the radio
> stations of the mind, so to speak, whereas I was thinking of the spontane-
> ous mind. . . . But at any rate I think he thought that my own method was
> much too involved with personal statement and ego: it's a legitimate objec-
> tion. (Ellingham and Killian 58)

While admitting a conflict in their stances toward the personal, Ginsberg
doesn't feel that their contextual practices are "actually very different in operation: as a practical matter of composition" (58) they both bring obsessive interests into poems marked by unanticipated juxtapositions. Although Spicer
would disagree that their methods are similar, he admits the inevitability of
leaving his own signature on a poem. Unlike Blavatsky, he doesn't claim that
words and images in his writing are unknown to him, but he does feel the
need to explain the apparent paradox that poems dictated from Outside still
sound recognizably like Jack Spicer. In a way that might have intrigued Smith,
he imagines art as occurring inside a memory theater, within which the spirit

of the poem (which comes from Outside) arranges all the words and knowledge the poet has gathered like so much "furniture." Once the furniture has
been collected, the poet cedes the space of the poem to what is Outside: "given
the cooperation between the host poet and the visitor—the thing from Outside—the more things you have in the room the better if you can handle them
in such a way that you don't impose your will on what is coming through."
Most poets, however, "can't resist, if they have all of these benches and chairs
in the room, not to arrange them themselves instead of letting them be ar-
ranged by whatever is the source of the poem" (Gizzi 9).

The theory that the source of the poem arrives from elsewhere to arrange
a series of objects bears a remarkable similarity to the compositional principle
at work in Smith's collections and artworks. Both artists hold that each passing moment creates its own context, which links composition to divination
as the age-old attempt to read the moment's imprint on an array of objects.[19]
Divination appealed strongly to Smith and Spicer, particularly in the form of
reading tarot cards. Smith created an entire deck of irregularly shaped cards
(*AM* 9) and wrote an unpublished series of poems about the cards, "Evensongs of Exstasy" (1977)[20]. Spicer outlined a book to write that would be entitled "Understanding Tarot Cards: A Short Manual on the Use of Tarot Cards
for Predicting the Future and Clarifying the Past." In Spicer's outline, a section of the book called "The Poetry of Chance" would offer a quasi-scientific
explanation for the efficacy of tarot divination "in terms of the difference
between randomness and nonsense in statistical theory" (Spicer, "Tarot" 27).
More important, Spicer advocates an approach to the cards that ties divination to contextual practice; his promised description of the deck would stress
"strongly the fact that the individual card has no meaning solely in itself but
only in relation to the cards around it and its position in the layout—exact
analogy to words in a poem." Like the poetics of dictation, tarot reading gives
meaning to a series of objects by virtue of their arrangement in the assemblage of a particular moment. For Spicer, words in a poem and poems in a
book acquire context by a serial rather than a narrative or thematic arrangement. As with Smith, pattern is paramount.

The poetics of dictation leads Spicer to compose assemblages quite different from Duncan's Grand Collage. If the Grand Collage describes a "poetry
of all poetries," Spicer's poetry resembles a collection of real objects such as
those Smith assembles. In his first serial book, *After Lorca* (1957), Spicer presents a set of poems, purportedly by Federico García Lorca, as "real objects."

These objects consist of translations and transformations of poems by Lorca, poems by Spicer posing as translations from Lorca, letters to Lorca, and an introduction written by the already dead poet.[21] The apocryphal quality of this book might intrigue Smith, as would the instructions for turning collections of objects into works of art in one of the letters to Lorca:

> Dear Lorca,
>
> I would like to make poems out of real objects. The lemon to be a lemon that the reader could cut or squeeze or taste—a real lemon like a newspaper in a collage is a real newspaper. I would like the moon in my poems to be a real moon, one which could be suddenly covered with a cloud that has nothing to do with the poem—a moon utterly independent of images. The imagination pictures the real. I would like to point to the real, disclose it, to make a poem that has no sound in it but the pointing of a finger. . . . [22]
>
> Things do not connect; they correspond. That is what makes it possible for a poet to translate real objects, to bring them across language as easily as he can bring them across time . . . every place and every time has a real object to *correspond* with your real object—that lemon may become this lemon, or it may even become this piece of seaweed, or this particular color of gray in this ocean. One does not need to imagine that lemon; one needs to discover it. (*CPJS* 133–34)

The concepts in this "letter" resonate harmoniously with many of Smith's principles. At base both Spicer and Smith employ an alchemical logic, believing they can affect the world by manipulating correspondences. They counsel the artist to avoid what Spicer calls "the big lie of the personal" (150) and engage objects found in the actual world, thereby making patterns and correspondences visible. In a Smith-like tone of oracular contrariety, Spicer claims in the letter to create a work of art that will dissolve into the gesture of disclosing the meaningful nature of what occurs moment by moment. Imbibing alcohol in quantities similar to the quantities of drugs and alcohol ingested by Smith, Spicer likewise invites a derangement that will make his contextual art attentive to what comes from Outside human control. Neither one cares at all for the imagination; the goal is to reveal correspondences among objects while performing a Zen disappearing act, in which the finger that points out the patterns that make up the real can vanish—leaving only the quivering lemon.

In a period of "heroic" personal expression in the arts, dominated by gesture and confession and the aching desire to concoct a personality, Smith and

Spicer—two difficult, learned, hermetic figures—move in a direction counter to many of their peers. Rather than project an identity, they seek to so hone their creative capacities as to disappear wholly into their work, thus leaving readers, viewers, or auditors equipped to see more than they had before encountering it. This ego-dissolving stance can be seen as one pole of a continuum that tracks visionary art from the confessional dreams and pleas of Ginsberg to the Grand Collage of Duncan, in which the individual mirrors the cosmos, and on to the impersonal dictation informing Spicer's books of poetry. The multifarious oeuvre of Smith provides a signal reference point for this entire range of stances and also for some of the ways in which assemblage has moved beyond the status of a formal principle and become a means of conducting life. Smith's restless, anarchic, polymathic creativity represents one of the salient examples of bringing into contextual practice an erotic poetics from the West Coast. Like Cage—whose upbringing and first work were on the West Coast—and like Ginsberg, Kerouac, and Creeley—all of whom had significant aesthetic breakthroughs while living there—Smith brought the anarchic and mystical qualities of West Coast culture into his highly original and influential assemblage projects. The standard critical bias toward the East Coast as cultural fountainhead has served to obscure the impact of West Coast aesthetic innovations on the explosive social movements of the sixties and seventies, whose residual consequences remain with us still.[23]

5

SURREALISM AND KABBALAH
IN SEMINA CULTURE
Wallace Berman Cultivates the Erotic
in California Poetry and Art

In "Spicer and the Practice of Reading," Peter Gizzi gives an extended comparison of Jack Spicer's constructivist poetic practice to that of the California
assemblage movement of the fifties and sixties, which was also known as Junk
or Funk Art. Invoking artists such as Wallace Berman, Bruce Conner, and
George Herms, Gizzi argues, "Seeing Spicer as an assemblage artist further
clarifies his program of dictation as composition. Within his constructivist
aesthetic, to insist on originality or newness in a poem is as absurd as to insist
that every object in an assemblage be made from scratch by the artist." Like
Kuspit, Gizzi draws attention to assemblage as an art of becoming, in which
the found material lives on in unforeseen ways: "Assemblage offers a way to
understand Spicer's insistence on poetic renovation, since assemblage itself
represents an ultimate posthumous life of objects, a place both within and
outside the dominant culture." In this sense, Spicer's poetry represents a kind
of secular monument, like Rodia's *Watts Towers*; "the absence of salvation in
Spicer's poetry makes room for a kind of salvage yard of lost songs and stories"
(Gizzi 225). Like many of the California poets and artists of the period, Spicer
reveled in a "salvage yard" that yielded both art materials and the means for
sustaining anarchic communities living on the fringes of society. Speaking of
these "artists of the survival" (*RB* 169) in a prose poem, Robert Duncan dedicates the poem to Shirley and Wallace Berman, who dwelt at the heart of the
California salvage yard that has come to be called "Semina Culture" (Duncan
and McKenna 9–15).

A pioneering California artist of the postwar era, Berman (1926–1976) was born in New York and grew up in Fairfax, the Jewish district of Los Angeles. As a zoot-suited high school student he was expelled for gambling and then became a fixture in the dynamic L.A. jazz scene. Although his first precocious pencil drawings graced the covers of jazz albums, he gravitated toward collage and assemblage, becoming one of the primary California practitioners of contextual art. Severely shaken when his first public exhibition, in 1957 at the legendary Ferus Gallery (Fig. 15), was deemed obscene and closed down, Berman moved to Northern California and helped launch the countercultural revolution in the arts that fostered communal living, anarchist politics, occult research, drug exploration, and sexual display.[1] One of the leading expressions of this communal artistic practice was the journal *Semina* (1955–1964; Fig. 16), which Berman printed on loose-leaf cards, stuffed into decorated envelopes, and mailed off to friends. *Semina* ran for nine issues as a contemporary "museum without walls," combining Berman's photos and collages with reproductions of work by other California artists and filmmakers and with an equal representation of poetry, mostly by California writers. Beginning with *Semina 7* (1961), the only issue devoted entirely to his own work, Berman's art became progressively more dominated by Hebrew lettering. His most well-known works, for instance, are the series of kabbalistically flavored collage-facsimiles, made up of multiple iterations of a hand holding a transistor radio, with each version of the radio face housing an occult, mundane, or erotic image. One of the indispensable artistic instigators of the hippie movement, Berman himself became an icon, appearing both in the collage on the cover of the Beatles album *Sgt. Pepper's Lonely Heart's Club Band* (1967) and as a communal farmer in his friend Dennis Hopper's film *Easy Rider* (1969).

Semina occupies a legendary place within the California art world as *the* club for those in the know. An experiment in private, improvised art distributed among friends, *Semina* can be compared to the fascicles and letters of Emily Dickinson a century earlier; both Dickinson and Berman sought through their hand-made, private creations—often sent out as "mail art"—to coalesce a community that was at odds with the official world. Within the charmed circle of the *Semina* coterie, distinctions between literature and art collapsed; poets drew and made collages, and artists and filmmakers wrote poems. Speaking for Berman, his wife Shirley asserts that he published *Semina* "because he loved poetry so much" (Starr 81). "We spent a lot of time reading poetry," she recalls, insisting that poetry was a more fecund source

FIGURE 15. Charles Brittin, "Wallace Berman at Ferus Gallery," 1957. Charles Brittin Archive, Research Library, The Getty Research Institute. Used with permission. (2005.M.11)

FIGURE 16. Wallace Berman, *Semina*, 1955–1964, hand-printed magazine. Courtesy L.A. Louver, Venice, CA.

of inspiration for Berman than two other art forms he adored, music and film; "His working process was to read poetry, all the new young poets" (70). By reading seriously California poets such as Robert Alexander, David Meltzer, Michael McClure, Robert Duncan, John Wieners, Philip Lamantia, Jack Hirschman, Bob Kaufman, Ray Bremser, and Kirby Doyle, Berman gained entrée into myriad modern and occult literary ideas and forms. In fact, his poetic explorations opened up fields of experience and experiment that took

Berman beyond what he was learning from the visual artists who congregated around him. In particular, the poets joined him in a lifelong fascination with surrealist writers and intermedia figures such as Jean Cocteau and Antonin Artaud. Shirley attests that the extended surrealist literary tradition gave Berman more instruction than did surrealist painting: "He was really more involved with [surrealist] poetry than he was with the artists—Baudelaire, Rimbaud, Mallarmé, and Cocteau" (70).[2]

Like two of the poets central to the San Francisco Renaissance, Duncan and Spicer, Berman admired Cocteau "as a Renaissance man, because he did so many different things" (70). This model of the artist whose work extends into a number of media and ultimately into an aesthetic approach to life had another exemplar in Artaud, who was renowned as both writer and psychic pioneer. Shirley affirms that Wallace "did love Artaud," and the Frenchman provoked an unquenchable fascination in many of the other *Semina* figures. Berman also joined the California poets and filmmakers for whom surrealism was a major preoccupation by undertaking a variety of occult investigations. Ultimately, these investigations flowered for Berman in the kabbalistic conjuring with Hebrew letters that became the signature of his visual art. In concert with Berman, the poets Duncan, Meltzer, and Hirschman all made Kabbalah a central feature of their artistic and spiritual practice. For poets and artists in the *Semina* context, their engagement with surrealism and Kabbalah resulted in an erotic poetics that extended contextual practice out from artistic circles and into the anarchist communities that sprouted like mushrooms in the California sixties.

California Context

In a time when the idea of performance art has become so ingrained in how we conceive of culture that an entire popular genre, reality TV, has emerged that is based on the premise of life and art being indistinguishable, it is not surprising that artistic figures hitherto confined to the margins of Beat culture such as Wallace Berman and Harry Smith—figures who consistently blurred the boundaries between life and art—have come to exert an irresistible fascination. It could be argued that Berman and Smith were early practitioners of postmodernism, staking a claim to aesthetic innovation by perspicaciously appropriating and arranging existing artifacts rather than by creating original masterworks. In actuality, though, the essence of their influence derives not so much from new appropriationist techniques as from personal magnetism—from what they thought, what they did, their attitude toward art and life, and their uncanny ability to shine a new light on events happening around them. Resolutely anticommercial, unconcerned with producing enduring artifacts for collection, Berman and Smith acquired the aura of living works of art; their presence and example likewise inspired creativity in others. Latter-day shamanic figures, they shared an erotic poetics with a number of common features: they refused to live their lives conforming to institutional norms or expectations, they made the conduct of life itself an ongoing artistic composition, they so conflated art and a hermetic spirituality that it's impossible to say which was the dominant factor in their work, they engaged in an all-consuming artistic and spiritual quest, and their personalities exerted an uncanny magnetism on other people.

In direct opposition to how the mind-numbing voyeurism of reality TV reduces the unpredictable personal forays of performance art to a media-manufactured spectacle, the contextual practice of Berman and Smith thrived on a productive secrecy. They shunned publicity and promoted the formation of self-contained, countercultural communities. This creative ability to draw "a new circle" (as Emerson puts it in his essay "Circles," 401), to see new possibilities and thus invoke a new context for a group of people, a group of ideas, or a group of objects, made them contextual pioneers. Just as Smith drew a new circle around the scattered remains of "race" and hillbilly music, creating not a folkloristic compendium but an endlessly mysterious assemblage of songs that speak to one another and cry out for participatory interpretation by listeners and later performers, Berman made the loose-leaf *Semina* a unique and instantly revisable artistic context, in which words and visual artifacts have equal priority—so that instead of the visual illustrating the literary, or vice versa, all of the artworks in each issue draw the viewer/reader into an aesthetic, spiritual, and often political context that solicits participation.

Through his mastery of the art of context, Berman became a distinct innovator in what must be seen as a broad cultural shift, one that has foundations in the phenomenological orientation of Romanticism. In the ensuing two centuries, as I have argued, changing modes of perception and cognition have given rise to an aesthetic approach to life, such that life can now be lived and understood as if it were an artistic composition. In the largest sense, this new practice of taking art as a model for the conduct of life is a symptom of the breakdown of traditional values in Western culture, especially those sanctioned by organized religion. The substitution of artistic for religious frames around lived experience took on a particular cast at midcentury on the West Coast, joining an abiding aesthetic combination of avant-garde provocation with esoteric philosophy and anarchist politics. This aesthetic stance has been quite potent in West Coast culture over the past half-century, inspiring in various ways large social movements as diverse as the Beats, the hippies, Punk, and New Age spirituality.[3] As was pointed out earlier, John Cage, a native Californian, brought this avant-garde, occult, and anarchist mix to New York, combining the "perennial philosophy" cooked up by Aldous Huxley and Christopher Isherwood in California with the Zen sensibility of D. T. Suzuki and the antiart aesthetic pioneered by Marcel Duchamp. Insisting that art and life should be ever more closely intertwined, Cage expanded what was largely a California impetus into a gigantic force within the world of art, both nationally and internationally. Although Cage and Smith gained renown after moving to New York City, it is important to remember that both grew up in a West Coast intellectual milieu saturated in mystical philosophies such as Theosophy, spiritualism, and Vedanta, a milieu that was also fertile soil for political movements such as anarchism and anarcho-syndicalism.

Wallace Berman occupies a place at the center of the midcentury California aesthetic because of the vital context he created for the flourishing of that aesthetic, a context he named "Semina." Semina is best conceived as an open-ended, traveling exhibition that manifested in a variety of forms: as nine sets of printed cards sent out to friends over a period of nine years; as installations of visual art and poetry organized by Berman in a number of physical spaces (for example, there was a "Semina Gallery"); as a nexus of mail art produced by many hands; and, more broadly, as a principle of association among people, objects, artworks, photographs, texts, experiences, and ideas. In other words, Semina is the name of an aesthetic context that generated a way of life. "From the first," notes Duncan, "the intent of *Semina* was not a choice of poems and art works to exercise the editor's discrimination and aesthetic judgment, but the fashioning of a context." Taking cues from the earlier movements of Dada and surrealism, Berman assembled a context that was at once aesthetic and existential, an outlaw project that sought escape from prevailing social and political norms. Declaring himself part of that context, Duncan claims that "in our conscious alliance with the critical breakthru of Dada and Surrealism . . . , we began to see ourselves as fashioning unnamed contexts, contexts of a new life way in the making, a secret mission" (*SP* 198).

If Semina is the name of a context that encompasses "a new life way" and "a secret mission," then it must be regarded as much more than the name of an artistic and literary magazine. Entering the Semina context involved dedicating oneself to an erotic poetics (in which aesthetic values become the basis for life decisions) and to the secret mission of overthrowing the mundane reality of the fifties and early sixties, substituting a transgressive, ecstatic mode of life. In her book depicting the Semina context, Rebecca Solnit takes for her title George Herms's *Secret Exhibition* (1957), an outdoor installation of assemblages viewed only by fellow artists Berman and John Reed. From Solnit's perspective, this secret exhibition symbolizes the values and strategies of the entire movement: "For them the making of art was an end in itself, a spiritual exercise, because there was no market or showcase for the result. Many works were made as gifts with a particular recipient in mind, but many more were made in the same spirit as jazz—for the joy of creation itself" (15–16).[4] This secret mission of Semina can be seen as a Beat project, and so Semina has been placed alongside other Beat activities in exhibitions such as *Forty Years of California Assemblage* (Ayres) in 1989 and *Beat Culture and the New America: 1950–1965* (Philips) in 1995. While participating in the larger currents of Beat culture, though, Semina's distinctive union of art and life took its own path through those currents, drawn less toward the quietism associated with Buddhism and more toward the provocation associated with surrealism. Semina was inspired especially by three aspects of surrealism: by works that depict a life lived according to aesthetic principles (such as André Breton's novel *Nadja*), by the interwoven artworks and lifestyles of fringe surrealist figures such as Artaud and Cocteau, and by the long French avant-garde tradition of aesthetic rebellion as a way of life. In the sense in which the Semina group understood it, surrealism also contained Dada. Berman's closest friend, Robert Alexander, testifies to the eye-opening journey back from surrealism to Dada that he and Berman undertook around 1949 or 1950: "Dada set us free. After Dada, everything else around us opened up. Everything blossomed like a flower, because we knew we could do anything. That made every creative act that said something a piece of art. You don't need a license anymore. You don't have to be a part of this school or that school. We got stuck in Dada for quite a while, Wally and I did" (Starr 65). Growing out of Dada and surrealist experiments with drugs, dreams, madness, and sexual transgression, Semina ultimately became the first hippie context, in which expanded perception and sexual display were celebrated as aesthetic achievements in their own right.

Although drugs and sex were stimulants for the Semina breakthrough, the major artistic vehicle for expanded perception and bodily display was collage. In this sense, too, Semina harks back to Dada and surrealism; just as collage had been used by those movements to generate iconoclastic, antireal actions that would, at the same time, coalesce into an artistic movement, so it was used by Semina as the basis for a new, transgressive social and artistic context (Duncan, *SP*).[5] Collage was practiced by Semina artists in their mail art, in sculptural works of assemblage, and in the assemblage of *Semina* itself. A groundbreaking exhibition, *Semina Culture: Wallace Berman and His Circle* (2005–2007), curated by Michael Duncan and Kristine McKenna, reveals for the first time how everyone in the Semina circle—including the poets—made collages and assemblages as part of an overall contextual practice. David Meltzer, another poet central to Semina, puts his finger on the contribution of a Harry Smith-like contextual practice to the new modes of awareness the group cultivated: "The Bermans attached themselves to the mysterious quality intrinsic in many things. Any object could be transformed into something of great interest; it was a matter of placing it in the right context. Wallace would say something was 'strange' or 'weird,' in that re-ordered perception, and by looking at it with greater intensity or assumption it would take on a new meaning" (Meltzer, "Door" 100). Berman and others in the Semina cohort—including artists who worked in collage and assemblage (such as George Herms, Jess, Bruce Conner, Joan Brown, Edward Kienholz, and Dennis Hopper) and poets with a surreal bent (such as Duncan, Lamantia, Meltzer, McClure, Hirschman, Wieners, Kaufman, and Ginsberg)—employed a contextual practice to bring "new meaning" to a mundane reality lived amid the detritus of California urban existence. In their affinity for surrealism, the Semina group, both poets and visual artists, entered the stream of what Kenneth Rexroth called "the international avant-garde," transposing the breakthroughs of European surrealism to the California milieu.[6]

With Artaud in Mexico

Antonin Artaud, poet, actor, theater revolutionary, and madman, was one of the renegade surrealists whose concepts and practices proved instrumental to Berman and the Semina poets. In particular, texts by Artaud that gained early translation, "To Have Done with the Judgment of God" and "Concerning a Journey to the Land of the Tarahumaras," became touchstones for the Semina group (Duncan, *SP*). As a young man, Artaud proclaimed, "Where others want to produce works of art, I aspire to no more than display my own spirit. . . . I cannot conceive of a work of art as distinct from life" (Esslin 5). After his death in 1948, Artaud assumed a role as international icon of the aspiration to live life as a continuous experimental performance; his influence on theater and performance art has been incalculable. One of Artaud's experiments that greatly impressed the Semina group was a trek to Northern Mexico for the purpose of ingesting peyote with the Tarahumara Indians. Artaud's 1936 report of his "Journey"—like Aldous Huxley's 1954 chronicle of mescaline experiments, *The Doors of Perception*—is one of the first modern depictions of psychedelic experience. Berman's friend, the artist and hermeticist Cameron (Marjorie Cameron Parsons Kimmel, 1922–1995), took peyote for the first time in 1954 after hearing Huxley speak. Her peyote session resulted in the "allegorical" drawing of sex between two kneeling nudes that was responsible for Berman's arrest and the closing of his Ferus Gallery exhibition (Starr 77–78; see Fig. 1).[7]

For many in the Semina group, Artaud's advocacy of peyote had a profound effect. Over and above the extensive influence of his "theater of cruelty," which emphasizes spectacle, bodily danger, and personal and social transformation, Artaud inspired imitation by describing graphically the effects of peyote and by invoking Mexico as a magical and forbidden realm. In an essay titled "Artaud: Peace Chief," Michael McClure hails Artaud as "more than a man of literature," adding, "He has turned his body into an instrument of science and become a being of history" (McClure, *Meat* 77). McClure found occasion to turn his own body into such an instrument early in 1958, when Berman left off five peyote buttons at his apartment (Cándida Smith, *Utopia* 247; Solnit 69). The morning after, McClure wrote "Peyote Poem," which Berman then printed as a single long sheet and made the sole contents of *Semina 3*, graced on its cover by a photo of two large peyote buttons. The poem depicts the ecstasy of expanded consciousness, in which an *I* witnesses itself intersecting with an external world in ways both fantastic and fleshly:

> I am separate. I close my eyes in divinity and pain.
>   I blink in solemnity and unsolemn joy.
> I smile at myself in my movements. Walking
>   I step higher in my carefulness. I fill
> space with myself. I see the secret and distinct

> patterns of smoke from my mouth
> I am without care part of all. Distinct.
> I am separate from gloom and beauty. I see all.

In certain ways, this report of McClure's echoes the famous visionary experience of becoming a "transparent eye-ball" that Emerson reports in his
essay *Nature*: "I am nothing; I see all; the currents of Universal Being circu-
late through me; I am part or particle of God" (10). Despite the similarity of
language used in describing them, though, the two visions result in different
outcomes; Emerson embraces his as confirming a Platonic tendency to see
transcendent forms as most real, while McClure is moved by his experience to
see the fleshly as inherently spiritual, an insight that sets him off on the path
of biological mysticism he has followed since that time.[8]

The Semina equation of Artaud with Mexico and drugs reaches a climax in
Semina 5 (1959), an entire issue dedicated to an Artaudian view of Mexico. The
complementary cover images (Fig. 17) of a huge pre-Columbian stone phallus
and a portrait of the classic poet/nun Sor Juana Inés de la Cruz articulate a

FIGURE 17.   Wallace Berman, Cover, *Semina* 5 (1959). © Wallace Berman Estate.

complex union of opposites that runs throughout the issue: both the images and the poems seek to blend antinomies such as male and female, voluptuous and ascetic, fleshly and spiritual. In this issue of *Semina*, sex, drugs, and an earthy spirituality associated with Mexico by both Artaud and the Semina group operate as catalysts to bring about a kind of alchemical conjunction of opposites. Artaud's invocation of this alchemical transformation can be seen on one of the cards that contains a translated excerpt from his "Le Mexique et la Civilization:"

> and to Mercury corresponds the movement,
> to Sulphur corresponds the energy,
> to Salt corresponds the stable mass
> even as the activity of fundamental sources
> manifests the Mexican thing, an image, its
> powers perpetually renewing itself.

By bringing elements fundamental to the conduct of alchemy, such as mercury, sulfur, and salt, into the Mexican landscape, Artaud portrays it as dynamic, transformative, and perpetually self-regenerating. Possessed of remarkable alchemical abilities, Mexico seems to represent for Artaud both an image in its own right and the power to create images. He acquired this sense of the assertive, transformative quality of the landscape during peyote sessions, when the mountains and stones took on biomorphic shapes: "I seemed to read everywhere a tale of childbirth amid war, a tale of genesis and chaos, with all these bodies of gods which were carved like men, and these truncated human statues" (Artaud 71). In another card from this issue of *Semina*, "I Mexico After Artaud," Kirby Doyle imitates Artaud's initiation into the dynamic powers of the Mexican landscape by throwing himself into the same crucible of madness that Artaud courted by ingesting peyote: "Stricken by my unconscious impotence, / Dizzy from intelligent spells of madness / Revealing the same thoughts, / I fall into Nature already prepared."

Other cards evince a similar sense of being "prepared" by Artaud. In particular, many depict states of derangement and insight achieved through the use of drugs. "Memoria" [*sic*] is Lamantia's paean to marijuana as a Mexican seeress, who "spoke sibyl sentences silver and cut the throats of time!" A photo by Berman of Lamantia injecting heroin on one card is matched on another by a poem of Kaufman's that ends with the lines, "O Mexico, give me your Easter Faced Virgin / And your Junk."[9] Likewise, in his "Peyote Poem,"

Wieners finds himself "inhabited by strange gods" and he wonders, "who / are they, they walk in white trenchcoats / with pkgs. of paradise in their pockets." The filmmaker Larry Jordan contributes a poem, "Rockets," that seems to chronicle a peyote-enhanced trip to Mexico:

> Motor oxydizing
> Space-raped Breugel sand oxydizing
>
> Blue sky oxydizing
> Peyoton cloud oxydizing
> Pepsi-cola oxydizing
>
> The undeceived rearview mirror
> blasting back an oxydized grey stripe.
>
> Burnt, skin & spirit, we returned
>
> More purified than we knew.

Through a drug-inspired vision of the world rusting away, Jordan partakes of the Mexican alchemy outlined by Artaud, in which breakdown and burnout are the first stages of an eventual purification and regeneration.

Just as there is a union of the opposing qualities of rust and purity in Jordan's poem, other cards in this issue of *Semina* portray Mexico as either dangerous or seductive or both. Reed invokes the ancient Mexican sense of the macabre with a drawing of a ferocious, partially skeletalized torso alongside a horrific poem presided over by vultures (Fig. 18). Poet and filmmaker Christopher Maclaine speaks in "Callejon García Villa Lorca" of the archetypal experience of Mexico as "a stone / flung into the otherness of time." Notwithstanding his invocation of the Spaniard García Lorca in his title, Maclaine sounds more like Mexican poet Octavio Paz when he portrays Mexico as a stone following an aberrant trajectory through history. John Chance imagines his own death, impaled on "Mexican green bull horns / Growing out of the Aztec Earth," in his poem "How I Died," while John Hoffman offers a more peaceful image of the ocean "clos[ing] the break of land / Into its time-deep crystal."[10] Meltzer envisions the dead Pancho Villa, whose ear "hangs like a rotted flower, / its blood nourishing the flies & / a disfigured unknown cactus." In contrast, McClure's reverie about Mexico has a gentle quality, invoking "pastel / adobe houses. Pink, Salmon, and Blue / piñatas and crinoline hems." Seemingly addressed to a lover, McClure's poem opens up to the feminine side

FIGURE 18. John Reed, Untitled ink drawing and untitled manuscript poem (*Semina* 5). © Wallace Berman Estate.

of the packet, in which Sor Juana, Mexico's first poet (translated by Lamantia), asks whether it is worse to be the seducer or the seduced, the prostitute or her client. Poet and filmmaker Ruth Weiss contrasts the "calendar-poster of saints" with "the open-legged girl [who] IS the / mother of your children," in order to illustrate what she calls "the two-sided coin" of Mexico. The feminine image of Mexico is rounded out by William Margolis in a sentimental depiction of "pious-shawled women / mourning poverty in the sun / impassively with their eyes." In sum, the Semina cohort finds Artaud's Mexico a context for exploration and escape, for breakdown and transformation. In this surrealistically mediated Mexico, the straitlaced reality of fifties America comes undone in the seductive embrace of otherness.

Kabbalah and Robert Duncan's *Letters*

Artaud was one of a number of surrealists, including René Daumal and Kurt Seligmann, who commandeered esoteric religious imagery for an assault on the reign of rationality. Author of an extensive *History of Magic,* Seligmann too made a profound impression on Lamantia. As a teenager in Los Angeles and New York, Lamantia had direct access to what he calls "the surrealist diaspora" of writers and artists who fled Europe during World War II: "Surrealism was what brought me to what you call hermeticism. . . . The key for me was my weekly lunch with the painter-engraver Kurt Seligmann, who graciously allowed me to look at his many volumes of very early, amazing alchemical texts. This was an unforgettable experience" (Meltzer, *Beat* 137).[11] Alongside alchemy, another major strand in the Western hermetic tradition, Kabbalah (literally, "tradition" or "transmission"), the mystical wing of Judaism, also held an enormous fascination for the surrealists. When trying to understand how repeated patterns in the Mexican landscape have a mathematical regularity, a regularity imitated in the patterns of the Tarahumara rituals and dances (another example of what Smith calls "the problem of rhythm in relation to thought"), Artaud turns to Kabbalah for an explanation: "There is in the Kabbala a music of Numbers, and this music which reduces material chaos to its prime elements explains by a kind of grandiose mathematics how Nature orders and directs the birth of forms she brings forth out of chaos. And all I beheld seemed to be governed by a Number" (71).

Kabbalah has seized the imagination of modern poets not only for its numerological magic but also because of the powerful, even cosmic, significance it accords to words. As Meltzer explains, "The Kabbalah, as much as poetry, is the study of and submission to the mysteries of the word. The language used by Kabbalists is so intricately dimensional that it is almost impossible to fully convey the simultaneous levels of meaning revealed in the simplest of words. It is said that one word is the seed of a particular universe, a system of interactions and realities as complex as the birth and death of a sun" (Meltzer, *Garden* xiii). The kabbalistic conception of a word as a cosmic seed is implicit in the term *Semina,* which points again to why poetry, with its insistence on the generative force of language, plays such a prominent part in the publication *Semina.* Of all the forms of magic outlined in Seligmann's *History of Magic* (among them, astrology, numerology, divination, casting of spells, mortuary magic, alchemy, Kabbalah, Tarot, witchcraft, and black magic), Kabbalah appeals most directly to poets because it is a kind of alchemy that engages with the basic materials of writing: the word, the letter, and the book. In Kabbalah all of the levels of occult "work"—magical practice, meditation and contemplation techniques, visionary excursions, and spiritual and psychological self-transformation—can be found, as they would be in any mystical system, but all derive from investigations of language and writing.

Kabbalah found its way into the Semina circle primarily through the advocacy of Duncan (Fig. 19), who heard it whispered of by his parents at theosophical meetings during his childhood (Kamenetz 9–10). The most important kabbalistic text, the *Zohar*, was read by Duncan's parents as one of the keys to the mysteries of the universe; from Duncan's own perspective, the *Zohar* ought to be read instead as "the greatest mystical novel ever written" (Meltzer, *Garden* x). Duncan's enthusiasm for Kabbalah made a profound impression on the Semina poets and artists, especially Berman, Meltzer, Hirschman, and to a lesser extent Lamantia. It is ironic that Duncan, raised as a Christian hermeticist, became the instigator of lifelong research by such Jewish figures as Berman, Meltzer, Hirschman, and Jerome Rothenberg into a Jewish form of mysticism. Meltzer, for instance, who edited a journal devoted to Kabbalah, *Tree*, and an anthology of kabbalistic texts, *The Secret Garden*, calls Duncan "my exemplar" in Kabbalah studies (x) and credits Duncan with introducing him to the works of Gershom Scholem, the modern scholar responsible for reviving interest in Kabbalah.[12] The story runs that in 1965 Meltzer was working

FIGURE 19. Wallace Berman, "Robert Duncan, Crater Lane," 1962. © Wallace Berman Estate.

in San Francisco at the Discovery Book Store, where Duncan and Jess would visit monthly to buy used books on the generous discount Meltzer gave them. One day, Duncan returned from the restroom indignant, waving a book in his hand and complaining, "Someone has left this library book in the bathroom! This book should not be taken out of circulation. Return it to the library immediately!" Meltzer began reading the book, Scholem's *Major Trends in Jewish Mysticism* (trans. 1954) to see why Duncan considered it so important, but found it deadly dull—until he reached the chapter on Abraham Abulafia, the thirteenth-century Spanish mystic who combined letters in musical permutations; there he recognized a poetic practice with direct bearing on his own. He then went back and devoured the entire book.[13]

The first meeting of Duncan and his partner Jess with the Bermans took place a decade earlier, in 1954 (*SP* 197), during a period when the triumvirate of Duncan, Spicer, and Rexroth dominated the San Francisco poetry scene. Nearly everyone in the Semina group—whether poet, artist, or filmmaker—was mentored by at least one of these poets. Duncan began drawing extensively on Kabbalah for his own poetry during the writing of the book *Letters* (1958), composed between 1953 and 1956, which was also the period when *Semina* was born. Although *Letters* has received relatively little critical attention, Duncan's recently reissued book is a remarkable achievement, for the impact it had on the Semina group and others on the scene at the time (including Norman O. Brown) as well as for discoveries he made within it that set the course for much of his subsequent poetry.[14] In an interview devoted to his excursions in Kabbalah, Duncan maintains that its study was so instrumental to the writing of *Letters* that "[e]ven the name *Letters* comes from the *Zohar* which I was reading in that period" (Kamenetz 13). In Kabbalah, as expounded both in the *Zohar* and in the earlier *Sefer Yetzirah*, the letters of the Hebrew alphabet are conceived of as the basic building blocks of the universe. Meltzer summarizes this notion: "The *Yetzirah* expresses the concept of God creating the universe through letters which hold the possibility of creation's entire vocabulary. The world is entered and invented through language rooted in alphabet systems. God translates Himself, condenses into alphabet. To know alphabet is to approach creation's workings. Within and without are the letters" (Meltzer, "Door" 93).

For Duncan, this creative activity of the letters is not literal but imaginative; in his conception, the poet participates through letters in the unending creative work of the cosmos. In accordance with his statement in the preface to *Letters* that "the lore of Moses of Leon in the *Zohar,* has been food for the letters of this alphabet" (xii), Duncan valued Kabbalah not as a believer but as a poet greatly nourished by it as a theory of the imagination: "It seemed to me," he says in the interview, "that in mystical traditions of Judaism, religion was passing into imagination." While maintaining an abiding fascination with Kabbalah, Duncan refused it his belief because his concern was not with certainty but with imaginative possibility; from his perspective, "imagination is the final ground of reality" (Kamenetz 13). Following the lead of the letter meditations in Abulafian *gematria* and the alphabetic puns in Joyce's *Finnegans Wake,* Duncan conceived of *Letters* as an exploration of the creative matrix that letters form in the imagination and the cosmos: "*Letters* is influenced toward a creative veil or world-cloth which would be identical with the maya in which it's woven all the way through. The warp and woof are connected and the figures emerge and disappear" (12). For Duncan, to work in art is not to strive for uniqueness or originality but to participate in this "Maya," this world weaving, and he passed along this sense of creative participation in every moment of life to those around him. As the poet Diane di Prima testifies, "Robert was probably one of the closest, most intimate lovers I ever had, even though we never had a physical relationship. I learned a lot of different kinds of things from him. One of the things I learned—in a way no teacher of Buddhism ever showed me—was how precious my life was. How precious the whole ambience of the time. A real sense of appreciating every minute" (Meltzer, *Beat* 17).

In the preface to *Letters,* Duncan describes this exquisite awareness as poised between creativity and self-consciousness (ix–x). Ultimately, it translates into the ability to uphold a balance between art and life, in which each penetrates but does not overwhelm the other. Duncan wanted to stand for the view that art and life are like warp and woof: both participate in and help create the design the artist makes. In his preface, Duncan singles out Artaud as an attractive but finally destructive example of someone whose life overcomes his art: "Artaud is torn apart by actual excitations which are intolerable to his imagination and to his material" (x). Duncan sounds this cautionary note in *Letters* and continues to sound it throughout his career. In his 1978 appreciation of Berman (who had died in a motorcycle accident two years earlier), he acknowledges the Semina group's romance with drugs and speaks parenthetically of his and Jess's "avoidance of the drug culture scene so that we did not cultivate [Berman's] Larkspur house." He recognizes, though, that there was also a creative side to that dangerously self-destructive scene: "The word 'junk' that in the 1950s would have meant the trashing of the drug heroin, in the 1960s came to mean the redemption of trash in the recognition of devotional objects, emblems and signs rescued from the bottom in the art of a new context" (*SP* 202). California Junk Art represented for Duncan a contextual survival practice, in which the artist, threatened by (self-)destruction, manages to reclaim an imaginative sway over a brutal reality. In the prose poem dedicated to the Bermans in *Roots and Branches* (a title that again alludes to Kabbalah by invoking its image of the Tree of Life), Duncan invokes the endangered "artists of the survival" and asks emphatically, "How to shape survival! In what art to survive!" (169).

When the "artists of the survival" engage in "a descent into the underground of the city and [a] programmatic use of forbidden drugs" (*SP* 200), Duncan views this Semina descent as part of "an alchemical process in which the *nigredo* or *melanosis*, 'the horrible darkness of our mind,' is the initial stage of a promised individuation." Through offering themselves, as Artaud did, to a psychic or artistic crucible, in which they would burn away within themselves the values of an unlivable society, the Semina group might hope to offer a new, creative vision for transforming that society. There was, in fact, an astonishing potency to this art of survival, whose discoveries continue to radiate far afield. "*Semina* is to be seen," Duncan proposes, "and the later work of Berman as themselves 'seminal,' as the seeding of 'that black, magically fecund earth,' as Jung describes the alchemical antinomy" (200–201). In their transformation of darkness and destruction into the potential for new creativity and community, the Semina group participated in the larger cultural phenomenon of the Beats. As Lisa Phillips notes, "The search for alternative consciousness, the mystical side of the Beats, goes hand in hand with their gritty realism and rebellion. These two sides—the ecstatic and the horrific, the beatific and the beaten, define the poles of Beat experience" (33). Even more directly than many of the other Beats, the Semina group combined mysticism, communalism, drug use, sexual frankness, and political protest into a survival art, which became in time a prototype for the hippie movement.

From Seeds to *Tree*

In the Kabbalah of Isaac Luria, which the Semina group read about in Gershom Scholem's *Major Trends in Jewish Mysticism*, the transformative art of survival is known as *tikkun olam*, the restoration of the broken world (265–86).

The sense of wholeness indicated by tikkun is essential to the Lurianic Kabbalah and is implicit in a number of other mythical kabbalistic symbols, such
as the Tree of Life and the figure of Adam Kadmon, the Cosmic Human Being.
Berman adopted another symbol of wholeness, the first letter of the Hebrew
alphabet, aleph, as his personal signet. Scholem points out that aleph is a silent
consonant that "represents nothing more than the position taken by the larynx
when a word begins with a vowel" (*Kabbalah* 30). Symbolically, aleph is the
silent source of all articulation, the seed of the entire alphabet, "and indeed
the Kabbalists always regarded it as the spiritual root of all other letters." The
Zohar recounts the most famous story concerning the letter aleph as the silent
source: "When the blessed Holy One wished to fashion the world, all the letters were hidden away. For two thousand years before creating the world, the
blessed Holy One contemplated them and played with them. As he verged on
creating the world, all the letters presented themselves before Him, from last to
first" (Matt 11). Each letter stepped forward in turn and asked the "Master of
the world" to "create the world by me" (12). The Holy One praised the virtues
of each letter on the basis of a particular word that it begins but refused to
create the world with it, until finally the letter *bet* entered and said, "Master
of the world, may it please You to create the world by me, for by me You are
blessed above and below" [*berakhah*, blessing, begins with bet]. The Holy One
agreed. The letter aleph had remained outside this scene in humility, at first not
wanting to assert itself where other letters had failed and then not wanting to
usurp the favor that had been granted already to bet. "The blessed Holy One
said, 'aleph, aleph! Although I will create the world with the letter bet [using
be-reshit, the first word of the Torah], you will be the first of all letters. Only
through you do I become one [aleph is the number one]. With you all counting
begins and every deed in the world" (16).

Aleph is the source of creation, although it remains inactive, incipient.
Berman stamped this originary letter everywhere, from his motorcycle helmet to *Semina 7*, entitled "ALEPH," an entire issue consisting of photography,
drawing, and writing by Berman and dominated by the letter aleph (Figs. 20,
21). Speaking of Berman's collages and assemblages, Meltzer notes the dia-
critical function of aleph in relation to mundane imagery drawn from print
sources: "Above the triteness and everydayness of this image continuum was
Aleph—the first letter of the Hebrew alphabet, which put everything into
a strange tension, because on the one hand you'd see the normative images
that newspapers and magazines use to increase circulation held at bay by this

BOXED CITY

My beautiful wife
Rearranges deaf photographs   talks
Rococo & dances off four walls
Son Tosh pencils the faithful
Image & ignores the subtle drama

Stoned in black corduroy I continue
To separate seeds
                    From the bulk.

BIRD
1920 - 1955

FIGURE 20. From *Semina* 7 (A) (1961). Text, photographs, collage by Wallace Berman.
© Wallace Berman Estate.

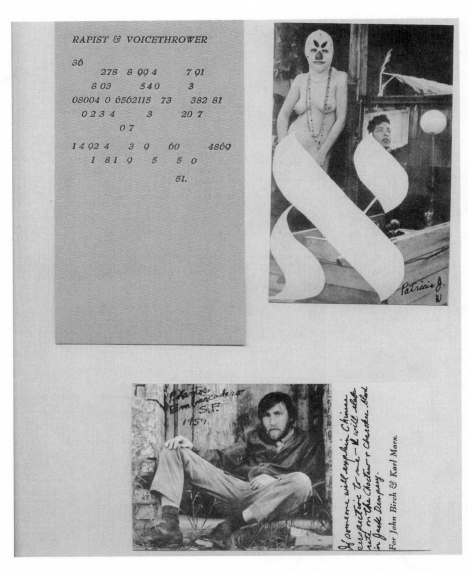

FIGURE 21. From *Semina 7* (B) (1961). Text, photographs, collage by Wallace Berman. © Wallace Berman Estate.

letter" (Meltzer, *Beat* 200). Berman's aleph accrued a transformative, sacralizing role, as though it were capable of reordering contexts and conferring blessings on a degraded, commodified reality. In *Semina 7*, a huge aleph is stamped alongside or on top of a variety of photographs: a woman strapped into an electric chair awaiting execution (on the cover); Berman's young son, Tosh, holding a rifle and wearing a Davy Crockett leather jacket; a vigorous stand of marijuana plants; a memorial collage for Charlie Parker; the bust of his wife, Shirley, with a large medallion between her exposed breasts; photographer Patricia Jordan nude, wearing a mask and beads; a saxophone being played; and a figure seen through a window in two poses. The obsessions of Berman's life—his family, his friends, his devotion to jazz, his love of sexual display, his outrage at society as death-inducing—are all stamped with the sacralizing signet of aleph.

Berman's aleph participates in an "intuitive Kabbalah" that blesses the most vital facets of his life (Meltzer, "Door" 100); it also has an elegiac quality by virtue of its iconic use so soon after World War II. Growing up in the Fairfax District of Los Angeles, Berman saw the Hebrew lettering of the Yiddish language displayed in shop windows and in newspapers. Invoking that world in the aftermath of the Holocaust, his aleph draws attention to the death of the Hebrew letter, not only because the Yiddish speakers of Los Angeles were dying out but also because the extermination of Jewish culture in Europe had incinerated the letters, both written and spoken, and rendered them ghostly. Like many of his gestures, in his living and in his art, Berman's depiction of Hebrew letters—on photographs, in assemblages, on parchment, and on massive stones and walls—is fraught with opposing motives: at the same time that the letters invoke suffering and disappearance, they promise redemption.

If Berman's relationship to Kabbalah is more intuitive than doctrinaire, two of the other members of the Semina group, Hirschman and Meltzer, have made it the focus of serious study and a centerpiece of much of their poetry. Author of an essay promoting "Kabbalah Surrealism," Hirschman has set about actively integrating these two major influences into works of poetry and painting that also have an aggressive political character. Like Duncan, Hirschman views Kabbalah as opening up the most explosive poetic potential in words and as translating religion into imagination. Of his favorite kabbalistic thinker, Abraham Abulafia, whom he has translated, Hirschman claims, "Abulafia was the poet who changed the Tetragrammaton and put the name of a poet in. He identified with David the poet, and that's who God was to him,

FIGURE 22. Jack Hirschman, *Black Alephs*. Cover collage by Wallace Berman. New York: Phoenix Book Shop, 1969.

ultimately" (Meltzer, *Beat* 118). The Tetragrammaton is the four-letter name of God, never to be uttered, the holiest word in the Hebrew language. Hirschman contends that because Abulafia recognized the tremendous creative potency of the kabbalistic manipulation of letters, he saw that the poet who writes verse as sublime as the Psalms becomes the equivalent to the One who creates the cosmos.[15] Like Berman, Hirschman is attuned not only to the spiritual but also to the graphic qualities of Hebrew letters, regarding them as hieroglyphs and as forms to be explored by calligraphy. Although Hirschman does not appear in *Semina*, he was a wholehearted participant in the Semina context. His first major collection of poetry, *Black Alephs* (1969), contains a cover collage by Berman (Fig. 22)—featuring a torn photograph of a bride and groom, with a kabbalistic diagram and two large alephs emerging from the tear—and three of Berman's Verifax collages as half-titles.[16] In addition to sharing Berman's fascination with the letter aleph, Hirschman also made artworks out of Hebrew letters. By smashing inked Hebrew block letters onto sheets of paper, Hirschman felt he was pushing the gestural aesthetic of abstract expressionism in a kabbalistic direction (Meltzer, *Beat* 118; Hirschman, "Letters").

Even more alluring for the Semina group than the heroic gesture cultivated by abstract expressionism was the improvisatory aesthetic of jazz. Meltzer has called his own poetic method "Bop Kabbalah," which corresponds nicely to Hirschman's "Kabbalah Surrealism" and to Kerouac's "spontaneous bop prosody." In an essay for a 1978 retrospective of Berman's work, Meltzer quotes a long passage from Abulafia comparing the manipulation of letters in kabbalistic meditation to an improvisatory musical composition ("Door" 96–97). Meltzer himself claims that bop and Kabbalah can blend into one mystical exercise: "They're based on sonic and rhythmic practices and utilizing systems, musical or alphabetical, that have, if you so choose, profound dimensionality to them" (Meltzer, *Beat* 213). After describing the many permutations of words inside of words that occur in kabbalistic gematria, Meltzer concludes that as a practice gematria follows the same regimen as jazz: "That's attention and submission and at the same time improvisation" (214). For both Meltzer and Hirschman, Kabbalah is less a form of biblical commentary than it is a wide-ranging poetics of linguistic assemblage. Rather than studying Kabbalah in order to deepen a traditional religious observance, they practice what might be called a "tantric Kabbalah" of physical and psychic experimentation.

In the early seventies, Meltzer published a magazine called *Tree*, which took up where *Semina* left off in the mining of Kabbalah for artistic stimulus.

Besides translations of and commentaries on kabbalistic texts, *Tree* published
from the Semina group writing by Meltzer, Hirschman, Wieners, McClure,
Herms, and Idell Romero (Aya Tarlow), and images by Berman, Herms,
Hirschman, and the actor Russ Tamblyn. Meltzer also reached out to a number of other poets looking to combine Kabbalah with surrealism, such as Jerome Rothenberg, Nathaniel Tarn, Clayton Eshleman, Robert Kelly, Richard
Grossinger, and John Brandi. With remarkable foresight, Meltzer also published the first selection to appear in English from Edmond Jabès's monumental *Book of Questions*, the Egyptian Jewish poet's consummate synthesis
of Kabbalah and surrealism, which interrogates the intertwined issues of Jew-
ishness, writing, and the Holocaust. In a long essay on the work of Jabès published in 1985, Duncan recognizes a poet whose *Book of Questions* shares the
same impulse to discover "meaning within meaning, words within words,"
that he first began to explore in his own *Letters*:

> The Book of Questions is meant to arouse, beyond the boundaries of apparent
> meaning, suspicions and rumors of meaning within meaning, words within
> words. Jabès writes in order to read, or reading is the order of his writing, and
> he brings us back again and again to this boundary of the presence of its being
> written in the presence of its being read—to the letter the eye sees even as the
> hand writes the word, to the rhyme or homophone the ear hears even as it at-
> tends the message of the voice in the book. (*SP* 208–9)

With the combination of Kabbalah and surrealism sponsored by *Tree* as
an example, it becomes clear just how instrumental the Semina group was not
only in modeling the hippie lifestyle but also in founding a new erotic poetics. Because Berman dedicated himself to an art in which letters and words
have equal power with visual images, the Semina context of writers, artists,
and filmmakers he convened effected a remarkable cross-fertilization. From
the fifties through the seventies, the joining of Kabbalah and surrealism fostered by Semina was at the base of much of the poetic production, the drug
and sexual experimentation, the group living, the filmmaking, and the collage and assemblage art of the West Coast. The erotic poetics of Semina draws
surrealism, the occult, and anarchism together in ways that turn the largely
private practice of assemblage into a communal mode of performance.

6

BEFORE CAESAR'S GATE,
ROBERT DUNCAN COMES TO GRIEF
The Vietnam War and the "Unengendered Child"

The Impasse

During the course of this book, Robert Duncan has emerged as one of the most far-sighted and articulate exponents of a contextual practice. With his dedication to a Grand Collage that encompasses not only collaborating locally with Jess but also participating in a "symposium of the whole" (*SP* 98) that draws charged artifacts from around the world and throughout history into a vast assemblage, Duncan makes a compelling case for a complexly hybrid artistic practice. Placing poetry and poetics at the core of a meaningful life as human being and as artist, he uses classic rhetorical devices (metaphor, metonymy, irony) to weave together artworks, experiences, history, science, mythology, and hermetic philosophy, creating endlessly reverberating assemblage structures. Like Emerson before him, Duncan finds correspondences everywhere, which allows him to bring together the most disparate materials to form a new context.[1] In addition, his profoundly erotic orientation toward poetry and life, fueled by thoroughgoing Freudianism, queer sexuality, mystical exuberance, and linguistic playfulness, makes him the consummate spokesman for a vitally engaging erotic poetics. Having turned to him often in the course of this book, I want to use the final two chapters to examine the limits of erotic poetics, making Duncan the primary example. During the Vietnam War, especially in the early seventies, this most exuberant proponent of contextual practice underwent an access of grief that interfered with his metaphorical imagination.

By investigating Duncan's crisis—occasioned by the war, by the disruption of his friendship with Denise Levertov, and by a deep-seated regret at never having been a father—we can see how an erotic poetics, which had enabled his vigorous pursuit of a contextual practice, can also help to describe how such a practice may break down under the force of stresses too powerful for an artist to assimilate fully.

Let us begin with the Levertov friendship, one of Duncan's most profound relationships. It commenced with the first poem of Duncan's *Letters*, "For A Muse Meant" (1–4), which was titled initially "Letters for Denise Levertov: An A Muse Ment" (Bertholf and Gelpi 3–4) when it was sent to her in June 1953, inaugurating their correspondence. Levertov misunderstood the mischievous punning in the poem as a parody and critique of her poetry, but Duncan assured her in his next letter that the poem is a gift in recognition of his excitement at encountering her work; the poem, he tells her, is "*for* you not about you" (Bertholf and Gelpi 5). She expresses relief at his explanation—"I certainly am glad you admire my poems because I've been admiring yours for 4 years now" (6)—and this correspondence initiates an alliance, mainly epistolary, of two decades' duration that, like Creeley's largely epistolary friendship with Olson, was a mainstay for each of the poets in their aesthetic development. The easiest way to gauge the weightiness of the Duncan-Levertov correspondence is to heft the volume in which it has been gathered, which runs to more than eight hundred pages. As a document exposing the passionate intensity of lives propelled by aesthetic concerns, the correspondence is unsurpassed. After observing the warmth of their affection and the perceptive criticism and comradely encouragement they afford one another, it is all the more dismaying to witness the demise of their relationship in the late sixties and early seventies. The catalyst was the Vietnam War, which in a larger sense marks the outer boundary for the age of contextual art. The erotic poetics that sprang to life in the aftermath of World War II began to break down under the pressures of the Vietnam War, the first conflict after the Civil War in which the United States turned in on itself in destructive conflagration. With the country at war with what it perceived as a communist proxy in Vietnam, and with American society in the convulsive throes of a generational conflict over the legitimacy of the war and the authority of the state, the erotic impulse was muffled by a blanket woven of rage, fear, and grief.[2]

In the case of Duncan, all three of these emotions made their way into his poetry, with grief proving to be the one over which he had least command.

The preface he wrote in 1972 for a new edition of an earlier book of poems, *Caesar's Gate*, contains a number of reflections on grief that are the impetus for the next two chapters. The first chapter is organized around Duncan's preface and the second around the potent image of Levertov as the Hindu goddess Kali in his poem "Santa Cruz Propositions." Duncan "came to grief" not only in experiencing and writing about grief during this period but also in the sense that he lost control of one of his most important faculties: the thoroughgoing perspectivism he had relied on throughout his career to search out "meaning within meaning, words within words" (*SP* 208), and to join opposite impulses together in a larger whole. In many ways a corrosive emotion, grief is one of the experiences least understood and valued in the modern world. Young people generally try to set it aside as an unpleasant sensation for their elders to take seriously, until they encounter a first truly irreparable loss. For most people, grief takes root in middle age with the deaths of parents and peers, becoming more tightly interwoven with living and with expectations for the future the longer one survives. Around the age of fifty, as the Vietnam War reached its height, Duncan found his erotic poetics overwhelmed by an onslaught of thanatos and its attendant state of grief.

When Duncan returned in 1972 to *Caesar's Gate* (1955), a book of poems written mainly in 1949 and 1950 (with collages by Jess), he resurrected an earlier work he had all but repudiated. The new *Caesar's Gate* (Fig. 23) has received little critical attention, which is unfortunate because it tells much about Duncan's state of mind while he was working on his crucial late book, *Ground Work: Before the War.*[3] In 1970, he suffered the loss of Charles Olson, the poet whom he regarded as the standard bearer for his generation. At the same time, Duncan, like Whitman during the Civil War, regarded the ravages of the Vietnam War as an attack on his own person, identifying with the national body and its fateful implication in an imperial war wreaking havoc on Southeast Asia and the United States alike. Another casualty of the war, his relationship with Levertov entered a destructive maelstrom, provoked by disagreement over the proper relationship among poetry, protest, and war. Even more intimately, the Vietnam War was the occasion for a long-buried source of grief in Duncan's life to rear its head: contemplating the war caused the homosexual poet to mourn the loss of a son he never had. Reaching more than twenty years into the past to the beginnings of the Cold War, Duncan revived the forgotten book, *Caesar's Gate*, as part of the work of moving beyond his Black Mountain period (which had ended with Olson's death); he engaged

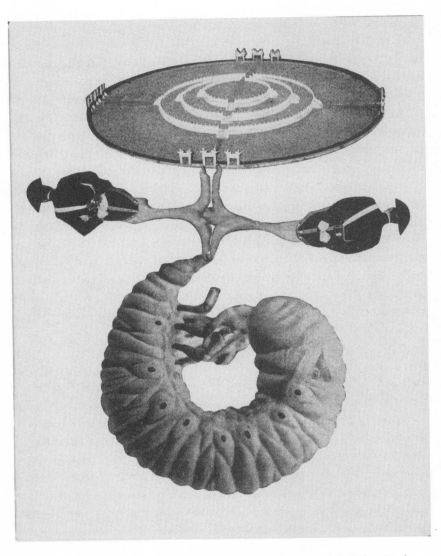

FIGURE 23. Robert Duncan, *Caesar's Gate*. Cover collage by Jess. Berkeley: Sand Dollar, 1972. © 2009 The Jess Collins Trust. Used by permission.

the earlier, unresolved encounter with thanatos exuberantly, intuiting that it would lead him to a poetry of maturity.

The greatly expanded 1972 edition of *Caesar's Gate* includes additional poems from 1949–50, some new collages by Jess, a new preface and epilogue, and a new poem, "Despair in Being Tedious," which Duncan later published in *Ground Work: Before the War*. In a letter to Levertov written in the tense period of their pulling apart, Duncan acknowledges a breakdown in his address to her and hints at a similar breakdown in the communicative function of the prose meditations that festoon the new edition of *Caesar's Gate*. "I'm sure much of what I wrote to you must have been rant," he confesses to her, "the kind of frantic talk jag that goes on when one loses sense of communication" (Bertholf and Gelpi 707). At the same time, he informs her that he has expanded *Caesar's Gate* dramatically by enveloping the relatively short book in ruminative writing on issues that obsess him in 1972:

> I have been wrapping up a new edition of *Caesar's Gate*—literally "wrapping up," for I've just finished a 1972 Preface of 42 pages and a Postscript of another 13. There will be, following the Postscript a 1972 POEM. The prose will annoy I guess—it tries me—and thinking of how trying my relentless going after the involutions of a subject has proved to be for you in the past, the Preface is almost over-doing that in writing. (708)

The overwrought "Preface" circles around a number of topics from the Cold War era of *Caesar's Gate*'s initial composition that have a renewed relevance for Duncan in 1972. He undertakes a "relentless" meditation on the issues of homosexuality, personal and poetic embarrassment, surrealism, and exoticism (with reference to an imaginary "Asia"), and he develops an "involuted" but profound reading of Federico García Lorca's poetry of war and lamentation. A brilliant critic, Duncan keeps turning over and approaching from different angles a nagging dissatisfaction with the poetry of *Caesar's Gate* and with what it reveals about him as a poet, hoping to breach an impasse that looms before him in the early seventies as he leaves the relative security of his Black Mountain period and moves into the uncharted, unaffiliated future that he proposes for *Ground Work*.

The impasse Duncan faces is figured by the image of "Caesar's Gate" itself. In a section of the "Preface" called "The Gate" (viii–xii), Duncan unravels the intertextual and emotional layers of the image. The "Caesar" is actually Alexander the Great, a proto-Caesar, whom Marco Polo, in his account of his

Asian travels, described as being unable to breach a particular narrow passage into Asia because it was flanked on one side by the sea "'and confined on the other by high mountains and woods . . . so that a very few men were capable of defending it against the whole world.'" Unable to break through, Alexander built a heavily fortified gate, which, "'[f]rom its uncommon strength . . . obtained the name of the Gate of Iron'" (x). In *Caesar's Gate*, Duncan adopts the image of the impenetrable passage that resists conquest and translates it into sexual and poetic terms. He explains how a poetic conquest had occurred during his writing of "The Venice Poem" (*First Decade* 81–107):

> *The Venice Poem* had defined the previous period between February and September of 1948 as one of a victory for me. It was the first time in my writing that I had both known what I had to do—something more in writing than knowing what you *want* to do—and known as I worked that I was able to do it. I saw the City of Venice in that poem as my own and the history of its empire as the history of an imperialism in Poetry in which I saw my own dreams expand. (ix)

The sexual conquest involved "falling in love in November of 1947 and 'winning' my lover from a rival, . . . impersonating the conqueror of a world falling into ruin in being conquered" (ix).[4] During the writing of *Caesar's Gate*, which followed upon "The Venice Poem," Duncan's sense of triumph was thwarted. Emotionally, his affair with Gerald Ackerman entered a bitter period of betrayals that ended in its dissolution. Poetically, he was unable to recapture the sense of contextual cohesion, "the full structural imperative of a form seeking to come into existence in the process of the poem" (xii), that he had discovered in "The Venice Poem." Two articles by fellow poets, Thom Gunn's "Homosexuality in Robert Duncan's Poetry" and Bruce Boone's "Robert Duncan and Gay Community," offer readings of *Caesar's Gate* as a book of erotic descent into a "sexual hell, where lust is continuous, and where neither body, mind, nor spirit can be satisfied. . . . This work, then, largely focuses on sexual fury, both self-mastering and self-defeating" (Gunn 148).

Duncan makes the infernal reference explicit in his 1955 "Preface" to the book, which commences with a section entitled "HELL": "To this point I came, willingly demoralized, to pray for grief, or for sleep, or for the tides of blood, for the worm to turn" [xlv]. Like the pilgrim in Dante's *Commedia*, Duncan stands before a gate whose counsel is to abandon all hope. The poems of *Caesar's Gate* portray an after-death state filled with hellish denizens: corpses, worms, cocoons, clay, demons, shadows, fire, ashes, sleep, decay, rats, beehives, stone statues, and moonlight. Unlike the pilgrim in the *Commedia*, however, Duncan does not merely observe or converse with the souls trapped in Hell; he identifies as one of them:

Upon Another Shore of Hell

O forbidden Dead, I too drift.
Coming near to your river, I hear you.
Dead voices that would take body
out of my blood, your love cannot heal
nor your touch comfort.

So am I—four months—like you—
loveless, driven by hatred as by rain
or by pain of cold, driven.

Is it true that the Christians,
rank on rank, stand
immortal in their love or
the love of a God? singing?

O holy Dead, it is the living
not the Divine
that I envy. Like you
I cry to be rejoind to the living.

(17)

Turning away in the third stanza from the paradise of immortal souls standing rank on rank singing their love for a Christian God, Duncan yearns instead to return to earth enlivened by mortal love. Both at the time of its composition and in retrospect, the poems of *Caesar's Gate* loomed up after "The Venice Poem" as expressions of a self-lacerating netherworld, a feeling-state representing an impassable obstacle like the Gate of Iron that blocked Alexander's further conquest. Interpreting the passage from Marco Polo cited above in the 1972 "Preface," Duncan explains more fully how the image of Caesar's Gate and the explorer's account of it resonate for him: "The passage, itself referring to the very difficulty of passage, a passage to Asia, but it was also—for this was the secret lure that Marco Polo followed—the passage from one time to another, from medieval Christendom to the Renaissance—the passage, like a passage in a dream, might be speaking of a sexual conquest, of making a pass or, deeper, of coming to a pass in making love" (x). The latter phrase suggests that the obstructed passage may refer in mundane terms to a physical impasse in anal intercourse. When Duncan returns to *Caesar's Gate* in 1972, though, the issue of "obstructed passages" has a compelling figurative significance for the progress of his poetry. Around the time of writing the "Preface," Duncan appears to have reached a crisis with regard to his major series of poems, *Passages*. After he had written the last numbered entry, "*Passages* 36" (dated December 17, 1971), the ordered continuity of the sequence began to dissolve. Unlike all of the previous entries, this one received no title; other poems that Duncan subsequently conceived of as participating in the series did not receive even a number but were merely designated in parentheses as "(*Passages*)."[5] Rather than relying on a simple notion of passages as signaling fluid motion, he observes in his meditation on Marco Polo that passages may be difficult or resistant, that they may involve a disjunctive leap from one historical era to another, that they may have the surrealist linkage found in the movement of dream imagery, and that they might well signal moments of crisis in love or in sexual intercourse.

On the initial page of the 1972 *Caesar's Gate*, which lists his books in print, Duncan announces publicly for the first time a new impasse in his poetry: "'I do not intend to issue another collection of my work since *Bending the Bow* until 1983 at which time fifteen years will have passed.'—Robert Duncan, 1972." He proposes the fifteen-year gestation as a new "Caesar's Gate" period, a time of perilous passage analogous to the years between "The Venice Poem" and *The Opening of the Field*:

> In *The Venice Poem*, I had, for the first time, known the full structural imperative of a form seeking to come into existence in the process of the poem that, at the same time, I was in my own work working in cooperation with, coming to acknowledge in the works of the poem. . . . But not again, it seems to me, until the conception of *The Opening of the Field* in 1956, almost seven years later, did I come into the fullness of that experience, and then the force of the poetics I had pursued had overtaken me. . . . *Caesar's Gate, The Book of Resemblances*, and *Letters*, are works of a phase in Poetry fearfully and with many errors making its way. (xii)

The poetry that Duncan wrote between "The Venice Poem" and *The Opening of the Field*, collected mainly in *Caesar's Gate* (written 1949–1950 and 1955), *A Book of Resemblances* (written 1950–1953), and *Letters* (written 1953–1956), did not partake of the "structural imperative"—that sense of all parts working together within an open-ended context—which Duncan first knew in "The Venice Poem" and which also informed his three Black Mountain books published in the sixties, *The Opening of the Field* (1960), *Roots and Branches* (1964), and *Bending the Bow* (1968). The three books of the fifties do not possess that sense of "imperial conquest," in which the form of the book and the poems within it all cooperate in a single conception. In 1972, Duncan was eager to write once again outside of a "structural imperative," in order to lay himself open to a new "phase in Poetry fearfully and with many errors making its way." He was seeking in *Ground Work* a transformation, an undisclosed "Asia," beyond the discoveries of the projectivist years, and so it made sense to return to the unresolved and thwarted forms and emotions lurking in *Caesar's Gate*.

In Duncan's August 24, 1972, letter to Levertov, quoted from earlier, he describes reentering the book by writing additional material as "wrapping up" *Caesar's Gate*, which has the senses both of enveloping and completing. The contents of *Caesar's Gate* would need enveloping because they are dangerous and colored by a grief that threatens to leak out uncontrollably into Duncan's world. This concept of wrapping up grievous contents rhymes with an image by one of Duncan's key source poets, Walt Whitman, whose influence can be felt through much of the "Preface" to *Caesar's Gate*. Whitman's uncannily haunting Civil War poem, "Vigil Strange I Kept on the Field One Night," casts the battlefield vigil held over a young soldier's body by an older comrade as an act of mourning for a lost child. Portrayed as a maternal father, the older soldier tenderly wraps the younger in his blanket and buries him where he fell:

> My comrade I wrapt in his blanket, envelop'd well his form,
> Folded the blanket well, tucking it carefully over head, and carefully under feet;
> And there and then, and bathed by the rising sun, my son in his grave, in his
>   rude-dug grave I deposited.

>   (Whitman 304)

Like Whitman, Duncan experienced a father's grief during the Vietnam War, a grief that both gay poets felt not only for all of the young men killed in battle but also for a particular sacrificed son, a son who was only imaginary. In the "Preface" to *Caesar's Gate*, Duncan replicates Whitman's double grief of watching young men die (now on television rather than in a field hospital) and of "wrapping up" an imaginary son, sacrificed by keeping faith with a nonprocreative homosexuality.

"Grief's Its Proper Mode"

Between Whitman and Duncan, the Spanish poet García Lorca stands as a mediating figure in *Caesar's Gate*. For poets of Duncan's generation such as Ginsberg, Spicer, Levertov, Paul Blackburn, LeRoi Jones (Amiri Baraka), Stephen Jonas, and Bob Kaufman, Lorca served as a crucial forebear. His poetry and life played a formative role in development of a gay poetry by Duncan, Spicer, Ginsberg, and Jonas, and it offered to African American poets, such as Jones, Jonas, and Kaufman, a remarkably resonant assessment of both the oppressed condition and the special gifts of Harlem's blacks.[6] Animating the concerns of both of these groups, *Poeta en Nueva York* (composed 1929–1930), Lorca's only book written outside Spain, has been regarded by U.S. poets since its publication in 1940, four years after the poet's death, as a work of prophecy. Shocked by his encounter with Whitman's democratic America at the moment of the Stock Market Crash, Lorca excoriates what he sees as a mechanistic loss of soul and a cult of death; he condemns the treatment of blacks, whom he views as "the most delicate, the most spiritual," and the most influential citizens of North America (*PNY* 189); and he searches for a redemptive vision in the countryside and in the example of sexual camaraderie afforded by Whitman.

In a preface he wrote in 1966 to a collection of his early poems, Duncan remembers reading *Poeta en Nueva York* in Spanish when it first appeared and then hearing it read aloud two years later. The incantatory rhythm of lines like "Negros. Negros. Negros. Negros" of "Oda al Rey de Harlem" haunted him and found their way into his 1942 poems "Toward an African Elegy" and "King Haydn of Miami Beach" (*Years* viii). In the "Preface" to *Caesar's Gate*, Duncan focuses on other aspects of the book. He notes, "The impact of Lorca's *Poeta en Nueva York* was . . . immediate, a voice speaking for my own soul in its rage it seemed" (*CG* xv), and he recalls that he and Spicer sensed in "1946 and 1947 as young poets seeking the language and lore of our homosexual longings as the matter of a poetry, that Lorca was one of us, that he spoke from his own unanswered and—as he saw it—*unanswerable* need" (xxii). Duncan read Lorca's most famous tableau of homosexual love, "Oda a Walt Whitman," as "charged with Lorca's passionate affirmation of Whitman's noble longing for homosexual love, even as it is charged with a loathing for homosexual lusts and commerce" (xxii). Composed of idealism and self-hatred, Lorca's queer ambivalence is distilled in the lines "Agony, agony, dream, ferment and dream. / This is the world, my friend, agony, agony" (*PNY* 161)—lines that express, according to Duncan and Spicer, a "terrible knowledge" about the homosexual life revealed "from the depths of a shared fate in experience" (*CG* xxiii).[7]

In 1972, Duncan reread *Poeta en Nueva York,* finding that "it speaks . . . for the very current of my own life." Especially, he confesses, "I come upon the poem 'Iglesia Abandonada,' whose lament touches upon another lament and still another" (*CG* xix). He devotes seven full pages of the "Preface" to meditating on the lamentation within the lament within Lorca's "Abandoned Church," subtitled "Ballad of the Great War." The poem begins with a stark declaration of loss: "Once I had a son named John. / Once I had a son" (*PNY* 35). Duncan points out that when the woman laments her lost son, "The cry echoes in the abandoned Church of a God who gave over His only Son to the sentence of Death that emerged from His own offended Wrath." At the same time, though, that Duncan depicts Christianity as a religion founded on wrath and a death sentence, he wonders, "Is it from a loss at the heart of Christendom, or is it from my own heart, that the loss of a son at the heart of this poem finds its echo?" (*CG* xix). He delays his answer to this momentous question for seven pages. Before answering it, he takes up Lorca's "Ballad of the Great War" as a vehicle to think about the social, psychological, and religious stakes in war and in the loss of sons. If the Christian religion celebrates the sacrifice of a son by an angry father, then how much is this religious predilection echoed in contemporary sociopolitical reality? In his jeremiads condemning the Vietnam War, such as the *Passages* poems that end *Bending the Bow* and begin *Ground Work,* Duncan berates the older generation that seems bent on sacrificing its youth for no good reason.[8] In the "Preface" to *Caesar's Gate,* he analyzes in a scathing passage this intent to offer up the sons to war:

> There is a suspicion that each generation in their degeneration as old men become obsessed by the threat of losing honor, even as they secretly brood over losing youth and manhood, and set up in place of their hearts the holocaust of a war in the works of their nations in order to make vivid, in the orgies of young men at their command slaughtered and slaughtering, the play of a terrible sentence long brooding and unutterable otherwise against Youth itself. At the depth of the intent, beyond all hostilities, there is always the mime of an aweful attention, the grief they seek to bring us all to in their surviving the death of those they feared would survive them. They write the poetry of a lament using the lives of others as we poets of the language pretend lives. (xix–xx)

This powerful indictment of the social and psychological forces at work in the generational conflict behind war does not stop with its terrible insights about human character. As always, Duncan takes his analysis one step further by looking for the poetics at the heart of the most fateful deeds of our time. In bringing us all to grief, the war makers not only slaughter their own sons, they also involuntarily provoke a lament—thus giving rise to a poetic act—that echoes throughout the land. Conversely, because poets are given the subject matter of war as an enabling feature of poetry, they cannot escape from the scene of war and from implication in its horrors. Commenting on a passage in the *Odyssey* in which Homer seems to be identifying with the disguised Odysseus, Duncan claims, "It is as if, for Odysseus/Homer, identity cloaked in identity, the City burned in order to furnish his *Iliad*, even as he sings it, with the verity of his weeping. In this vision, Christ dies upon the Cross—'I had a son who was called . . .' a woman somewhere laments—in order for a sufficient grief to come into a poetry" (xxi). It is indeed an ironic but "awe-ful" accusation of poetry to acknowledge that war's destruction supplies it with the tragic note that provokes full-throated song.

At this point in the "Preface," Duncan moves on to read more of "Iglesia Abandonada" and to discuss it in the context of Lorca's essay "Theory and Function of the *Duende*" and of his play *Yerma* concerning a barren wife. But I want to pause over the phrase "sufficient grief," which had already appeared in "*Passages* 36," a poem from *Ground Work* composed in mid-December 1971, slightly before the "Preface." The title to the poem includes a parenthetical deictic reference to its first lines ("THESE LINES COMPOSING THEMSELVES IN MY HEAD AS I AWOKE EARLY THIS MORNING, IT STILL BEING DARK, December 16, 1971"), claiming in effect that the lines were composed involuntarily, arising from the dream world as something like an auditory hallucination. These lines speak of surrender to an insistent grief that has not yet been identified, and by putting them in italics Duncan makes that insistence more emphatic:

> *Let it go. Let it go.*
> *Grief's its proper mode.*
>
> *But O, How deep it's got to reach,*
> *How high and wide*
> *it's got to grow,*
> *Before it come to sufficient grief . . .*

(*GW* 84)

The phrase "sufficient grief" can be found in the first two lines of the last stanza of D. H. Lawrence's "Priapus": "Grief, grief, I suppose and sufficient / Grief makes us free" (*Selected Poems* 62). An avid reader of Lawrence, Duncan does not find, though, that grief leads him to freedom but rather to an emotional precipice. When reading "*Passages 36*" aloud, he would impart a keening quality to the lines cited above—one that I can't recall hearing in any other poem—giving full voice to the repeated long vowels, *o*, *e*, and *i*, and coming to a pause at the middle "*O*." Chanting these vowels, he evoked enough pathos by the end of the refrain that "sufficient grief" seemed almost attainable. Almost, but not quite, for a consuming grief of this sort is finally unfathomable: "I know," Duncan goes on to say in the poem, "but part of it and that but distantly" (84). As in many of his poems, this one unfolds by way of probing an initial vatic utterance, using its impetus to marshal an assemblage of charged passages. The first direction Duncan turns in seeking a referent for the grief is toward "a catastrophe in another place," which he identifies as originating both "distantly" (the catastrophes of the time: the Vietnam War and famine in Bangladesh) and "within" the mind itself. An attentive reader of Duncan's poetry would also hear in the phrase "a catastrophe in another place" an allusion to the primary catastrophe of his life, the death of his mother in childbirth. This catastrophe recurred from childhood on in his "Atlantis Dream," a dream that ends when a flood rushes into a cave and obliterates the dreamer and the world; it can be found represented in such poems as "Often I Am Permitted to Return to a Meadow" and "A Poem Beginning with a Line by Pindar."[9] In the terms set forth in *Caesar's Gate*, written at the outset of the Korean War, the catastrophe takes place in "Asia," which is both an actual continent and a locus for Duncan's grief.

"The End of an Old Friendship"

As the text of "*Passages 36*" unfolds, the war in southeast Asia comes to represent "the despoiling of nature, of earth, / of animal species, and mankind among them, / with hatred" (*GW* 84), provoking the expressions of outrage, shame, and horror that swirl throughout the poem. By its end, though, when the refrain "*Let it go. Let it go. / Grief's its proper mode*" returns, the search for "sufficient grief" in a time of catastrophe finds a focus in Duncan's breakup with Levertov over the place of poets and poetry in resisting the Vietnam War: "It was about the end of an old friendship, / the admission of neglect rancoring, /

mine of her, hers of what I am, / and festering flesh was there" (*GW* 86). The image of "festering flesh" seems extreme, but Duncan had come to identify it with Levertov through his mistrust of the graphic portrayals of Vietnamese victims in her poetry. In the "Introduction" to *The Letters of Robert Duncan and Denise Levertov*, Albert Gelpi traces the stages of their friendship, including its regrettable demise: "The episode that wrecked the friendship beyond repair" (xxv), he claims, occurred when Levertov read an excerpt from a 1969 interview with Duncan, in which he asserts that there is a sadomasochistic strain to her protest poetry. Speaking to James Mersmann, Duncan says,

> She'll be writing about the war and suddenly—in one of the earlier poems that's most shocking ["Life at War"]—you get a flayed penis. . . . Suddenly you see a charged, bloody, sexual image that's haunting the whole thing, and the war then acts as a magnet, and the poem is not a protest though she thinks she's protesting. (xxvi)

Duncan portrays Levertov in similar terms in "Santa Cruz Propositions" (*GW* 40–50), a long, apocalyptic poem directed at the social malaise of the period. Written in diary fashion while he was teaching at the University of California at Santa Cruz and attending a course of lectures by Norman O. Brown, "Santa Cruz Propositions" is a collage that contains newspaper clippings about the local murders of a wealthy doctor and his family by a group of "revolutionary" hippies.[10] The poem is rife with threatening female figures, including "Madame Defarge of the Central Committee" from *A Tale of Two Cities*, who seeks unending vengeance in the name of the Revolution. In the last section of the poem Duncan finally admits, "But it is Denise I am thinking of" (48), and he presents her in mythological guise:

Out of the depths of the Woman's love,

SHE appears, Kali dancing, whirling her necklace of skulls,
trampling the despoiling armies and the exploiters of natural resources
under her feet. Revolution or Death![11]

(49)

Having been shocked at seeing Levertov captured by a television news crew while speaking at an antiwar rally, Duncan pictures her in a violent apotheosis as Kali, the powerful Hindu goddess of destruction, wearing a red miniskirt, and he also describes her as "Madame Outrage of the Central Committee." Her vociferous denunciations at the rally had transformed her, he feels, into an unknown figure: "She changes. / Violently. It is her time. I never saw that dress before. / I never saw that face before." With dramatic finality, Duncan depicts this terrifying vision of Levertov as a turning point in his life: "This Night / opens into depth without end in my life to come" (49).

Duncan was most likely prepared to perceive Levertov as an avatar of Kali by his deeply sympathetic viewing of the films of Kenneth Anger. Along with several other mythopoeic filmmakers whom Duncan knew well—Stan Brakhage, Larry Jordan, James Broughton, and Bruce Conner—Anger was one of the prominent independent filmmakers in San Francisco with whom he associated most closely. Duncan's friendship with Anger endured for decades, and he meditates on issues in Anger's cinema in a key series of poems in *Bending the Bow*, "Moving the Moving Image, *Passages* 17," "The Torso, *Passages* 18," "The Earth, *Passages* 19," and "An Illustration, *Passages* 20 (Structure of Rime XXVI)" (with a dedication "*for* Kenneth Anger"; *BB* 60–69).[12] Anger transforms recognizable personalities into mythical figures in his films, in exactly the way Duncan imagines it is happening with Levertov. In Anger's *Inauguration of the Pleasure Dome* (1954), for instance, Anaïs Nin appears as Astarte and the red-haired artist and occultist Cameron has a dual role as Kali and the Scarlet Woman. By means of stark juxtapositions in an Eisensteinian montage technique, Anger films such as *Scorpio Rising* (1964), *Invocation of My Demon Brother* (1969), and *Lucifer Rising* (1967–1981) also equate contemporary popular culture and politics with the unleashing of demonic forces.

Like a character in an Anger film, Levertov appears to Duncan as the Devouring Mother (in opposition to the Weeping Mother of "Iglesia Abandonada"), a nightmarish figure that promises murder and destruction in a hellish damnation he fears he cannot escape—a darkness "without end in my life to come." This vision of Levertov ignites a vertigo that touches on primal terrors. In "*Passages* 36," after speaking of the "end of an old friendship" in which "festering flesh was there," he goes on to compare the conflict with her to struggling as an adolescent with his adoptive mother over his identity—as poet and as homosexual: "It was very like that coming to know / my mother was at war with what I was to be" (*GW* 87). In the midst of the Vietnam War, a chasm opens in which Duncan experiences his rupture with Levertov as similar to the life-and-death battle for identity in adolescence. Levertov joins his mother as primary female figures that provide him with life-giving sustenance but also threaten to annihilate him. As in the poem "My Mother Would be a Falconress," where Duncan imagines himself as a falcon tearing away from and exacting revenge on his mother ("I tore at her wrist, at the hold she had for me, / until the blood ran hot and I heard her cry out"; *BB* 53), he acknowledges in *"Passages* 36" that the cycle of revenge apparent in conflicts such as the Vietnam War also exists within his own mind, "itself exacting revenge and suffering revenge" (*GW* 84). By the end of *"Passages* 36," declining to "grow tolerant / of what I cannot share and what / refuses me" and approving the finality and necessity of his break with two of the central figures in his life, he has "let go" completely his attachment to these women: "In Truth 'tis done. At last. I'll not / repair" (87). The five disyllabic units, each followed by a pause, reinforce the sense of finality, as though this were a slow-paced funeral dirge.

In her later "Some Duncan Letters—A Memoir and a Critical Tribute," Levertov ponders issues that precipitated their conflict (Levertov 194–230). She notes that their friendship was grounded in the mutual confirmation of a shared poetic enterprise, in which Duncan acted as a "mentor" (205) in what she calls the "ethics of aesthetics" (210)—that is, the conviction that aesthetic decisions must be seen as ethical choices. For Duncan as an inveterate Freudian, ethical choice involves not only conscious volition but also taking responsibility for unconscious desires and aversions. Levertov protests, however, that his obsession with the unconscious and the shadowy causes him to devalue individual volition and commitment: "unfortunately, though his 'digging for meanings' results in many felicities and resonances in his own work, the method often makes him a poor reader of others, a reader so intent upon shadow that he rejects, or fails to see, substance" (223). She too finds that the destruction of their friendship can be traced from his "misreading" of her line "implosion of skinned penises into carcass-gulleys" as being rooted in her own psychic economy. Interpreting her poem in that way, he "misses the obvious," she argues: the reason this poem imagined such atrocities being committed in Vietnam is because "I considered myself morally obliged to attempt to contemplate, however much it hurt to do so, just what that violence can be" (222). Beyond poetic testimony to her outrage, she directed her "grief, rage, shame and frustration" into political action, in which she experienced "unforeseen blessings" (225) in "a new sense of community as one worked, or picketed . . . with comrades" (226). "As a good Anarchist from his youth up," Levertov explains, Duncan seldom allowed himself the solace of participating in group action: "Duncan himself suffered, surely, a greater degree of frustration than we [Levertov and her husband Mitchell Goodman] did, because we lightened that burden for ourselves by taking on the other burden of action" (225). To corroborate her sense that Duncan's grief was unabated, she quotes from a letter of his to her from the midsixties:

> Jess and I have decided that we will wear black armbands (as the Spanish do when some member of their immediate family has died) *always* and keep a period of mourning until certainly the last American soldier or "consultant" is gone from Viet Nam—but may it not be the rest of our lives? until "we" are no longer immediately active in bringing grief to members of the family of man. (224)

The bottomless grief each poet felt during the Vietnam War was compounded by hurt feelings as their opposition regarding "the ethics of aesthetics" hardened—"each of us," Levertov says, "taking fierce, static, antagonist 'positions,' he of attack, I of defense" (228).

"Sunless"

The grief provoked by war and by his break with Levertov is joined by another source of grief for Duncan at this time. In the "Preface" to *Caesar's Gate*, he strives to direct his discussion of Lorca, who becomes in many ways a surrogate for himself, into a region of grief he has explored less fully. Speaking of his own sexual frustration and attraction to madness during the original writing of *Caesar's Gate*, Duncan says he arrived at a juncture where, in order to avoid madness, "I would have, ultimately, to name the grief myself" (xviii). Instead of offering a name for his grief from that earlier time, he undertakes the work of naming in the "Preface" itself. Speaking of "Iglesia Abandonada" and the play *Yerma*, he remarks, "[I]n Lorca's poetic theater, there appear now women who rage in the fury of a denied passion, a not having a son that is their fate. The poet has given up his own bearing a son in his bearing his art" (xxiv). It seems to me that this last sentence specifies the unnamable core of Duncan's grief at this time, a grief at not having (at not "bearing"—the female role) a son. This grief, which involves the sacrifice of parenthood in the service of art, Duncan shared with both Lorca and Whitman. The inconsolable loss these poets experience has not only an immediate locus but also a global bearing on psychological health. For instance, in the psychological stages of life conceived by Erik Erikson, the stage where one becomes a parent and cares for future generations is designated "generativity," and one must pass through a "crisis" of generativity in order to progress to the final life stage of "wisdom."[13]

In the throes of such a crisis, Duncan has difficulty admitting to mourning an unborn son. Looked at in light of the virulence of his quarrel with Levertov, his emotional reticence regarding parenthood in the "Preface" is all the more striking. Rather than say more about the source of his grief, though, Duncan spends the next two pages of the "Preface" reading *Yerma* as the tragedy of a barren woman, whose childlessness destroys her marriage and brings her in compensation the mysterious gypsy spirit of the duende—which arrives only when death is in the air. At this point, Duncan breaks off his exposition without warning and inserts a poem (initially slated for inclusion in *Ground Work* but later withheld), marking it off by a rule both before and after:

"CHILDLESS" I wrote in a notebook over a year ago

"*Sunless*" means
having no son. Let's be done with it.
The Son grows in the heart
the word I dared not speak. The Word

shakes the poem-center.

(*CG* xxvi)

Duncan does not gloss this eruption into his interpretation of Lorca, moving on instead to address the issue of sexual perversity in "Oda a Walt Whitman." This silence leads one to conclude that the insertion of "CHILDLESS" in the "Preface" constitutes the deeply troubled admission by a homosexual man of the endless bereavement he suffers as a result of forsaking biological continuity. In Whitman's "Vigil Strange," the maternal soldier, "bathed by the rising sun," deposits his "son" in the grave. In Duncan's poem the womblike images of the son growing in the heart and of the Word shaking the "poem-center" point to a forsaken maternal impulse; likewise, Duncan draws on the same ageless pun that Whitman employs when he explains that "'*Sunless*' means / having no son." To have no son is to be without a light rising from the future. Becoming aware of this situation renders Duncan speechless, afraid to name the source of his grief.

Strikingly, he shares this unending, unspeakable mourning for the "unengendered child" with Lorca as well. In the "Introduction" to *Poet in New York*, Christopher Maurer cites several poems of Lorca's, including "Iglesia

Abandonada," that revolve around an anguished void: "In the void that is at the center of his swirling images, in the eye of the storm, in the resonant hollow of the well, is an absent child" (xxix). Maurer goes on to observe: "One of the unresolved tensions in the book, as in Lorca's life, is this: on the one hand, grief for the 'unengendered child'; on the other, the calm certainty, expressed in the 'Ode' [to Walt Whitman], that not all men were destined for procreation" (xxxi). Duncan did not seem to possess such a calm certainty. In fact, when he was married briefly and unhappily in the forties and made his wife pregnant, the fetus was aborted. The abortion doomed the marriage, but Duncan had already begun another homosexual affair. If his wife had delivered a boy, however, he would have been of draft age during the Vietnam War.[14] In "This Form of Life Needs Sex," Allen Ginsberg too contemplates his lack of progeny, recognizing that "Between me and oblivion an unknown / woman stands," whom he would have "to accept . . . if I want to continue the race." In this poem, Ginsberg is consumed not by grief but by fear and repugnance: to bring forth a new generation, he would have to "bury my loins in the hang of pearplum / fat tissue / I had abhorred / before I give godspasm Babe leap / forward thru death" (*CPAG* 292).

In "Changing Perspectives in Reading Whitman" (1970), Duncan engages the poetic progenitor that he shares with Lorca (and Ginsberg) and explores further the issue of the unengendered child. Like many commentators, Duncan recognizes that even though Whitman declares in the "Children of Adam" poems "'The oath of procreation I have sworn—my Adamic and fresh daughters'" (*SP* 83), and states apocryphally to J. A. Symonds, "'I have had six children—two are dead—One living southern grandchild,'" nowhere in the poems that proclaim his desire for women does he express anything like the longing and loss that charge the poems treating male lovers. What Duncan notices in Whitman's male love poems "is a homosexuality in distress, not only in its cry for a mate . . . but in its generative loss." This "generative loss" is so compelling, for both Duncan and Whitman, that Duncan judges Whitman's "longing for a woman not as lover but as mother to his fathering desire" as sincere—a judgment Ginsberg might well echo (although there is admittedly a comic quality to Ginsberg's poem). Duncan sympathizes when Whitman admits the "'greed that eats me night and day with hungry gnaw, till I saturate what shall produce boys to fill my place when I am through'" (83), claiming that an "old agony of the heart" (84) is behind it. In Whitman's less-than-romantic desire to inseminate a "what" (his neuter term for a womb), he enters the same dilemma as Ginsberg with regard to intercourse with a woman.

Quoting one of the key passages from "Song of Myself," "'Urge and urge and urge, / Always the procreant urge of the world,'" Duncan contends that in this passage as in Whitman's vision of saturating "what will produce boys," the elder poet's preeminent concept of procreation is ejaculatory. Understanding Whitman's phallic dilemma, Duncan reads his verse as proposing the sperm themselves for children in an ejaculatory fantasy: "the jetting of a multitude in which one spermatozoa may come to the consummation of its egg, a host jetted forth to live the lifetime each its own as a sperm." "Here again," Duncan notes, "we find the terrible perturbation of the suns, seeds of sons Whitman never fathered, 'swelling, collapsing, ending, serving their longer, shorter use.'" These interlocking images of phallic procreation—sperm, suns, seeds, and sons—bind Duncan closely to the agonies of Whitman and also, he recognizes, to those of Lorca. He imagines the two earlier poets as antiphonal voices singing of the unfulfilled longing to create a son: "'Urge and urge and urge . . . 'Agonía, agonía, sueño, fermento y sueño . . . agonía, agonía,' Lorca will reply, a poet who was himself obsessed with the longing of a woman to give birth, to have a child, and denied fulfillment" (84).[15]

The renunciation of marriage and fatherhood by these homosexual poets joins the complex series of emotional equations we have been tracing in Duncan's poetry and life. Just as he had turned his back on his mother in order to remain true to his vocation as poet, so he turns his back on Levertov to remain true to his belief that the poet cannot maintain a purely denunciatory position with reference to the wars of his or her time but must admit to being implicated in them. These renunciations of important women in his life can also be equated with Duncan's turning his back on marriage and on "childbearing" by choosing to remain true to his homosexuality. But Duncan's homosexuality did not conform to the Apollonian ideal that Lorca praised; in the "Preface" to *Caesar's Gate*, Duncan admits to a history of the sort of promiscuity that Lorca lashes out against in "Oda a Walt Whitman": "I am sick at the thought of it, but I too must be one of those *maricas de las ciudades* [faggots of the cities] Lorca inveighs against" (xxvii). Nonetheless, Duncan also practiced a kind of renunciation like that the Spanish poet praises by crowning Whitman a "chaste" Apollo (*PNY* 159): many homosexual men have fathered children, but Duncan turned aside from that path, pursuing instead a homosexual "procreativity" comprising love and sex with men and creation in poetry. Although he had accepted long ago his fate as homosexual poet, Duncan now finds that this fate involves a sort of backward relationship to Christian Mystery: instead of celebrating the Son as the Word, Duncan realizes that he "dare not speak" the word "son," for it names a grief nearly impossible to bear—a grief that "shakes the poem-center" in ways so threatening to his poetic vocation that he begs, "Let's be done with it."

In the "Preface" to *Caesar's Gate*, Duncan professes to join not only the poet Lorca and the women in his poetry and plays but also (ironically) the politicians and generals conducting the Vietnam War in making a sacrifice of the son. Orthodox Christianity celebrates this sacrifice as God's ultimate gift to humanity, but from his gnostic perspective Duncan sees not only sacramental blessings flowing from the death of Christ but also a history of generational destruction, in which old men in authority arrogate to themselves the divine image and sacrifice their sons to maintain their own sense of power and immortality. With this deeply tragic sense of history and concomitant admission of the personal sacrifice he has made by remaining "sonless," Duncan cannot credit the efficacy of the revolutionary antiwar politics that Levertov pursues, for he sees the politics as also consumed by war and the sacrifice of sons—but without the acknowledgment of guilt that he feels tragedy demands. As he reminds her, intending to make her aware of the delusion he sees in her ferocious desire for peace, "THERE HAS BEEN NO TIME IN HUMAN HISTORY THAT WAS NOT A TIME OF WAR" (Bertholf and Gelpi 661). A confirmed Heraclitean, Duncan believes that "War is the Father of all" (*FC* 111). Among the great variety of his responses to the Vietnam War and to the personal crises it evokes—no matter how prophetic or denunciatory or vengeful or fearful his writing becomes—an underlying tone of bereavement sounds, for which "grief's its proper mode."[16]

7

IN ROBERT DUNCAN'S
"ANIMA REBELLION," DENISE LEVERTOV
MEETS THE GODDESS KALI

The Erotic Mother

Duncan's seemingly obsessive return to the disturbing contents of *Caesar's Gate* in the 1972 "Preface" does not represent a departure in his method. A profoundly exegetic poet, he not only read previous poets such as Whitman and Lorca with probing insight but also engaged often with his own earlier work, in both cases commenting on images left uninterpreted in the original and adding new perspectives suggested by the context of the moment. This procedure can be seen in his essays, ranging from his 1959 comments on "The Homosexual in Society" (1944) to his many dated revisions and commentaries to chapters of *The H.D. Book*, and it also can be found at the heart of many of his poems. Duncan was a dedicated analyst, especially attuned to the contradictory or paradoxical valences of images from mythology, and he went to great lengths in both his prose and poetry to ferret out dialectical values in such charged figures as Hermes or Isis, adopting a Freudian reading style that turns suggestive images in many directions in order to reveal their latent contents. In his essay on Whitman, Duncan reaffirms this erotic poetics while discussing Whitman's presentation in "Out of the Cradle Endlessly Rocking" of "the ecstasy of orgasm" as a return to the instinctual origins of life; this vision demonstrates, Duncan claims, that Whitman "had been a forerunner of Freud in this conviction that the whole question of sexuality 'strikes far deeper than most people have supposed'" (*FC* 82).[1]

Given the persistence and subtlety of Duncan's erotic poetics, a method deeply informed by Freud and rivaling him at times in creativity and penetration, it is striking that Duncan does not offer a more nuanced treatment of the goddess Kali, whom he invokes to condemn Levertov in "Santa Cruz Propositions." With her highly charged attributes of sexuality, horror, and maternity, Kali is exactly the sort of figure whose lore one would expect Duncan to research and to bring to bear upon his dependably revelatory reflections on desire and fate. Curiously, though, in the poem and in letters to and from Levertov in response to the poem, Kali remains for Duncan a remarkably one-dimensional figure of opprobrium, which this psychoanalytically gifted and self-aware poet refuses to investigate for what it might reveal about psychic energy in general or about his own fears and desires.[2] To draw out other facets of the disturbances haunting Duncan during the early years of writing *Ground Work: Before the War* (which include his revising *Caesar's Gate*), I would like to undertake a more extended reading of Kali as an erotic image in Indian and Western culture and in Duncan's own psychic economy, a reading that he surprisingly left unattempted.

To do so involves pursuing a number of strands of exposition. First, it is important to peer into the deeply erotic lore of Kali, not just in iconographic terms but also with reference to her impact on the religious imagination in India and the West. Presenting this lore also helps us consider how Kali and other horrific appearances of the divine in South Asia are converted through esoteric means into salvific images. Such traditions capable of making the transit from the horrific to the enlightening foster a hermeneutic approach that can be contrasted with Duncan's uncharacteristic inability to interpret this particular form of the mother goddess as a multifaceted psychic force. Observing the variety of ways one can respond to the menacing mother goddess opens up new perspectives on Duncan's relations to his own mothers (his birth mother and his adoptive mother) and on his unfulfilled desire to "bear" a son. In a letter to Levertov and in a later interview with Robert Peters and Paul Trachtenberg, Duncan indicates that around the time of writing "Santa Cruz Propositions" he was suffering from "an inner disturbance with what the Jungians call the *anima*," a disturbance in which Levertov was implicated (Bertholf and Gelpi 711).[3] His prose poem "The Museum," he tells her, also concerns this disturbance, and an analysis of the poem will reveal how his difficulties with maternity and with what he calls in the letter "offended womanly powers" produce a corresponding poetic disturbance. His painful encounter with the wrathful goddess Kali signals a complex psychic disruption, an "anima rebellion" (Peters and Trachtenberg 101), in which his tremendously ambitious poetic assemblage does not fail altogether but verges on coming to grief.

There are three primary perspectives from which I would like to view Kali: that of her place in Hindu mythology and ritual, that of Western appropriations and responses to the goddess, and that of psychoanalysis. These three perspectives have been suggestively linked by religious scholar Jeffrey J. Kripal, author of *Kali's Child: The Mystical and the Erotic in the Life and Teachings of Ramakrishna* and editor, with Rachel Fell McDermott, of *Encountering Kali: In the Margins, at the Center, in the West.*[4] The latter volume presents the latest research on Kali from religious, anthropological, postcolonial, psychoanalytical, feminist, and new media scholars. Like all major mythological figures, Kali has a long, multifaceted history; most likely a tribal goddess two millennia ago, she gradually became incorporated into both the Brahmanical and the tantric traditions. Kripal and McDermott offer a capsule summary of her attributes: "Kali is commonly perceived as a goddess who encompasses and transcends the opposites of life. She is, for example, simultaneously understood as a bloodthirsty demon-slayer, an inflictor and curer of diseases, a deity of ritual possession, and an all-loving, compassionate Mother." Her worship occurs in a number of geographically peripheral regions of South Asia, especially in Bengal, where she is represented with shocking intensity, "wearing fetuses for earrings, decapitating men, sticking her tongue out for all to see, wearing a garland of chopped-off heads and a mini-skirt of human arms, and living in cremation grounds." She is often shown astride a corpse, which is sometimes considered the god Shiva—who may also sport an erect phallus. "To make matters ever more complex, despite all of this, her devotees still insist upon affectionately addressing her as 'Ma' ('Mother')" (4).[5]

Encompassing dualities, Kali combines ferocity and eroticism and enacts the roles of dominant sex partner and all-giving mother. These paradoxical attributes inform the two prominent modes of worshipping her: the tantric mode (which has been undertaken traditionally by men) and the mode of the devotee (available to both men and women). Transgressing the most sacred cultural taboos, tantric rituals include meditation in cremation grounds, ingesting "unclean" substances, and ritual intercourse, often with nonspousal partners. Kali is central to tantric spirituality because her attributes embody both the forces that the tantric "hero" (the successful practitioner of a tantric discipline) strives to overcome and the means for such overcoming: "The figure of Kali conveys death, destruction, fear, terror, the all-consuming aspect of reality. As such, she is also a 'forbidden thing,' or the forbidden par excellence, for she is death itself." The tantric hero faces Kali fearlessly and endeavors to transform her into a means of salvation: "It is she, when confronted boldly in meditation, who gives the *sadhaka* [spiritual aspirant] great power and ultimately salvation. In Kali's favorite dwelling place, the cremation ground, the *sadhaka* meditates on every terrible aspect of the black goddess and thus achieves his goal" (30). Like the tantric hero, the devotee of Kali can reach this same goal but by taking a different route. The devotee and the hero both acknowledge the undeniable truths that Kali represents: "namely, that life feeds on death, that death is inevitable for all beings, that time wears all things down." The devotee, though, overcomes fear by taking the role of a child and regarding Kali as a mother, thus embracing in the fullest sense the hard truths figured by the goddess—"no matter how awful, how indifferent, how fearsome she is" (32–33).

A controversial image of divinity within India over the course of centuries, Kali became notorious in the West in the nineteenth century, once British missionaries were allowed to evangelize in India. Kali was singled out by missionaries as the consummate embodiment of bloodthirsty and highly sexualized savagery, whose sway over her minions justified British rule. A Scottish missionary, for instance, "portrays Kali's worship as the quintessence of hideous idolatry and superstition: 'Of all the Hindu divinities, this goddess is the most cruel. . . . [Her] supreme delight . . . consists in cruelty and torture; her ambrosia is the flesh of living votaries and sacrificed victims; and her sweetest nectar, the copious effusion of their blood'" (Kripal and McDermot 174). Hugh B. Urban asserts that these images of Kali appealed to and colored the British imagination, both in fiction and in "factual" reports: "They are, in [Michael] Taussig's sense, mimetic projections of the colonizer's simultaneous fear of and secret desire for the native Other, the mixed repulsion and attraction to his untamed savagery, sexuality, and animal violence. . . . For Victorian novelists, the image of Kali was a powerful projection of their own sexual desires and anxieties, objectified in the mirror of an exotic Other" (182). This orientalized view of Kali has continued in the West as the dominant one down to the present day, and it informed Duncan's portrait of Levertov as much as it has the images of Kali in popular films, such as the Beatles's *Help* (1965) and *Indiana Jones and the Temple of Doom* (1984).

In contrast to Duncan, Ginsberg was drawn to the goddess rather than repulsed by her, exploiting for political purposes the attributes of Kali that frighten Western commentators. In "Stotras to Kali Destroyer of Illusions" (1962; *CPAG* 298–300), he equates Kali with the Statue of Liberty in a parody of a Hindu devotional poem: "O Freedom with gaping mouth full of Cops whose throat is adorned with skulls of Rosenbergs / whose breasts spurt Jazz into the robot faces of thy worshippers grant that recitation / of this Hymn will bring them abiding protection money & dance in White House" (*CPAG* 299). Accompanying the poem, his "Notes for Stotras to Kali as Statue of Liberty" (*Indian Journals* 13–20) make apparent Ginsberg's extensive knowledge of the lore and paradoxical qualities of Kali, garnered especially during his travels in India. His fascination with Kali as the ferocious mother can be seen at work also in the collage poem "Wichita Vortex Sutra" (1966), where he alludes to her three times during a litany of the "Powers of imagination" summoned to bolster his prophecy of "the end of the War!": Kali appears first in the name of the yogi, "Kali Pada Guha Roy whose yoga drops before the void"; then she is evoked as mother goddess when the poet calls forth "Sri Ramakrishna master of ecstasy eyes / half closed who only cries for his mother"; and finally the image of "Durga-Ma covered with blood / destroyer of battlefield illusions" refers to Kali through a mythologically related form of the goddess as warrior (*CPAG* 414–15).

The more rounded version of Kali that Ginsberg presents still manifests what Urban identifies as "sexual desires and anxieties," and these reactions to the goddess beg to be treated with the tools of psychoanalysis.[6] A psychoanalytic understanding of Kali must begin in India, with the caste Hindu family structure in which a young girl leaves behind her birth family in order to join an alien household presided over by her mother-in-law: "The young wife's isolated, subservient role in the joint family is such that she may i) indulge her infant son, ii) form erotic attachments to the child, and iii) unknowingly display repressed rage toward the infant"; this creates an image of mothers as "both loving and hating, nurturing and destroying, and . . . this is the psychological root of the salience of the symbol of the fierce goddess" (McDermott and Kripal 212). In Freudian terms, the fierce mother is also a castrating mother, which accounts for the sword Kali brandishes in one of her four hands (213). This fierce mother figures centrally in Duncan's psychological makeup, as a glance at his most celebrated poem, "My Mother Would Be a Falconress," with its portrait of the mother as huntress, makes abundantly clear. We will return to issues pertaining to Duncan's mother(s) below, but for now I want to emphasize that tantric lore encourages the successful hero to confront and vanquish the goddess as castrating mother. Kripal argues that Tantra resembles psychoanalysis in that each confronts its culture's deepest and most pervasive taboos, taboos having to do with "death, sexuality, pollution, and the dissolution of the socialized self" (196). Just as the successful *tantrika* transgresses taboos and converts the energy released into spiritual power, psychoanalysis confronts the repressed power locked in psychic complexes in order to dispel fear and promote understanding and freedom. In this sense, "psychoanalysis can be poetically described as a kind of Western Tantra, as a century-long meditation on the powers of sexuality, the body, life, death, and religion" (197). This encounter between psychoanalysis and Tantra, discussed earlier in the example of Norman O. Brown's *Love's Body*, epitomizes erotic poetics as it arose in the postwar period; it is especially evident in the eroticized spirituality of Robert Duncan's writing.

"An Emptiness in God"

A Freudian tantrika constantly responding to eros, Duncan deserves the epithet of "tantric hero" for his brave and unending confrontation with cultural taboos concerning the most carefully policed psychosexual complexes. Who but a dedicated Western tantrika would have the courage to invite upon himself overwhelming legal wrath and social ostracism by advertising his sexual orientation in "The Homosexual in Society" in 1944? This is just one example among many of Duncan's daring to confront and transform for his own purposes the most entrenched sexual, political, social, religious, and poetic norms, using psychoanalysis as a weapon to battle the repression concealed in the commonplace and release erotic energies. Surveying the sober certainties of his time and place, Duncan was never content to accept any of them, employing the Freudian discovery of the unconscious as a lever to pry the unacceptable out from underneath the accepted; as he wrote in "A Poem Beginning with a Line by Pindar": "I see always the under side turning" (*OF* 64).

In *Caesar's Gate*, Duncan invokes directly a famous text from Tibetan Buddhism (also known as Vajrayana), one of the principal tantric traditions. The action of *Caesar's Gate* takes place in an after-death realm, which Duncan equates not only with Dante's Hell but also with the Bardo state—the period after death and before rebirth—as it is described in *The Tibetan Book of the*

Dead (or *Bardo Thodol*). The Bardo state occupies the forty-nine days be-tween death and rebirth, during which the soul moves through three stages: the vision of light at the moment of death, the meetings with peaceful and wrathful deities, and the descent into birth. At any point along this journey, the soul can recognize its own essential nature, achieve Buddhahood, and step out of the cycle of birth, death, and rebirth. *The Tibetan Book of the Dead* was first published in English in 1927 and became an important text in the theosophical tradition in which Duncan was raised. In the 1955 "Preface for *Caesar's Gate*," he speaks of writing "a poetry of hell" that partakes of a pro-found erotic abjection, of "a soul-shriveling," in which he can rely only on "visions of this state, this bardo realm, to sustain me" (*CG* xlv). One of the bitterly ironic poems in the book makes this realm explicit in its title: "He Entertains at a Dinner Party in the Bardo State" (35).

A central feature of the middle Bardo state in the *Bardo Thodol* is the en-counter the soul makes with wrathful deities, which have to be recognized as hallucinations, as karmic thought forms arising from the complexes of the individual personality (Evans-Wentz 34). When understood as hallucina-tions, the wrathful deities revert to their former state as beneficent beings: "[A]fter the cessation . . . of the Peaceful and Knowledge-Holding Deities, who come to welcome one, the fifty-eight flame-enhaloed, wrathful, blood-drinking deities come to dawn, who are only the former Peaceful Deities in changed aspect" (131). Ordinary people are deluded into fearing and fleeing the bloodthirsty forms, but an initiate of Vajrayana, "as soon as he sees these blood-drinking deities, will recognize them to be his tutelary deities, and the meeting will be like that of human acquaintances. He will trust them; and becoming merged into them, in at-one-ment, will obtain Buddhahood" (132). During a lifetime of concentration and meditation, one acquires the focusing power to effect such transformations; for the tantric traditions this attentive acuity represents a major goal. In South Asian religious thought, the most influential story of the meditative conversion of the horrific into the salvific occurs in the eleventh book of the *Bhagavad-Gita*. In the climax of the most revered Hindu scripture, Lord Krishna grants an overpowering vision of his cosmic form to the princely warrior Arjuna. Perceiving the entire universe as existing inside the god, Arjuna is horrified to see all beings—including the warriors arrayed for the *Mahabharata*'s epic battle, which hasn't yet begun:

Rushing through
your fangs

into grim
mouths,
some are dangling
from heads
crushed
between your teeth. . . .
You lick at the worlds
around you,
devouring them
with flaming mouths;
and your terrible fires
scorch the entire universe,
filling it, Vishnu,
with violent rays.

Arjuna asks in dismay, "who are you / in this terrible form?" Krishna responds, "I am time grown old, / creating world destruction, / set in motion / to annihilate the worlds" (Miller 101–3). Krishna's cosmic form turns out to be not a static icon of the universe but rather a kinetic motion picture of time as devourer. Horrific and stomach-churning, the vision also grants ecstasy and reassurance, for Arjuna has prepared through dialogue with Krishna over the course of the first ten books of the *Gita* to endure a direct encounter with the force of divinity—if only for a brief moment.

Duncan's erotic poetics generally thrives on the psychic capacity to convert the fearsome into the ecstatic, combining theosophical invocations of Asian classics that he encountered in childhood, such as the *Gita* and *The Tibetan Book of the Dead*, with a relentless Freudian pursuit of the multivalent powers of unconscious images. The poems of *Caesar's Gate*, however, arise out of such deep abjection that he elects to portray the Bardo state not as one of opportunity for enlightenment but rather as one of stasis, of impeded life. In effect, he combines the concept of the Bardo state with Dante's notion of Hell as the realm of arrested spiritual development, a realm in which "a forfeiting of the goods of the intellect" ("*il ben de l'intelletto,*" *Inferno* III.18; *CG* xlv) renders conscious self-transformation impossible. One of Jess's collages for *Caesar's Gate*, "Upon Another Shore of Hell" (*CG* 16; Fig. 24)—which accompanies a poem of the same name about being trapped in death (discussed in the previous chapter)—seems to depict this state of blocked transformation. The main figure in the collage is a Japanese sculpture of the Buddha, looming gigantically over the small women before it. This photograph is altered slightly by the addition of two eyeballs in unexpected places and by what looks like the mirrored surface on the faceplate of a motorcycle helmet in place of the Buddha's face. As a reflective surface, the mirror refuses entrance to the contemplative peace of the statue. The mirror is shattered, though, suggesting not only a denial of access to the self-transformative powers of the Buddha but that the possibility of such transformation has been violently abrogated.

FIGURE 24. Jess, *Upon Another Shore of Hell*, 1955. Illustration for Robert Duncan, *Caesar's Gate*. Berkeley: Sand Dollar, 1972. © 2009 The Jess Collins Trust. Used by permission.

The 1949–50 representation in *Caesar's Gate* of the breakdown of Duncan's tantric heroism echoes again in 1972 as he takes up the book during a period of prolonged torment, a time in which the goddess Kali arises as a feminine-inspired image of implacable wrath and destruction that he cannot master. In the poems of *Caesar's Gate*, he had named the realm of liberated desires "Asia" and then placed it beyond his reach by making the impenetrable Caesar's Gate the primary image of the book. In this sense, "Asia" joins the Bardo state and Kali as charged images that signal a psychic disturbance in his writing. Engaging them, he fails to enact the wished-for transformation, whose thwarting evokes self-loathing in response to the inability to convert grief, fear, and wrath into spiritually empowering emotions. A short poem from 1972 with the suggestive title, "And Hell Is the Realm of God's Self-Loathing" (*GW* 52), projects the poet's attitude onto God and thus closes off again the possibility of emotional conversion. If from a psychological or tantric perspective "God" represents the principle of endless transformation, then Duncan seems to have reached during this period an impasse in which that principle is voided. The poem that he writes to close out the 1972 edition of *Caesar's Gate*, "Despair in Being Tedious" (*CG* 72–73; *GW* 13–14), reflects back on the time when he wrote the poems of the first edition and his obsession with "Asia" and "an emptiness in God":

Despair in Being Tedious

A long way back I look and find myself
as I was then I am, a circling man
in a seizure of talk that he hears too as he goes on.

. . . .

I do not know if I am bound
to run upon this wheel, wound up,
excited in a manic spiel of wheel in wheel,

or if I'm free to talk wherever they are free
to listen. A long way back I look,
and I was often disheartend there where I was.

Returning found the room deserted,
an empty space of Asia that crept into me.
I tried to die and did not. The hurt

was an empty place in meaning I turnd from.
That God was Asia I tried to say. Some were tired of it
and left, but there was too much that I had left to say.

. . . .

What did I have to say? The talk was of Asia
and an emptiness in God that men have known
in deserts and in times like we are in.

What was I come to? As I come to,
your eyes have left me, and they stray
to find some exit from where we are.

"*In Asia . . .*" There is a desolate possibility
I strive to get across. You gather up your things apart from me.
You do not follow, and I am lost therein.

There is in me a weary stretch I mean to say
some urgency that draws the matter out
I cannot come to, and I want company.

. . . .

The place is closing and I am alone I fear.
It's twelve to two.
I have come to myself. Good night.

I will not need your help
me Lord. From here
Great Asia beyond the horizon of my sight

goes on to nowhere I cannot say
and in that continent as I go
the hour stretches year on year.

(*GW* 13–14)

Such an extended recollection of a specific moment in his life is rare in Duncan's poetry. In this poem, he claims an identity with the person he was when writing *Caesar's Gate* in 1949 and 1950: "as I was then I am." He portrays himself as an outcast, boring other patrons at a bar with his "manic spiel," and wonders if his compulsion to talk incessantly is equivalent to being bound on a wheel—which is the Buddhist image for *samsara*, the unending cycle of birth and death that one can escape only through enlightenment. "Asia" is first mentioned in the sixth stanza as "an empty space that crept into me." It was "an empty place in meaning" so painful that he contemplated suicide: "I tried to die and did not." Asia represents not only physical desire but a spiritual desire to convert abject experiences into meaningful ones, as becomes apparent when Duncan proposes "That God was Asia," only to draw out the equation between God and Asia by declaring both empty "in times like we are in." In the next stanza, the speaker awakens alongside a lover trying "to find some exit from where we are." "*In Asia*," the speaker asserts, and finds his desolation confirmed again by the lover's retreat. In his utter aloneness, he will not let go of the urgent disturbance that holds him in thrall: "There is a weary stretch I mean to say / some urgency that draws the matter out / I cannot come to, and I want company."

Throughout much of the poem, Duncan's syntax is uncharacteristically simple, consisting mostly of declarative sentences, but in the last two stanzas the syntax twists and turns in strange ways. The first sentence reads, cryptically, "I will not need your help / me Lord." The initial line comprises a complete utterance, which is only ambiguous because the referent of "your" is unclear. As it turns into the second line, though, the syntax becomes much more clotted. The sentence seems to be making a number of declarations at once: "I will not need your help." "I will not need *your* help, but help me Lord." "I will not need your prayerful 'Help me Lord.'" "I will not need your help, my Lord." "I will not need, but help me Lord." The paramount question regarding this sentence is whether the addressee is a believer whose spiritual ministrations Duncan refuses or God himself: whose help does he profess not to need—and with or without conviction? The last sentence is longer and even more convoluted and mysterious: "From here / Great Asia beyond the horizon of my sight // goes on to nowhere I cannot say / and in that continent as I go / the hour stretches year on year." There are a number of paradoxes in this sentence: "Great Asia" is beyond the horizon of his sight, and yet he is somehow traveling in that continent; although "Great Asia" stretches beyond the horizon, it "goes on to nowhere"; the phrase "nowhere I cannot say" looks like a double negative that should resolve to "somewhere I can say," but it seems instead to refer more literally to an unutterable nowhere; as the speaker travels through space in an imagined Asia, an hour of time "stretches year on year," as though a momentary fantasy had become an endless repetition compulsion. The purposefully ambiguous syntax in these final two stanzas of the poem mimics a profound confusion, in which God and Asia, past desires and present grief cannot be disentangled.

God, Asia, desire, manic speech, and self-loathing: these vast signifiers all seem to bear upon Duncan's grief and his inability to convert negatives into positives. He becomes trapped in a "nowhere I cannot say," a double negative that does not resolve to a positive but instead retains its twin aspects of negation: "nowhere"—the emptiness in God and Asia; and "I cannot say"—the inability to communicate signaled by a "manic spiel" that turns away listeners. Duncan analyzes this condition of being nowhere and not able to communicate in "A Song from the Structures of Rime Ringing as the Poet Paul Celan Sings" (*GW* 12), the poem just prior to "Despair in Being Tedious" in *Ground Work*.[7] Identifying with the emptiness of God and the inaccessibility of desire in Celan's poetry, Duncan declares, "Something has wreckt the world I am in." The poem tries to define *what* has wrecked the world but keeps coming up against irresolvable negatives:

> Something is there that is it. Must
>   be   nothing ultimately   no
> thing.   In the formula derived
>   as I go
> the something is   Nothing   I know
> obscured in the proposition of No-thingness.

Duncan joins Celan in a dizzying world of nothingness, in which trauma seems so all-encompassing that it lacks an origin and dissolves the solid world of things; inhabiting this void, the poet turns language inside out while seeking a means of communicating the trauma. The dilemmas of communication in Celan's poetry result in an interrogation and breakdown of language that parallels his endless ruminations on the unspeakable experience of the Holocaust. By identifying with Celan, Duncan signals confrontation with a trauma of like severity for him as an individual, a trauma whose expression is beyond him. At the center of the poem, Duncan comments on this inexpressibility in a one-line stanza: "It is totally untranslatable."

"An Anima Rebellion"

The inaugural trauma of Duncan's life, in which birth and death were unalterably fused, was the death of his mother as a result of giving him birth. Thus, for Duncan the locus of trauma resides in the conjunction of birth and death. If the mystical impulse is in the view of Freudians an attempt to return to the womb, then the death of Duncan's mother can be seen as the ultimate "Caesar's Gate," for hers is a womb of bliss to which he can *never* return. The next conjunction of Mother with trauma in Duncan's life concerns his relations with his adoptive mother, whom he naturally identifies with his birth mother. Peter O'Leary remarks on this conflation in his reading of "A Sequence of Poems for H.D.'s Birthday," in which he singles out this prose passage: "How long my mother waited for me, all her life long, like someone waiting at last to see once more a friend or a son coming from afar before she dies. No, the second mother, waiting in doubt and in hope for me for six months when I was hidden" (*RB* 14). As O'Leary points out, "What is remarkable about this poem—and this passage—is that Duncan conflates the trauma of his mother dying in birth with the trauma of his adoptive mother not giving birth at all but waiting for an appointed baby. In both cases, a menacing fate is at work in which Duncan is the center" (56). In the passage, Duncan not only conflates his two mothers and their anxious waiting but also, by imagining how they must have felt, identifies with them—as one who wishes to bear a son but finds himself, as he later expresses it, "CHILDLESS." In *Gnostic Contagion*, O'Leary rightly makes much of Duncan's uneasy bond with his mother(s), stating, "The conflict Duncan experienced with his mother was quite intense, and much of his poetry is informed by that tension" (56). It also informs his conflict with Levertov and, especially, his depiction of her as the mother goddess of birth and death, Kali. His grief during the most violent period of the Vietnam War plunges him into a vertiginous birth-and-death trauma, which leaves him, as he puts it, "nowhere I cannot say."

In the poems of *Caesar's Gate*, Duncan portrays the womb as a one-way gate of birth and death. "The Conqueror's Song," for example, ends with these lines:

Go to sleep, go to sleep.
You will waken again.
The Gate is still closed
and the soul wastes away.

Be angry like the lions
who roar like paind men,
suck at their sex
and crumble like clay,

filling the air with their rage.

(54)

The sexually frustrated souls in this poem seem to be longing for death—or banging on the door of the womb, as though wanting to retreat back into the final Bardo state. The lowest and last of the three Bardos is known as the *Sidpa Bardo*, "where the dead man, unable to profit by the teachings of the [two previous Bardos], begins to fall prey to sexual phantasies and is attracted by the vision of mating couples. Eventually he is caught by a womb and born into the earthly world again" (Jung, "Commentary" xli). In his speculations on the traumatic relations of birth and death in "The Conqueror's Song," Duncan seems to recall the unconquerable Sidpa state, "characterized by the fierce wind of *karma*, which whirls the dead man along until he comes to the 'womb-door.' In other words, the *Sidpa* state permits of no going back, because it is sealed off ... by an intense striving downwards, towards the animal sphere of instinct and physical rebirth" (xlii). In the *Caesar's Gate* poems there is no specific mention of the Mother, but it must be she whose locked womb provokes the rage of the fellating (or self-fellating) men whom she excludes.

When Duncan tries to convert some of the fateful powers of birth and death associated with the Mother into poetically available energy, he often invokes Mnemosyne, goddess of memory and mother of the muses, and approaches her from the perspective of a tantric Freudian:

> Back of the Muses, so the old teaching goes, is Mnemosyne, Mother of the Muses. Freud, too, teaches that the Art has something to do with restoring, re-membering, the Mother. Poetry itself may then be the Mother of those who have destroyed their mothers. But no. The image Freud projects of dismembering and remembering is the image of his own creative process in Psychoanalysis which he reads into all Arts. Mnemosyne, the Mother Memory of Poetry, is our made-up life, the matrix of fictions. Poetry is the Mother of those who have created their own mothers. (*H.D. Book* I.2 28)

This passage from *The H.D. Book* reveals Duncan's desire to destroy and dismember his mother(s) and his compensatory need to identify with his mother(s) by creating a new mother through poetry. In this way, he could be said as poet to give birth to his mother. During the period of crisis that holds our attention, though, he cannot seem to enact the compensatory moves that are hallmarks of his erotic poetics. Speaking to Levertov about "A Seventeenth Century Suite," he admits,

> I read thruout these poems, as in "The Museum" and in the second part of "Santa Cruz Propositions" how much you have been fused in my projection

of an inner disturbance with what the Jungians call the *Anima*. After my taking that *She* to be so specifically you in Passages 36, in the following section [Section 9 of "A Seventeenth Century Suite"] the persona proliferates and shows flashes of offended womanly powers. (Bertholf and Gelpi 711)

In his interview with Peters and Trachtenberg, Duncan speaks of this same offense to "womanly powers" with reference to "The Museum" (*GW* 63–65) specifically: within that prose-and-verse poem, "The figure of a poetess appears, as arising from my psyche, at a time when I was suffering from an anima rebellion" (Peters and Trachtenberg 101).[8]

"The Museum" is a "Grand architecture that the Muses command," an imagined physical space that houses the female force of creativity (the anima). In certain ways, the Museum is a space like "Asia" in "Despair in Being Tedious": just as "Great Asia beyond the horizon of my sight // goes on to nowhere I cannot say," the space of the Museum "is an horizon coming in from what we cannot see to sound in sight that is female." Duncan replaces the double negative of "nowhere I cannot say" with a similarly irresolvable "what we cannot see," which then presents itself as a synesthetic "sound in sight that is female." The aporia beyond the horizon of "Despair in Being Tedious" becomes an aporia within the Museum that is female. It is striking that Duncan represents this female aporetic power of the muses as *shadow* and *stone*, both images of death. He speaks of the Mother multiplying into the women "in a run of alcoves—shadowd radiance upon shadowd radiance," and then offers a threatening instance of "a Woman that is a company of women": "The shadow she stands in is the shadowing of the heart's ease." He also tells of being "Entirely shadowd. Entirely gazing. A route of seeing carved in stone" (63). Near the end of the poem, he states that, "The Muses are of stone to be riven from stone" (65).

In the course of his lengthy, illuminating discussion of Duncan's "My Mother Would Be a Falconress," O'Leary cites Freud on the effect of unremitting grief, using terms that are directly pertinent to "The Museum": "Freud, in 'Mourning and Melancholia,' is . . . explicit about what the melancholic is suffering from, usually a loss of love, either real or perceived, which has its best example in the death of a parent—or in a disappointment suffered at the hand of a parent." This is exactly the state in which we find Duncan with respect to each of his mothers—a state where, according to Freud, the ego splits in two, with one half identifying with the lost object. In other words, Duncan replaces Mother with ego, but a split ego that is both itself and the shadow of its lost object. The processes of shadowing and stony objectification we have seen in "The Museum" mimic the terms of Freud's description of melancholia: "Thus the shadow of the object fell upon the ego, and the latter could henceforth be judged by a special agency, as though it were an object, the forsaken object." O'Leary's comment on this passage is pertinent: "What . . . had been a normal human conflict—the suffering of a loss—has become a critical cleavage between the ego and the ego submerged in melancholia" (156).

As the dominant temper of "The Museum," melancholia is linked with the Mother and the grief she invokes: "And every mammal weeping I hear, drip upon drip, as if alone, resounding there. And birds and reptiles weeping. Cell upon cell, in each, this shadow. In each, this Muse of a commanding Art. In each, this falling into Time, drop by drop. In each this eternal gaze. In each, this ultimate Woman." This lugubrious sounding of lonely self-enclosure under the Woman's command reaches a crescendo when the poem presents "poetesses [who] advance to sing once more as Sappho sang . . . that Love that breaks us from what we are" (*GW* 64). At the point of introducing the Sapphic poetesses, the prose swerves into an italicized verse that, while referring to Sappho's portrayal of eros as bittersweet, reaches for the keening quality we heard in the "*Let it go*" refrain of "*Passages* 36":

> . . . *irresistible force, bitter, sweet, that even now*
> *strikes us down, you have awakend what we feard we were, and,*
> *men and women, we are lost in you. Pain*
>   *enters Being*
>   *drop*
>   *by drop.*

(64)

In the Peters and Trachtenberg interview, Duncan glosses this nearly unbearable suffering evoked by the "poetesses," referring in his gloss to three female literary figures: "[T]hree of my own personal icons, Ophelia, Desdemona, and Virginia Woolf I envision as death-pale. And since neither Ophelia nor Desdemona were writers that means that my obsession with them has killed the womanly writer inside me. And what's happened? This male Robert, this raging Othello, has taken over" (101). Stepping into the realm of Shakespearean tragedy, Duncan not only invokes the tragic fates of the women in *Hamlet* and *Othello* in the interview, but he also draws attention to the Kali-like figure of Lady Macbeth in "*Passages* 36" by declaring at the end of the poem, "'tis done" (*GW* 87), which echoes her "What's done is done" and "What's done cannot be undone."[9] Grief (represented by Ophelia and Desdemona) and rage (represented by Othello and Lady Macbeth) walk hand-in-hand in a melancholia in which gender conflict is deeply implicated. Duncan goes on in the interview to explain, "Two years ago I published a poem[,] The Museum, announcing this. The figure of a poetess appears, as arising from my psyche, at a time when I was suffering from an anima rebellion." In order to make clear what he means by "an anima rebellion," he recalls a time in the forties when he turned against the effeminate mannerisms that had gained him a position within a glittering demimonde: "In order to reject that period in high society where I found my effeminacy socially and acutely painful, I had to assert a more masculine identity. I felt literally sick, as though I'd eaten food waiting to be vomited forth. That masculine self, secure within me, now began to control situations and dominate them and to come on strong" (101). This visceral need to hold at bay his identification with the feminine has re-occurred, he maintains, during his battle with Levertov, and it feeds on deep reservoirs of grief, rage, shame, and fear.

In the midst of his grief-fueled rage against Levertov, Duncan experiences an anima rebellion, in which the inner female poet—also known as the Muse, also known as the Mother—turns against him in menacing fashion. In "The Museum," he portrays the Museum at one point as "the Labyrinth at Knossos," which harbors a Minotaur whose gender has been converted to "Woman." He then proceeds to depict her as something like an Aztec priest, who in sacrificing her victim "will not devour the heart but holds it high in her command." He also addresses her as "the Bestial Muse" and as "the devouring *Impératrice* at the heart of the Museum" (*GW* 63). These images of a bloodthirsty, domineering Mother bring us back to the fearsome, voracious figure of Kali.

And now it's time to return for one final look at the passages in "Santa Cruz Propositions" where Duncan depicts Levertov as Kali's avatar:

out of the depths of the Woman's love,

SHE appears, Kālī dancing, whirling her necklace of skulls,
trampling the despoiling armies and the exploiters of natural resources
under her feet. Revolution or Death!
Wine! The wine of men's blood in the vat
of the Woman's anger, whirling,

the crackling—is it of bones? castanets?
tommyguns? fire raging in the ghettos? What
is the wrath of Jehovah to this   almost blissful Mother-Righteousness
aroused by the crimes of Presidents?

"And I know such violent revolution has ached my marrow-bones,
my soul changing its cells"
—so immediately the lines of her poem come into mine.

She changes.
Violently.   It is her time.   I never saw that dress before.
I never saw that face before.

["When she is in the depths of her black silence," he told me,
"Phone right away. Don't think you know what to do to help her.
She is dangerous."]

Madame Outrage of the Central Committee
forms a storm cloud around her where she is brooding. This Night
opens into depth   without end in my life to come.

The Four Winds come into the Womb of Her Grievance.
Every woman   an Other   I fear for her.

She has put on her dress of murderous red.
She has put on her mini-skirt   and the trampling begins.
She has put on her make-up of the Mother of Hell,
the blue lips of Kore, the glowering
pale of the flower that is black to us.
She has put on her fashion of burning.

(*GW* 49)

In this passage the full horror of Duncan's anima rebellion shines forth. This
vision of Kali seems to ally her with both Revolution *and* Death, for that rally-
ing cry from Levertov's journal poem of Vietnam War protest, "Staying Alive"
(*To Stay Alive* 21–84), appears here as another motto of destruction. Duncan
finds in Levertov's righteous anger at political figures an unacknowledged
mirror to his own rage: who is it who sees in the culture at large "despoiling
armies," "exploiters of natural resources," "tommyguns," "fire raging in the
ghettos," "crimes of the Presidents"? The bitterness with which he accuses her
of "an almost blissful Mother-Righteousness" echoes his own grief-inspired

bitterness at the commanding presence of the Mother who "was at war with what I was to be" (*GW* 87). And the Mother of Hell is the Mother who stands on the other side of Caesar's Gate, guarding with implacable fierceness the birth door from the abandoned son's return.

"Creative Strife"

When possessed of the remarkable self-awareness afforded him by his thoroughgoing erotic poetics, Duncan insisted that we acknowledge everything that seems inimical to us as part of the fabric of the "creative veil or world-cloth," as he called it in *Letters* (12). In his most Heraclitean essay, "Man's Fulfillment in Order and Strife," he argues, "The very life of our art is our keeping at work contending forces and convictions. When I think of disorders, I often mean painful disorders, the disordering of fruitful orders that form one's own work. This is the creative strife that Heraclitus praised, breaking up, away from what you knew how to do into something you didn't know, breaking up the orders I belong to in order to come into alien orders, marches upon a larger order" (*FC* 112). It was just such "disorders" that Duncan courted by returning to the old book *Caesar's Gate* as a part of his venturing into "alien orders" after the completion of his Black Mountain period. In "Man's Fulfillment," written in 1968, Duncan offers an extended gloss on the disorders of one of his most virulent poems against the Vietnam War, "Up Rising, *Passages* 25" (*BB* 81–83). Introducing the poem, he admits that in his scathing denunciation of President Johnson and of a vengeful and rapacious America he "came close to the demotic voice" (*FC* 129), as he later accuses Levertov of doing, yet he argues that "the poem belongs, in the scope of the larger poem-series it appears in, not to the history of the United States, but to a larger structure of ideas. For not even *Man* for me can represent the term of World Order" (130), which contains all forms of life in a Grand Collage or "symposium of the whole." Duncan recognizes that even what he calls in "Santa Cruz Propositions" "the despoiling armies and the exploiters of natural resources" cannot merely be "trampled" on, as he imagines Levertov/Kali doing in the poem, for their very real threat of annihilation can be an urgent spur toward a kind of apotheosis of assemblage in the vision of "an ideal World Order, the universe as a triumphant work of art" (120).

When invoking the expansive context of a "poem-series" or a World Order, Duncan fully acknowledges the power of evil: "It is the attack everywhere upon the potential intellect of Man, the contempt for the vision of the world ecology and animal life and for Man's work and identity therein, that brings us to the brink." But he also points out that this attack by death-dealing forces and the sense of crisis it evokes "is made in every generation of Man. The bend of the bow, Heraclitus called it. Freud, in our day a Heraclitean, saw the bow bent between Eros and Thanatos." In Duncan's estimation, a successful erotic poetics will be able to take in and imaginatively inhabit the entire spectrum between eros and thanatos, "seeing as if with 'God's' eye a release of Man's fullest nature from its bonds" (120). During the period of the climax of the Vietnam War, especially between 1970 and 1972, Duncan seems to afford thanatos the most comprehensive release. In the larger perspective of his career, however, eros acts with equal if not greater energy, often overcoming thanatos—as was suggested by designating Duncan a tantric hero. The point, though, is not to seek to transcend death by denying the centrality of grief to human life. As Peter Homans demonstrates in *The Ability to Mourn*, loss and grief reside at the very inception of Freud's psychoanalysis, and the same can be said of the inception of Duncan's poetry. Loss furnishes the aching need to which a prodigious creativity responds. An erotic poetics can help us see contending forces of eros and thanatos at play not only in Duncan's work but also in that of many artists of the postwar period, when the practice of assemblage offered a new means for those seeking to preserve the erotic in a world besieged by thanatos.

CONCLUSION

Jerome Rothenberg's "Symposium of the Whole"

Assemblage

In 1968, Jerome Rothenberg published an unprecedented book, *Technicians of the Sacred: A Range of Poetries from Africa, America, Asia, & Oceania,* a work of assemblage art in the form of an anthology. With affinities to two earlier groundbreaking anthologies, Donald Allen's *The New American Poetry* (1960) and Harry Smith's *Anthology of American Folk Music* (1952), *Technicians of the Sacred* presents a convenient culmination point for a survey of contextual practice. In actuality, the anthology can been seen as a kind of threshold, not only a synopsis of erotic poetics in a compendious assemblage but also a transition into the related cultural and artistic movements of the seventies and eighties, such as multiculturalism, ethnopoetics, conceptual art, minimal art, performance art, and investigations of the relationship between orality and literacy. In *Technicians,* Rothenberg also enters the mythological storehouse that Duncan relies on so intensely, exploring world mythology less as a repository of psychological states than as a repertoire of stories about what it means to be human.

For all his justly celebrated internationalism, Rothenberg owes a major portion of his poetic horizon to the Black Mountain poets, especially Charles Olson, Robert Creeley, Robert Duncan, and Paul Blackburn. Duncan in particular had a signal impact on *Technicians,* and Rothenberg memorializes it in essays and interviews through invoking the phrase "symposium of the whole," a phrase he plucked from Duncan's essay "Rites of Participation," first published in *Caterpillar* 1 and 2 (October 1967, January 1968). Duncan imagines the "symposium" to be a new collocation that joins human beings in consanguinity not only with animals but with all earthly cells—a coming together in "one fate" brought about by the ecological imperatives of our time. He prophesies a global community that has "gone beyond the reality of the incomparable nation or race, the incomparable Jehovah in the shape of a man, the incomparable Book or Vision, the incomparable species, in which identity might hold & defend its boundaries against an alien territory" (*SP* 97). Such a community would not be hierarchical, as in Plato's *Symposium* (in which Socrates urges an ever more rarified sublimation toward ideal Forms), but would be rather a model of equality and wholeness: "To compose such a symposium of the whole, such a totality, all the old excluded orders must be included. The female, the proletariat, the foreign; the animal and vegetative; the unconscious and the unknown; the criminal and the failure—all that has been outcast and vagabond must return to be admitted in the creation of what we consider we are" (*SP* 98). Accepting Duncan's invitation to speak for a radically expanded totality, Rothenberg characterizes the symposium of the whole as "a complex redefinition of cultural and intellectual values: a new reading of the poetic past and present" (*Symposium* xii) in which "culture" is thought of ethnographically and poetry is defined broadly as the creative verbal address to present circumstances, whatever they might be. He coins a new term for this encompassing, inclusivist aesthetics—"ethnopoetics"—and titles the anthology of essays he edits with Diane Rothenberg, *Symposium of the Whole: A Range of Discourse Toward an Ethnopoetics* (1993; Fig. 25). Ethnopoetics is proposed as a site of dynamic interchange between contemporary poetry and that of the most far-flung times and places, reincorporating endeavors seen as "nonliterary," such as ritual, shamanism, and bodily display, back into poetry.

Rothenberg and Duncan first met in San Francisco in 1959, when Rothenberg came out from New York to consult with Lawrence Ferlinghetti on the City Lights publication of his second book, *New Young German Poets* (1959), a volume of translations.[1] This publication signaled immediately Rothenberg's dedication to a model of poetry as a world phenomenon, beyond the confines of the United States or the English language. In fact, when Allen began assembling materials for his foundational anthology *The New American Poetry* (1960), he told Rothenberg that he wouldn't be included because he was "an international poet."[2] Duncan suggested to Rothenberg that his internationalism ought to include his own Jewish identity: "[T]he first indication I had that I should possibly be going in that direction was a conversation with Duncan

SYMPOSIUM
OF THE WHOLE

A Range of Discourse Toward an Ethnopoetics

Jerome Rothenberg & Diane Rothenberg

FIGURE 25. Jerome Rothenberg and Diane Rothenberg, eds., *Symposium of the Whole*. Cover collage by Wallace Berman. Berkeley: University of California Press, 1983.

back around 1959 or 60. . . . [H]e was dropping all sorts of hints to me about the possibility of . . . [ellipsis in original] That I was giving up too much in ignoring the Jewish identity, which was something that must have been with me in a very deep sense since my first language was Yiddish" (Alpert 114). The other poet who insisted that Rothenberg confront Jewish identity was Paul Celan, whom he had translated already in *New Young German Poets*. Rothenberg reports that "Celan was crazy on the question of being Jewish and when I met him in Paris . . . he kept questioning me on that, challenging my credentials to work on his poetry . . . : was I 'Jewish' enough to do them?" (Alpert 115). The circle turned again when Rothenberg introduced Duncan to Celan's poetry, via his translation of "Shibboleth" in the magazine he edited, *Poems from the Floating World*. In a letter of May 25, 1959, Duncan mistakenly assumes that "Shibboleth" is a sentimental Stalinist poem; Rothenberg corrects Duncan's misreading of the lines, "that dark / and twin redness, / Madrid and Vienna," pointing out that for Celan the conquest of these cities represented not defeat for international communism but the beginning of the fascist terror (May 28, 1959). Over time, Duncan developed a profound admiration for Celan, whom he invokes powerfully in "A Song from the Structures of Rime Ringing as the Poet Paul Celan Sings" (*GW* 12). It was Duncan, finally, who introduced Rothenberg to Gershom Scholem's epoch-making *Major Trends in Jewish Mysticism*, which opened up for Rothenberg, as it did for so many other Jewish poets, a window onto the texts and practices of Kabbalah.[3]

When editing *Technicians*, Rothenberg took cognizance not only of Duncan's example but of the entire climate of twentieth-century avant-garde poetry and the arts. In the body of the anthology, for instance, he asserts analogies between the tribal and the modern by selecting translations or retranslations that display formal characteristics of the New American Poetry: recourse to vernacular and erotic rather than "poetic" diction, avoidance of articles and punctuation, extensive use of abbreviation, and lineation based on breath rhythms—including multiple indentations. These qualities bespeak a "hip," up-to-date style that brings the translations into the purview of contemporary poetic habits. The "Commentaries" section of *Technicians* follows Allen's practice in *The New American Poetry* of appending back matter to create new contexts for the primary work. In its enlarged second edition, *Technicians* contains 186 pages of commentary, consisting of ethnographic accounts and modern and contemporary works of poetry and art. The dual aims of the commentaries are to document the original performative circumstances of the translated poetry and to demonstrate specific affinities between works of "primitive" and archaic poetry and those of avant-garde poetry and performance art.[4] In a suggestive table that maps out his expanded vision of poetry in 1968 (xxii–xxiii), Rothenberg makes explicit a set of analogies between "primitive" poetry and a whole range of avant-garde practices:

(1) the poem carried by the voice: a "pre"-literate situation of poetry composed to be spoken, chanted or, more accurately, sung; compare this to "the post-literate" situation, in McLuhan's good phrase, or where-we-are-today;	written poem as score public readings poets' theaters jazz poetry 1960s rock poetry etc
(2) a highly developed process of image-thinking: concrete or non-causal thought in contrast to the simplifications of Aristotelian logic, etc., with its "objective categories" & rules of non-contradiction; a "logic" of polarities; creation thru dream, etc.; modern poetry (having had & outlived the experience of rationalism) enters a post-logical phase;	Blake's multi-images symbolisme surrealism deep-image random poetry composition by field etc
(3) a "minimal" art of maximal involvement; compound elements, each clearly articulated, & with plenty of room for fill-in (gaps in sequence, etc.): the "spectator" as (ritual) participant who pulls it all together;	concrete poetry picture poems
(4) an "intermedia" situation, as further denial of the categories: the poet's techniques aren't limited to verbal maneuvers but operate also through song, non-verbal sound, visual signs, & the varied activities of the ritual event: here the "poem" = the work of the "poet" in whatever medium, or (where we're able to grasp it) the totality of the work;	prose poems happenings total theater poets as film-makers etc dada

(5) the animal-body-rootedness
of "primitive" poetry: recognition of a
"physical" basis for the poem within a
man's body—or as an act of body &
mind together, breath &/or spirit; in
many cases too the direct & open
handling of sexual imagery & (in the
"events") of sexual activities as key
factors in creation of the sacred;

(6) the poet as shaman, or
primitive shaman as poet & seer thru
control of the means just stated: an open
"visionary" situation prior to all system-
making ("priesthood") in which the man
creates thru dream (image) & word
(song), "that Reason may have ideas to
build on" (W. Blake).

lautgedichte (sound poems)

beast language

line & breath
projective verse etc

sexual revolution etc

Rimbaud's voyant
Rilke's angel
Lorca's duende

beat poetry
psychedelic see-in's, be-in's etc

individual neo-shamanisms, etc works
directly influence by the "other" poetry
or by analogies to "primitive" art: ideas
of negritude, tribalism, wilderness, etc.

The correspondences Rothenberg highlights in this chart suggest a number
of models for poetry beyond the then-current standard of the self-contained
lyric that dramatizes the dilemmas of a self-reflexive subject: (1) poetry as
public performance addressed to a specific occasion, (2) poetry as a vehicle for
probing states beyond the conscious mind, (3) poetry as convening a creative
social context, (4) poetry as participating in intermedia or multimedia events,
(5) poetry as instigator of erotic engagement, and (6) poetry as a shamanic or
visionary activity. Likewise, this chart identifies six qualities that "primitive"
and avant-garde works may share: emphasizing oral poetry and performance,
thinking through images rather than through rational discourse, tending toward minimalism, participating in intermedia art, insisting on the primacy
of the body and the erotic, and demonstrating how shamanism underlies poetry. For Rothenberg, this greatly enhanced poetics reincorporates into the
modern world long-buried human capacities. In this sense, he takes a position
similar to that of the Freudian Left (such as Reich, Marcuse, and Brown), in-
viting the return of the repressed in both political and psychological terms; he
links *Technicians* to "the recovery in our time, of the 'long forbidden voices'

invoked by Whitman over a century ago, the 'symposium of the whole' set forth in Robert Duncan's 'rites'" (*Pre-Faces* 119). Like Duncan and Whitman, Rothenberg summons a "sense-of-unity" (*Technicians* xxviii) that highlights shared forces within tribal and avant-garde poetries—forces of darkness, of the body, of the unconscious, and of the visionary. By setting the poetry of the most far-flung cultures into juxtaposition with the modern arts, Rothenberg creates a Grand Collage whose sense of wholeness allows it to claim the status of "a poetry of all poetries" (*BB* vii).[5]

In Duncan's poetics, the Grand Collage makes its strongest appearance within the composition of his poems. The poems of the *Passages* sequence, for instance, which begins in *Bending the Bow* and continues in *Ground Work*, act as assemblages of cited materials and contribute to the larger assemblage of the sequence. By increasing the scale of citation from passages to entire poems, Rothenberg creates not poems or sequences but anthologies, garnering him a reputation as one of the great anthologists of our time. He composes anthologies as an act of *poesis*—not to establish or reinforce a canon but rather to introduce new possibilities into literary creation and new ways of thinking about literary study. The dazzling array of his provocative anthologies includes *Technicians* (1968, 1985), *Shaking the Pumpkin: Traditional Poetry of the Indian North Americas* (1972), *America A Prophecy: A New Reading of American Poetry from Pre-Columbian Times to the Present* (1973), *Revolution of the Word: A New Gathering of American Avant Garde Poetry, 1914–1945* (1974), *A Big Jewish Book: Poems & Other Visions of the Jews from Tribal Times to Present* (1978), *Poems for the Millennium: The University of California Book of Modern and Postmodern Poetry*, Volumes I and II (1995 and 1998), *A Book of the Book: Some Works and Projections about the Book and Writing* (2000), and *Poems for the Millennium, Volume III: The University of California Book of Romantic & Postromantic Poetry* (2009). Rothenberg's anthologies do a variety of things:

> [B]ecause I don't like to write discursive prose or essays, I find the anthology is a vehicle for saying certain things about poetry that I really can't manage to say otherwise. . . . Through selection, through juxtaposition, through presentation of types of poems, through defining by pointing at something. The presentation of examples is a kind of definition. And it's a fantastic big form sometimes—like collage but on a super scale. (*Alpert* 101)

Within *Technicians*, for example, Rothenberg makes two kinds of juxtapositions. In the body of the anthology, he collects poems from every sort of tribal and archaic culture under the headings "Origins & Namings," "Visions & Spels," "Death & Defeat," "The Book of Events (I)," and "The Book of Events (II)," in order to point out common poetic strategies in disparate cultural situations. In the "Commentaries," he makes analogies between works from the body of the anthology and those of modern and contemporary poetry and art. Through selection, juxtaposition, and recontextualization in his anthologies, Rothenberg questions received assumptions about the scope of poetry and the conduct of literary history.[6] The anthologies intervene actively, calling into being fields of inquiry (such as ethnopoetics), operating as manifestos (arguing for a "tradition" of avant-garde poetry), and standing forth as works of art.

In New York in the early sixties, Rothenberg joined with a number of performance artists exploring a new contextual practice, including most particularly the Fluxus group, whose publisher, Dick Higgins, issued two of Rothenberg's books. What ultimately became the *Technicians* anthology received an impetus from a conversation with Higgins about Rothenberg's sense of "the closeness of primitive rituals (when stripped-down to the bare line of the activities) to the 'happenings' & 'events' he [Higgins] was presenting." More generally, it drew sustenance from the Artaud-inspired explorations of "primitive" rites and images by groups such as the Living Theater. In this context, Rothenberg reports that the anthology "grew directly out of a pair of 1964 readings of 'primitive & archaic poetry' at The Poet's Hardware Theater & the Café Metro in New York," in which the readers included Rothenberg, David Antin, Jackson Mac Low, and Rochelle Owens (*Technicians* xxxi).

From the perspective of assemblage, *Technicians* also bears comparison to Smith's *Anthology of American Folk Music*. Like Smith, whom he thanks for assistance in the "Pre-Face" to *Technicians*, Rothenberg chooses the works in his anthology because of their aesthetic toughness and challenging imagery, not their "representativeness":

> My intention from the start was to find translations that would "translate," i.e., bring-the-work-across or be a living work in English, & that's a very different thing from (in the first place) looking for representative "masterpieces" & including them whatever the nature of the translations. I also have (no question about it) my own sense of what's worth it in poetry, & I've tried to work from that rather than against it. I haven't gone for "pretty" or "innocent" or "noble" poems so much as strong ones. (xxxi)

The anthologies of Smith and Rothenberg have had such staying power because they were composed as works of art, whose component parts are enigmatic, often disturbing, and sometimes even uncanny. Acknowledging these qualities, Greil Marcus characterizes Smith's anthology as depicting "That Old, Weird America" (*Republic* 87–126), while Rothenberg invokes Bronislaw Malinowski's term "the coefficient of weirdness" (*Technicians* 21–22) to describe the poems that appeal to him. Both Smith and Rothenberg see their anthologies as provocations—breaking the professional decorum of the fields of literature or folklore by presenting rough, unpolished, vernacular works with harsh, erotic, or shocking subject matter—as attempts to make something happen.

From Rothenberg's perspective, the act of juxtaposition central to collage also governs much "primitive" and archaic poetry. One of the first pieces in *Technicians*, "Bantu Combinations," juxtaposes pairs of disparate statements: "1. I am still carving an ironwood stick. / I am still thinking about it. // 2. The lake dries up at the edges. / The elephant is killed by a small arrow. // 3. The little hut falls down. / Tomorrow, debts . . ." (16). In the commentary, Rothenberg calls these couplets "[e]xamples of plot-thickening in the area of 'image': a conscious placing of image against image as though to see-what-happens." He likens these "combinations" to the haiku and the sonnet, contending that, "In all these the interest increases as the connection between the images becomes more & more strained, barely definable." Citing a statement from *Life of a South African Tribe* (the source for the poems), that "Sometimes the imagination is so subtle that the result is almost incoherent," Rothenberg counters, "Not subtlety, though, but *energy*: the power of the word and image." The energy released by strong juxtapositions generates, he contends, a mysterious "light"—not "the light of logic & simile" but a more profound one "to which (for the first time) the word 'vision' might be said to apply" (455).

Similar in some ways to the "Bantu Combinations," the "Aztec Definitions" are also composed in short units:

Ruby-Throated Hummingbird
It is ashen, ash colored. At the top of its head and the throat, its feathers are flaming, like fire. They glisten, they glow.

Amoyotl (a water-strider)
It is like a fly, small and round. It has legs, it has wings; it is dry. It goes on the surface of the water; it is a flyer. It buzzes, it sings.

Bitumen (a shellfish)
It falls out on the ocean shore; it falls out like mud.

(20)

In the commentary, Rothenberg points out that these texts were collected by Fray Bernardino de Sahagún only a quarter-century after the fall of Tenochtitlan and that they constitute "a kind of glossary of 'earthly things'—the elders' minds & words are drawn toward definitions of the most ordinary debris of their lives." Rothenberg asserts that Fray Bernardino "led them to a reconsideration, to an assemblage of 'things of New Spain.'" Among the "everyday debris" of their ruined civilization, "the mind finds release in a strange new encounter; free of ritual & myth [The-System]; it approaches its objects as if for the first time testing their existence" (461; brackets in original). Rothenberg sees a powerful analogy between the Aztec "definitions" and contemporary poetry because each occurs within a civilization that has split apart and released the debris of its material and verbal life for recombination into striking works of assemblage.

Erotic Poetics

Assemblage operates for Rothenberg and Duncan as more than a formal principle; it is a means for gathering unaffiliated energies and tying them into a new whole governed by the erotic. When Duncan speaks of the Grand Collage as "a poetry of all poetries," he does so within the context of a discussion of the erotic as the central node of life energy. The discussion occurs in a section of the introduction to *Bending the Bow* entitled "*IT*," which begins: "Where you are *he* or I am *he*, the trouble of an Eros shakes the household in which we work to contain our feeling in our extending our feeling into time and space" (*BB* vi). Eros participates in this troubling paradox of containment and extension, of concentration upon the love object (the beloved *he*) and expansion of the power of love endlessly outward. Duncan speaks of this primal Eros as *It*, invoking thereby Freud's term for life energy, the *Id*. From Duncan's perspective, poetry is the erotic art par excellence in which the Id shines forth through the words of the poem and through its structure as a collage:

> In the poem this very lighted room is dark, and the dark alight with love's intentions. *It* is striving to come into existence in these things, or, all striving to come into existence is It—in this realm of men's languages a poetry of all

poetries, *grand collage*, I name It, having only the immediate event of words to speak for It. In the room we, aware or unaware, are the event of ourselves in It. (vii)

In this dense passage, many things are intertwined: poetry, love, selfhood, Grand Collage, and the energy of life. For Duncan, the poetic form that he chooses, the Grand Collage of created images from across time and space, mirrors or participates in the erotic energy underlying not only the experience of love but all of life. In other words, Grand Collage is inherently erotic; it creates new wholes that move inward to concentrate upon a central node— or egg or seed, as he often calls it, invoking the Semina context—and that move outward to encompass the largest scale imaginable.

The erotic is at the core of Rothenberg's poetics as well, and his invocation of the "symposium of the whole" likewise participates in a vision of erotic concentration and expansion. He views the erotic as guiding the expression of bodily, ritual (communal), and mystical states in tribal and archaic poetries, operating at each of these levels to intensify experience and shatter rigid forms of control. Ultimately, this erotic poetics constitutes what Rothenberg calls, on the masthead of the ethnopoetics journals he edited, *Alcheringa* and *New Wilderness Letter*, the "*mainstream* of poetry that goes back to the old tribes & has been carried forward by the great subterranean culture" (*Pre-Faces* 31). Like Duncan and Gary Snyder, Rothenberg believes that a countercultural, "shamanistic" impulse arose during the Paleolithic era, that it can be found in the erotic, visionary, and gnostic impulses woven into all of the great archaic civilizations, and that it continues into the modern era in more-or-less isolated tribal cultures and in the mystical countercultures of the world's major religions during the past thousand years. This tradition attracts the poets by its transgressive quality, its ability to pry open social and mental constructs through provocation and vision, through eruptions of an uncontrollable Id.

For both Duncan and Rothenberg, ethnographic accounts of Australian Aboriginal mythology and ritual mark a highly imaginative and explicit upsurge of the erotic into human society. In "Rites of Participation," Duncan discusses Aboriginal mythology extensively with the help of the Freudian anthropologist Géza Róheim. He cites Róheim's lengthy etymological treatment of the term *alcheringa*, ultimately rendered as "dream time" (*SP* 105), and the term also becomes the key to Rothenberg's ethnopoetics. According to Róheim, the Dream Time represents, in Freudian terms, the mythical time of the libido, in which the parts and effluents of the human body are cathected upon the landscape. Duncan notes how, in both Freudian psychology and Aboriginal mythology and ritual, "the body of man and the body of creation" are brought together "by a 'sexual obsession' (as Jung calls it)":

> The "b[r]east, anus, semen, urine, leg, foot" in the Australian song, chant or enchantment, that is also hill, hole, se[a], stream, tree, or rock, where "in the Toara ceremony the men dance around the ring shouting the names of male and female genital organs, shady trees, hills, and some of the totems of their tribe," are most familiar to the Freudian convert Roheim.

Duncan believes that the erotic, the psychological, the ritual, and the mystical cannot be separated, contending that "The 'blood' of the Aranda, the 'libido' of the Freudian, may also be the 'light' of our Kabbalistic text" (106). At every level, he insists, the erotic underlies and intensifies the lived experience.

In *Technicians*, Rothenberg extends Duncan's erotic poetics by reworking translations of Aboriginal performance poems to emphasize the unabashedly erotic imagery that generates a visionary mythology. Near the outset of the anthology, for instance, in the section of "Origins & Namings," he titles a selection from the *Djanggawul Cycle*, "Genesis II." The selection begins:

[**Song 159**]

> Go, take that hot stone, and heat it near her clitoris:
> For the severed part is a sacred *djuda rangga*. Covering up the clitoris within the
>   mat, within its transverse fibre, within its mouth, its inner peak . . .
> Go, the people are dancing there, like *djuda* roots, like spray, moving their bod-
>   ies, shaking their hair!
> Carefully they beat their clapping sticks on the *mauwulan* point . . .
> Go, stand up! See the clansfolk beyond the transverse fibre of the mat!
> They come from the Sister's womb, lifting aside the clitoris, coming out like
>   *djuda* roots . . .

                                                        (9; ellipses in original)

In the commentary, Rothenberg emphasizes the sexuality of the songs from the *Djanggawul Cycle*: "A heavy ripeness, the swelling & bursting of a teeming life-source, colors Australian views of the creation." This streaming libidinal energy stands revealed in the Aboriginal songs as the erotic basis for human culture: "the *Djanggawul Cycle* is the best example the present editor knows, of the celebration of human sexuality & birth in the work of genesis." He contrasts the Aboriginal recognition that sexual display is the basis of culture to the occlusion of that recognition in normative Western culture: "The body of the sacred sister, heat around the clitoris, the budding tree roots, spray & blood, a swarming sense of life emerging—not two-by-two, in pairs, but *swarming*—was turned-from in the West, reduced to images of evil" (447).

Rothenberg objects most to how such an imaginative constriction brings about a diminution of life energy, which he terms "sacredness." In stark contrast, a Gabon Pygmy song in *Technicians*, "All Lives, All Dances, & All is Loud," offers a straightforward example of a people at home with exuberance and able to express a "sacred" kinship with all living things through song, dance, and mimicry:

The fish does . . . HIP
The bird does . . . VISS
The marmot does . . . GNAN

I throw myself to the left,
I turn myself to the right,
I act the fish,
Which darts in the water, which darts
Which twists about, which leaps—
All lives, all dances, and all is loud.

(36, first third of the song)

Rothenberg begins his commentary on this song with the following exclamation: "UNIVERSAL PRIMITIVE & ARCHAIC VISION OF ALL LIFE IN MOTION & SHARING A SINGLE NATURE WHICH IS SACRED." He then adduces three analogies for the Pygmy song: a statement by Ernst Cassirer that "primitive man" has a "deep conviction of a fundamental and indelible *solidarity of life* that bridges over the multiplicity and variety of its single forms"; "A SONG OF THE BEAR" (Teton Sioux), which runs "my paw is sacred / all things are sacred"; and a citation from William Blake, "For everything that lives is holy" (476–77). In all of these examples, the concept of the sacred refers not to objects cordoned off from the realm of everyday life, but rather to the inherent nature of each object in the world.

For Rothenberg, the phenomenon of shamanism is the clearest model for an erotic poetics grounded in a conviction of the sacredness of all things: "Here is the central image of shamanism & of all 'primitive' thought, the intuition (whether fictive or not doesn't yet matter) of a connected & fluid universe, as alive as a man is—just that much alive" (487). With Duncan, Rothenberg shares an enduring fascination with the figure of the shaman, especially in the role of proto-poet. Over the course of his writing career, Duncan came to conceive of the shamanic ascent to other worlds as an image for entering the writing of other people (such as Dante, the Metaphysical Poets, Rumi, and Baudelaire in *Ground Work*) in order to compose his "derivative" poetry. In more literal terms, Rothenberg values the shaman as a primary figure for poetry: "the shaman can be seen as protopoet, for almost always his technique hinges on the creation of special linguistic circumstances, i.e., of song and invocation" (485). The term *technique* alludes to the title, *Technicians of the Sacred*, which "itself is a take-off from Eliade's 'specialist of the sacred' who masters the 'techniques of ecstasy'" (*Symposium* 59). Rothenberg found the two phrases in Mircea Eliade's *Shamanism: Archaic Techniques of Ecstasy* (trans. 1964), which became one of the most influential texts for ethnopoetics. In their mutual interest in shamanism, Duncan and Rothenberg emphasize several qualities they see as defining a universal erotic poetics of the sacred: the shaman as a lone figure who visits other worlds in order to bring back poetry addressed to the ills of society; the shaman as able to move through a variety of life forms, tying him or her to an underlying sense of the interconnectedness of all beings; and the shaman as confronting death, darkness, and disease without flinching, recognizing that "negative" forces cannot be avoided but must be confronted.

The figure of the shaman also appeals so strongly to Duncan and Rothenberg because it represents for them the integrity of individual experience against the forces of statehood, organized religion, and even artistic conformity. The poets share an anarchist orientation, which always prefers the powers of the creative individual to those of institutions and which believes that communalism (or tribalism) preserves the fullest potential for human experience. The commitment to communalism over institutions also manifests in a respect for the vernacular, which, for Rothenberg in particular, is a central feature of his avant-garde poetics. The avant-garde has been faulted in some quarters for being an elitist enterprise, but Rothenberg highlights its vernacular quality and its embeddedness in everyday life. *Technicians* takes a huge step in this direction by demonstrating how the most innovative and challenging works of the avant-garde can be seen as analogous to works by tribal peoples. Rothenberg begins the 1967 "Pre-Face" with the heading, "PRIMITIVE MEANS COMPLEX," arguing that just as there are no primitive languages (from the perspective of linguistics), there are no primitive poetries, given the imaginative and intellectual sophistication evident in every culture:

> No people has sat in sloth for the thousands of years of its history. Measure everything by the Titan rocket & the transistor radio, & the world is full of primitive peoples. But once change the unit of value to the poem or the dance-event or the dream (all clearly artifactual situations) & it becomes apparent what all those people have been doing all those years with all that time on their hands. (xxv)

The intelligence and sophistication Rothenberg appreciates in tribal poets reflect their care in infusing the visionary and the aesthetic into the conduct of everyday life. In this sense, they can stand as models for an avant-garde bent on providing an aesthetic infusion into the conduct of contemporary life.

Rothenberg's expansion of the contextual practices of Duncan, Smith, and Allen into a full-fledged ethnopoetics amounts to a model for how others have carried forward the contextual innovations of the major figures in this study.[7] For instance, Bob Dylan combined the songs in Smith's anthology with the writing of Ginsberg and Kerouac to inaugurate the music of the baby boom generation, and the Grateful Dead merged Smith's anthology with the mystical and surreal poetics of Semina culture to help create the musical, sexual, psychedelic, mystical, and communal ethos of the nascent hippie movement. You could even say that Creeley's pioneering engagement with people and objects in the present setting and his awareness that the setting itself must be taken into account makes him a forerunner of the Gestalt psychology of Fritz Perls and Paul Goodman, which became one of the mainstays of the human potential movement fostered by the Esalen Institute, among others.[8] As in the case of Brown's *Love's Body*, the erotic poetics of these contextual practices had intellectual, social, and political consequences that spread into the surrounding culture, continuing to exert a countercultural pressure.

As a work of the late sixties, *Technicians* takes much from its time, drawing on the emergent aesthetic and cultural strands of concrete poetry and sound poetry, minimalism, conceptualism, performance art, multiculturalism, and theoretical investigations of the interplay of orality and literacy. Likewise, it rests on a tradition of the vernacular in American poetry, which Rothenberg traces back to Whitman, Pound, Stein, and Williams, and which he sees continuing in Olson, Duncan, Creeley, Blackburn, Snyder, and Antin, among others. Drawing together the vernacular innovations of these poets, *Technicians* also heralds a more recent movement in American literary studies intent on opening "American" literature out from the geographical boundaries of the United States and from the self-conscious attempt to close itself off from the other literatures and cultures of the world in pursuit of an illusory essence of "Americanness." Rothenberg's unique contribution to this latter movement can be seen in his positioning of American poetry face-to-face with the European avant-garde and also with the most far-flung poetries of the world in time and space. If we imagine *Technicians* as imparting an image of a world poetry, then it would be one characterized not by formal qualities or national traditions but by imaginative approaches to the central preoccupations of human life—such as birth, death, love, war, food, shelter, disease, and cosmology—through a spicy contextual practice both vernacular and erotic.

REFERENCE MATTER

NOTES

INTRODUCTION

1. Descriptions of the exhibition and the trial can be found in Solnit 18–23; Cándida Smith, *Utopia* 216–31; Philips 127–30; and Krull 24–27. Judge Kenneth Halliday had earlier found Henry Miller guilty of obscenity.

2. For other provocative studies that take a cross-media and sociopolitical approach to the arts of the period and touch on some of the figures whom I discuss, see Belgrad; Cándida Smith, *Utopia*; Kane; Leland; MacAdams; Philips; and Solnit. None of these studies makes what I am calling contextual practice the central object of inquiry.

3. The rise of art-as-religion, for example, has been chronicled by Charles Taylor in his philosophical genealogy of modernism, *Sources of the Self.* Taylor notes that "for many of our contemporaries art has taken on something like the place of religion": "There is a kind of piety which still surrounds art and artists in our time, which comes from the sense that what they reveal has great moral and spiritual significance; that in it lies the key to a certain depth, or fulness, or seriousness, or intensity of life, or to a certain wholeness" (423). George Leonard has also written an enlightening study of how poetry and art have taken over the functions of philosophy and religion, beginning with the Romantics and culminating in John Cage.

4. This definition uses *collage* as a master term for a variety of practices in the modern arts, including montage, assemblage, frottage, readymades, and bricolage. See Perloff (246) for a discussion of collage as the most felicitous general term.

5. Adorno: "All modern art may be called montage" (cited in Bruns 8); Antin: "For better or worse 'modern' poetry in English has been committed to a principle of collage from the outset" (Bové 49); Perloff: "collage, perhaps the central artistic invention of the *avant guerre*" (xvii). The major critical explorations of collage in the twentieth century can be found in Adamowicz; Antin, "Some Questions"; Brockelman; Janis and Blesh; Perloff; Plottel; Poggi; Seitz; Brandon Taylor; Waldman; Wescher; and Wolfram. Hoffman has an excellent selection of key essays on collage.

6. See Jenkins for a nuanced comparison of Lowell and Pollock.

7. See Perchuk and Singh for a volume of revised essays from the Getty symposium.

CHAPTER 1

1. Among the 252 works in the *Art of Assemblage* show, only three artists have more than two or three works: Kurt Schwitters (35), Joseph Cornell (14), and Marcel Duchamp (13).

In a long, intricate footnote to *Into the Light of Things*, George Leonard points out that although Duchamp denied the influence of his readymades (which he exhibited as purely anti-aesthetic objects) upon Neo-Dada, his invention of an art of found objects had already been reconfigured by newer artists such as John Cage into an art of assemblage (230–34).

2. For a discussion of the new aesthetics of action and spontaneity after World War II, see Belgrad.

3. Jess's *Nadine* (1955), a window frame containing a shade on which images are collaged, appeared in *The Art of Assemblage* exhibition and catalog (111).

4. In the catalog *Translations by Jess*, Duncan provides an extended meditation on the erotic poetics of the "Translations" series. The essay is reprinted in *SP* 178–93.

5. Brown also shares with Duncan an early exposure to Theosophy, although Brown's acquaintance with it came during his adolescence and was due to his mother's enthusiasm for the occult (Neu 18–19), while Duncan's entire adoptive family was involved in Theosophy during his childhood and early adolescence. For a comparison of Duncan's early involvement in Theosophy with that of Harry Smith, see Chapter Four.

6. Brown's side of the correspondence is housed in the Duncan papers at the Poetry Collection, University at Buffalo. Duncan's side is presumably housed with Brown's (uncatalogued) papers at University of California, Santa Cruz. Lisa Jarnot, Duncan's biographer, has given me the information for this narrative of Duncan's friendship with Brown.

7. *The Opening of the Field* was brought out ultimately by Grove Press in 1960.

8. For recent assessments of Brown's work, see Greenham, and Pendell.

9. See Robinson.

10. It is curious that on both occasions when he cites this passage of prose poetry from "XVII: At Home," Brown lineates it as verse. See Duncan, *Letters*, p. 30.

11. In 1960, the year after he met Duncan, Brown met another poet (and potter), M. C. Richards, with whom he reportedly fell in love. Richards had been at Black Mountain College and "was the fleshly embodiment of the whole alternative 'scene' of poetry, music, and the arts. She gave him reading lists and introduced him to a number of sources and topics . . . , including Buddhism, surrealism, Owen Barfield, and other authors who later appear in *Love's Body*" (Pendell 68–69).

12. Duncan's meditations on *Love's Body* are offered in "Ground Work" as a prelude to his poem "Santa Cruz Propositions" (*GW* 40–50), which he dedicates in draft form, "for N.O.B. expounding the texts of Vico and Joyce in the copulation of a third unreveald text" (Ground 11). For more on "Santa Cruz Propositions," see Chapters Six and Seven.

CHAPTER 2

1. Tomkins's profiles were collected in *The Bride and the Bachelors: Five Masters of the Avant-Garde* in 1965; Kramer's profile was expanded in 1969 as *Allen Ginsberg in America*; and the first *Paris Review* anthology of interviews, *Writers at Work*, appeared

in 1958 (Cowley). Other series of interviews with writers include those conducted by David Ossman for WBAI and collected in *The Sullen Art* (1963) and those conducted for *Contemporary Literature* and collected in Dembo and Pondrom, *The Contemporary Writer* (1972). See Rasula, *American Poetry* 572–75, for a list of books of interviews with poets and collections of essays by poets, from 1963 to 1990.

2. "Containment was the name of a privileged American narrative during the cold war. Although technically referring to U.S. foreign policy from 1948 until at least the mid-1960s, it also describes American life in numerous venues and under sundry rubrics during that period: to the extent that corporate production and biological reproduction, military deployment and industrial technology, televised hearings and filmed teleplays, the cult of domesticity and the fetishizing of domestic security, the arms race and atoms for peace all contributed to the containment of communism, the disparate acts performed in the name of these practices joined the legible agenda of American history as aspects of containment culture" (Nadel 2–3).

3. See Fredman, *Grounding*, for a discussion of the "groundlessness" of American culture and the poetic devices developed to address American self-exile from tradition.

4. I have discussed Creeley's poem "This World" as an example of how his poetry takes context as a primary subject matter. See *Grounding* 134–39.

5. In "Projective Verse," Olson states that the principle of "field composition" is that "FORM IS NEVER MORE THAN AN EXTENSION OF CONTENT. (Or so it got phrased by one, R. Creeley, and it makes absolute sense to me . . .)" (*Collected Prose* 240). Creeley coined the phrase in a June 5, 1950, letter to Olson (Olson and Creeley 79).

6. For a discussion of phenomenological conjecture in Creeley's writing, see my *Poet's Prose* 62–64.

7. See Olson, *Maximus to Gloucester*, for the letters and poems Olson wrote to Gloucester's local newspaper.

8. Picking up on remarks of Antin's that compare Creeley to Wittgenstein (Antin, "Wittgenstein" 159–62), Hank Lazer compares Antin and Creeley as talk artists, referring their practice back to that of Chautauqua speakers such as Emerson and Thoreau (176–78).

9. "Olson once told me that the initial sign for the pronoun *I* was a boat. Insofar as *I* is a vehicle of passage or transformation, its powers are clear" (Creeley, *Essays* 563).

10. Emerson presents a version of this Epicurean astonishment near the beginning of his essay *Nature*: "If the stars should appear one night in a thousand years, how would men believe and adore; and preserve for many generations the remembrance of the city of God which had been shown! But every night come out these envoys of beauty, and light the universe with their admonishing smile" (9).

11. For two excellent meditations on the use of audiotape in postwar literature, see Davidson, *Ghostlier* 196–223, and Hayles.

CHAPTER 3

1. See Bernstein's "The Second War and Postmodern Memory" for a provocative discussion of the effects of the war on later poetry. Bernstein ends with a direct response

to Adorno: "I would say poetry is a necessary way to register the unrepresentable loss of the Second War" (217).

2. For materials about Smith's life and work, see *AM*; *Self*; Daniel; Foye; and Philip Smith. For commentary on *The Anthology of American Folk Music*, see Cantwell 188–238; Marcus, *Invisible* 87–128; Marcus, "Folk"; and Ward 136–57. For commentary on his films, see Sitney 235–58, and Sexton.

3. The symposium website is located at http://www.getty.edu/research/scholarly_ activities/events/harrysmith/.

4. Smith's friend Bill Breeze states, "Smith was one of the first American artists to exhibit at the Louvre, around 1951, in a two-man show with Marcel Duchamp; apparently it was his hand-painted films, and not his paintings, that were exhibited" (*AM* 8). Rani Singh, director of the Harry Smith Archives, says that evidence has not been found to support this statement. There is no question, though, of Smith's intense interest in Duchamp.

5. Cantwell (204–6) discusses the *Anthology* as a "memory theater" built on the model of Fludd's mnemonic library for encouraging thought, knowledge, and rhetoric. The illustrator who drew "The Divine Monochord" was Johan Theodor de Bry.

6. In the field of visionary filmmaking, Smith was a major innovator, but he was by no means the first of his kind. His most direct precursor was Oskar Fischinger, who was for Smith an important example of the relationship between abstract painting and film. "You can tell how much I admire Fischinger," Smith says: "the only film of mine that I ever gave a real title to was 'Homage to Oskar Fischinger'. . . . I learned concentration from him. . . . Something so wonderful happened in [his film *Motion Painting*], and in those paintings, something so much better than all the Pollocks and other stuff that the museums fight to get hold of" (Moritz 168).

Likewise, although Smith was a signal pioneer of the concert light show, he was by no means the only one. For a history of the light show and its relationship to psychedelia, see Grunenberg (21–43) and Iles.

7. The film Ginsberg refers to is *Mirror Animations, Film #11*.

8. Reznikoff is the principal subject of Fredman, *Menorah*. Discussions of *Testimony* can be found in Bernstein, *My Way* 197–228; Davidson, *Ghostlier* 149–70; Fredman, *Menorah* 22–23, 46–48; Hindus; Holsapple; Shevelow; Sweney; and Vescia 31–62.

9. In "American Folk," Marcus describes the uncomprehending reactions of Princeton University professors to a first hearing of the *Anthology*.

10. Jess was one of many assemblage artists inspired by the Watts Towers: "My father, in most everything a reactionary, one day taking the family 'for a drive,' took us from home in Long Beach out to Watts to see 'the Towers.' . . . As a student engrosst on becoming a Chemist (but still repressing a desire to become an artist) I filed this salient experience away for later sustenance" (Schaffner 15).

11. For a book-length study of the *Watts Towers*, see Goldstone and Goldstone. Recent considerations of it include Cándida Smith, "Quest" 28–32; Schrank; Whiting 139–65; and Davis 230–32. Davis chronicles in *The Visionary State* the vernacular architecture of California's metaphysical movements, much of it governed by assemblage principles.

In his treatment of the *Watts Towers*, he cites a different passage from the Duncan poem discussed below.

12. A poet with close connections to Duncan, Ronald Johnson modeled an entire book-length poem, *Ark* (1996), on the structure of the Watts Towers, a photograph of which graces the cover of the book. Johnson's book consists of three divisions, "The Foundations," "The Spires," and "The Ramparts," each with thirty-three sections.

13. Later in *Roots and Branches*, Duncan dedicates *Structure of Rime* numbers XIX, XX, and XXI to Shirley and Wallace Berman, to their son Tosh (dedication in Duncan's notebook in the Duncan Archive, not in printed version), and to Louise and George Herms, respectively (169–71). "*Structure of Rime* XIX" begins with a phrase that applies to all of these artists, including Rodia: "The artists of the survival" (169). See Chapter Five for further discussion of assemblage as an art of survival.

In *Holy Land*, his exquisite memoir in poet's prose, D. J. Waldie recounts the emotional and spiritual toll of growing up in the grid of "mean regular houses" that defined the landscape of much of postwar Southern California.

14. The prose narratives were initially published in 1932 in Louis Zukofsky's *An "Objectivists" Anthology* and in William Carlos Williams's magazine *Contact*. They were collected in an Objectivist Press book of seventy-one pages, *Testimony*, which appeared in 1934 with an introduction by Kenneth Burke.

15. The thesis of Cantwell's *When We Were Good* is that the folk music revival of the sixties, instigated by Smith's *Anthology*, was a transformation of the leftist political and cultural milieu of the thirties. See also Denning for an extensive treatment of the cultural legacy of the Popular Front of the thirties. Reznikoff's prose *Testimony* (1934) has been placed in the context of thirties documentary art by Davidson (*Ghostlier* 149–70), Kadlec, Sweney, and Vescia.

16. For an analysis of the power of the raw, raspy quality of singing found in the blues, in flamenco, in jazz, and in much of African music, see Nathaniel Mackey's revelatory essay, "Cante Moro" (181–98).

17. Smith anticipated the modus operandi of sampling in contemporary Hip Hop, where minute intervals of soundscape are sampled from prior recorded music in order to evoke a historical moment and style.

18. See Crow, "Lives of Allegory," for a comparison of Dylan and Warhol as allegorists.

CHAPTER 4

My "Forms of Visionary Collage: Harry Smith and the Poets" was delivered as a paper at "Harry Smith: The Avant-Garde in the American Vernacular," a symposium organized by the Getty Research Institute and held April 20–21, 2001, at the Getty Center, Los Angeles, and it was originally published in Andrew Perchuk and Rani Singh (eds.), *Harry Smith: The Avant-Garde in the American Vernacular*, 2010 (225–51).

1. See Ginsberg's review of Kerouac's *The Dharma Bums* for a defense of this method and a citation of Kerouac's "Essentials of Spontaneous Prose" (Ginsberg, *Prose* 342–48).

2. The Five M's refer to five forbidden substances or antinomian acts required of a tantric practitioner: *madya* (wine), *maithuna* (intercourse), *mamsa* (meat), *matsya* (fish), and *mudra* (grain).

3. For an insightful account of Ginsberg's journey to India, which became the model for its time of Western immersion in India and its religions, see Baker.

4. Is the fantasy of destroying the "human universe" a subconscious expression of competition with Charles Olson, whose 1951 essay "Human Universe" was republished in *Evergreen Review* 2.5 (Spring 1958)?

5. Luis Kemnitzer, like Smith an inveterate record collector, told me in April 2001 at the Getty Research Institute's symposium on Harry Smith that he remembers being in the same room with Duncan and Smith in spring or summer 1948. (For more of Kemnitzer's reminiscences, see the reissued *Anthology* booklet, 29–31.) In a biographical sketch of Smith, Ed Sanders also mentions a letter a friend of Smith's wrote to Duncan urging him to meet with Smith (9). A letter a decade later (probably 1958) from Michael McClure to Duncan speaks of Smith and of Smith's close friend and former employer, the Kabbalist Lionel Ziprin, in terms that make it clear Smith was known to Duncan. Vouching for artist and filmmaker Bruce Conner, whom Duncan has not yet met, McClure says, "He's also scrupulously honest. He likes to be in the swing of things, and is interested in poetry as a painter can be. Also he is in contact with Themistocles Hoetis and Lionel Ziprin right now. (Lionel used to be a pretty fair poet, contributed to ZERO, now is an occultist. Harry Smith was working for him when I was in NY)" (McClure, Letter).

6. The context of this passage is Duncan's reflection on Max Ernst's juxtaposition of a huge variety of writers and artists within a list of favorites. Ernst's forays into erotic collage were tremendously attractive to Duncan, Jess, and Smith. In 1952, Duncan gave Jess a copy of Ernst's surrealist collage book *Une Semaine de bonté*, which was to have an important influence on the "paste-ups" that Jess was just beginning to create (Auping 48).

7. Harry Smith's family background in theosophy is documented in Daniel 11–13; Duncan's can be found in Faas 17–29, with further discussion in O'Leary 74–77. Norman O. Brown identifies with Duncan's upbringing: "I too have a theosophical mother" (Brown, "Homage" 14).

8. See the Conclusion for a treatment of Duncan's "symposium of the whole" in the context of the anthologies of Jerome Rothenberg.

9. For critical discussions of Duncan's relationship to architecture, see Maynard 216–75, Collis, and Oudart.

10. Thomas Evans gives an extended description of the house as "a densely inhabited assemblage of resources and pleasures" (Schaffner 98–99).

11. O'Leary discusses this painting (69–70), and Duncan meditates on Jess's *Translations* series in "Iconographical Extensions: On Jess" (*SP* 178–93). See also Schaffner for an extended argument that Jess's relationship to books offers the key to understanding his art (15–72).

12. Faas titles the chapter of his biography of Duncan that treats this period "The Shaman Poet" (81–92), and Maynard discusses the project in relation to Surrealism (102–23). O'Leary (130–32, 144–51, 160–67) uses the figure of the shaman as a central in-

terpretive device, drawing on the scholarship of Mircea Eliade, as part of his exploration of Duncan's poem "My Mother Would Be a Falconress" (*BB* 52–54).

13. In the original text, a young woman and her uncle "came to a lonely spot" and "saw a man who was naked." This man says to them: "'I instructed you in the past about the sacred pack. "You are to make it," I told you in the past. I do not suppose you recognize me. "Owl" is what I am called,' they were told. 'This is how I am,' they were told. To be sure, they saw an owl" (Michelson 39).

14. These points about the oneiric quality of Smith's films were offered in email correspondence (2001) by Rani Singh, director of the Harry Smith Archives. See also *Self* 106, 139.

15. The shaman who carries the sacred pack has destroyed a Sioux war party, leaving only one survivor, whom he sends home and commands, "'You will often tell the story. If you do that you will be able to marry those you love. You will continue to marry. But you shall fear me. If I even see you, you will then die'" (Michelson 65).

16. See Robin Blaser's classic essay on Spicer, "The Practice of Outside" (Blaser, 113–63). For Spicer's biography, see Ellingham and Killian. Significant treatments of Spicer's poetics can be found in Damon (especially 142–78); Davidson, *San Francisco Renaissance* (especially 150–76); Feld; Finkelstein, *Utopian* (especially 68–82); Gizzi; Spanos, 1977; and Silliman (147–66).

17. Sources for contact between Spicer and Smith: Sanders 9; Killian 4.

18. See Mayhew (106–21) for a careful consideration of Spicer's relationship to Lorca.

19. Jung called this the principle of "synchronicity," which treats time as "a concrete continuum which contains qualities or basic conditions that manifest themselves simultaneously in different places through parallelisms that cannot be explained causally, as, for example, in cases of the simultaneous occurrence of identical thoughts, symbols, or psychic states" (Jung, *Memories* 400).

20. Thanks to Philip Smith for showing me a copy of the manuscript. The only two published poems by Harry Smith I have seen were printed posthumously as "(Think of the Self Speaking)," apparently dated "10-4-76" and "10-7-77."

21. Eshleman identifies the instances where Spicer's translations from Lorca become partially or wholly compositions of his own. In addition, Eshleman sees Spicer's serial poems as instances of collage: "a collage is a kind of serial poem" ("Lorca" 47).

22. Compare Marianne Moore's famous call in her poem "Poetry" for "imaginary gardens with real toads in them" (Moore 135). Spicer regarded Moore as "his heroine" (Ellingham and Killian 147–48) and in *After Lorca* worked permutations on the phrase (Gizzi 221).

23. See Cándida Smith, *Utopia*, for a convincing treatment of the thesis that the innovations of the assemblage artists and poets of postwar California were instrumental in creating the basis for the broader countercultural movement of the sixties and seventies.

CHAPTER 5

1. For recent treatments of the historical importance of Ferus Gallery, see Bernstein and Varnedoe, and especially McKenna.

2. For visual representations of the art scene in which Berman participated, see the photographs in Berman, Krull, and Martin and Krull. See Grenier for a year-by-year catalog of the Los Angeles art scene, 1955–1985, and Whiting for an investigation of Los Angeles art in the sixties.

3. See Everson for a poet's attempt to define a West Coast "archetype," comprising pantheism and violence, which he claims influences the major writing produced in the region.

4. Solnit, Cándida Smith, and Duncan and McKenna offer indispensable discussions of the *Semina* movement.

5. Philip Lamantia, one of the Semina cohort and also one of the most dedicated American surrealist poets of the second half of the twentieth century, recalls Berman's fascination with surrealism as a movement: "Something he was very emphatic about when he talked about poetry, he seemed to be particularly impressed by the surrealist movement. 'They're the only group,' he said, 'that has remained together for'—by that time, late fifties, 'forty years'" (Phillips 76).

6. In his famous "San Francisco Letter" in the 1957 "San Francisco Scene" issue of the *Evergreen Review*, Rexroth states, "Of all the San Francisco group Robert Duncan is the most easily recognizable as a member of the international *avant garde*" (10). In a 1969 interview, speaking of Philip Lamantia, Rexroth expands the membership of Bay Area poets in the international avant-garde: "Philip represents as all of us represent something that for many years has been an absolute obsession with me—and that is the returning of American poetry to the mainstream of international literature" (Meltzer, *Beat* 248).

7. For more on Cameron, who was the wife and spiritual guide to Jack Parsons (one of the founders of California Institute of Technology's Jet Propulsion Lab) and who also played the Scarlet Woman in Kenneth Anger's film, *Inauguration of the Pleasure Dome* (1956), see Michael Duncan's exhibition catalog, *Cameron*.

8. McClure describes and reflects on his peyote experiences in *Meat* 23–33.

9. This photo is one of five on the cover of Lamantia's *Narcotica*. Underneath the photos, the author's name is listed as "Lamantia—Artaud."

10. John Hoffman died in Mexico in 1952. His poetry was read by Lamantia at the famous Six Gallery reading where Ginsberg premiered *Howl* (October 7, 1955). An unpublished book of Lamantia's from this period, *Tau*, has been published recently for the first time alongside the poems of Hoffman (Caples).

11. For an extensive discussion of Lamantia's relationship to surrealism, see Frattali.

12. Duncan's conception of the *Zohar* as a novel was influenced by a statement of Scholem's: "The Zohar is written in pseudepigraphic form, almost, one might say, in the form of a mystical novel" (*Major Trends* 157). Eric Selinger discusses Duncan's role in exciting interest in Kabbalah among the Semina poets and Rothenberg (255–57).

13. This story was told to me by Meltzer at the Berkeley Art Museum, October 29, 2006.

14. For a fuller discussion of Duncan's achievement in *Letters*, see my review of the reissued edition ("Letters").

15. See Abulafia's 144 "Permutations of the Tetragrammaton" in Meltzer, ed., *Secret Garden* 136. For further discussions of Abulafia's influence on Meltzer, Hirschman, and Rothenberg, see Meilicke, "Abulafianism"; Meilicke, "California Kabbalists"; and Meilicke, *Rothenberg* 59–91.

16. Berman also provided a mystico-erotic collage, set on a grid of Hebrew letters, for the cover of Hirshman's *Cantillations* (1974).

CHAPTER 6

1. For a sustained comparison of Duncan with Emerson, see Fredman, *Grounding* 94–130.

2. See the essays exploring the poetic and political conflicts between Duncan and Levertov in Gelpi and Bertholf. For an expanded version of a major essay in this collection, see Dewey 113–54.

3. For a spirited response to the 1972 *Caesar's Gate*, see Eric Mottram's letters to Duncan in Evans and Zamir.

4. The impact of his homosexuality on Duncan's poetry and poetics forms a major topic of critical commentary. For particularly nuanced views, see Davidson, *Ghostlier* 171–95; Hewett; and Keenaghan.

5. There is a "*Passages* 37" (*GW* 55–56), entitled "O!" but Duncan places it prior to "*Passages* 36" in *Ground Work: Before the War*. None of the *Passages* poems printed after "*Passages* 36" carries a number. Finkelstein remarks that the dissolution of the ordered sequence of *Passages* marks an important shift in Duncan's late work, reflecting a new sense of urgency occasioned by his confrontation with mortality ("Late Duncan" 352, 369 note 13).

6. In his fascinating essay on the duende in poetry and music, "Cante Moro" (*Hinge* 181–98), Nathaniel Mackey begins the task of tracing Lorca's influence on American poets. See especially pp. 184–90. Jonathan Mayhew carries this task much further in *Apocryphal Lorca*, his important book-length study of Lorca's influence on the New American poets. In addition to discussing the figures I have mentioned, he makes a convincing case for Lorca's impact on Frank O'Hara and also considers Jerome Rothenberg's extensive translations and adaptations of Lorca.

7. Spicer translates Lorca's "Oda a Walt Whitman" in *After Lorca* (*CPJS* 126–30).

8. For a sweeping account of Duncan's Vietnam War poetry, see Mackey, "Gassire's Lute: Robert Duncan's Vietnam War Poems," *Hinge* 71–178.

9. See discussions of the Atlantis dream in Davidson, "A Book of First Things"; Featherston; and O'Leary 85–92, 95–96.

10. In his review of the Duncan-Levertov correspondence, "A Cold War Correspondence," Davidson notes that the poem was written in fall 1970, even though Duncan predated it to October 1968 when he published it in *GW* (550–51).

11. In a lecture, "Homage to Robert Duncan," Brown offers a comment on this specific passage: "Dionysos in Amerika" (16). In his later years, Brown saw his work as an attempt to bring the worship of Dionysos, with both its ecstatic and its destructive sides, into the modern world. His lecture on Duncan is a collage of quotations, mainly from

the poet, which celebrates Duncan's dedication to a sublime poetry that goes beyond the poet's own capacities and that partakes of spiritual and political forces affecting the society at large. From Brown's perspective, "Poems are real events in real history" (14). As he goes on to elaborate, referring to Duncan's "The Truth and Life of Myth" and Whitman's famous equation of the book with the man, "The Truth and Life of a Man. The New American Poetry: who touches this touches a man. Or a woman in wartime, like HD. Or ED; whose Life had stood—a Loaded Gun" (15).

12. See Kane (29–50) for a discussion of *Passages* 18, 19, and 20 as responses to Anger's *Fireworks* (1947). *Fireworks* is referenced explicitly in these poems, but they, and *Passages* 17, also draw upon Duncan's viewing of other films by Anger.

13. See Kotre for an attempt to work out a theory of generativity.

14. Thanks to Duncan's new biographer, Lisa Jarnot, for alerting me to these points. The fact of the abortion is corroborated in Faas 139.

15. In a discussion of Duncan and Whitman, Damon proposes a homosexual poetic generativity that favors "*dis*semination over *in*semination" in which "the role of sperm expands" beyond procreation to further the democratic, "manly adhesiveness" celebrated by Whitman (148–51).

16. Many young poets who were of draft age during the Vietnam War found a father figure in Robert Duncan, whose "generativity" manifested in a legendary generosity toward poets of that generation. One of his most gracious acts to me personally was to volunteer in 1975, when he heard that I would translate Lorca's *Poeta en Nueva York*, to read and comment on all of the drafts—which he did religiously. He told me that it had always been an important book for him and tried to educate me to its nuances by pointing out how the unavoidable pain of being homosexual was embedded within it. In my midtwenties, I felt that his interest in my poetry and translation was like that of a concerned father, and I wondered what such a relationship could mean to him. I had no idea that Lorca's book had become a primary signifier of his grief at being "sonless."

CHAPTER 7

1. The quotation within the quotation is from Whitman.

2. Kali is mentioned in seven letters: *445* (RD), 657; *446* (DL), 658; *447* (DL), 658–59; *450* (DL), 662; *451* (RD), 663–64; *454* (RD), 689; *462* (RD), 701. In the course of explaining the image to Levertov, "Duncan accuses her of being Kali, blames her for not being Kali, and instructs her in how Kali should behave" (Lacey 170).

3. Jung's definition of the psychological concept of the anima: "Every man carries within him the eternal image of woman, not the image of this or that particular woman, but a definitive feminine image. This image is fundamentally unconscious, . . . an imprint or 'archetype' of all the ancestral experiences of the female, a deposit, as it were, of all the impressions ever made by woman" (*Memories* 391).

4. In addition to the editors of *Encountering Kali*, two of the contributors to that book, David R. Kinsley and Sarah Caldwell, have also produced groundbreaking works on the Hindu goddess Kali.

5. Kinsley offers another synthesis of the iconography of Kali: "The goddess Kali is

almost always described as having a terrible, frightening appearance. She is always black or dark, is usually naked, and has long, disheveled hair. She is adorned with severed arms as a girdle, freshly cut heads as a necklace, children's corpses as earrings, and serpents as bracelets. She has long, sharp fangs, is often depicted as having clawlike hands with long nails, and is often said to have blood smeared on her lips. Her favorite haunts heighten her fearsome nature. She is usually shown on the battlefield, where she is a furious combatant who gets drunk on the hot blood of her victims, or in a cremation ground, where she sits on a corpse surrounded by jackals and goblins" (McDermott and Kripal 23).

6. This is Kripal's *forte*, both in *Kali's Child*, where he uncovers the homoeroticism and complicated maternal relations that color the nineteenth-century Hindu saint Ramakrishna's mystical life and teachings, and in his essay "Why the Tantrika Is a Hero: Kali in the Psychoanalytic Tradition" (McDermott and Kripal 196–222).

7. See Kaufman for a reading of this poem in a post-Holocaust context.

8. I attended an emotionally taxing reading by Duncan at the University of California, San Diego, in the spring of 1973, whose program consisted of a constellation of poems around the themes of war, grief, self-loathing, and anger at his mother, which includes most of the poems we are discussing: "A Lammas Tiding," "My Mother Would Be a Falconress," "An Owl Is an Only Bird of Poetry," "An Essay at War," "A Song from the Structures of Rime Ringing as the Poet Paul Celan Sings," "And Hell Is the Realm of God's Self-Loathing," "Despair in Being Tedious," and "The Museum." This reading is listed as item I62 in Bertholf's bibliography of Duncan (375).

9. Thanks to Robert Kaufman for drawing my attention in correspondence to Duncan's Shakespearean allusions. Kaufman also hears an echo to Lear's sense of tragic catastrophe in the lines of "Despair in Being Tedious" that refer to being bound on a wheel of fate: "I do not know if I am bound / to run upon this wheel, wound up, / excited in a manic spiel of wheel in wheel" (*GW* 9).

CONCLUSION

1. His first book publication was also a translation, with David Antin, of Martin Buber's *Tales of Angels Spirits & Demons* (1958).

2. Rothenberg speaking at the Kelly Writers House, April 29, 2008. He also said of Duncan, "In Duncan I found a poet ten or twelve years older who incorporated twentieth-century poetry from a range of places. Charles Olson and Gary Snyder were too much Americanists, but I was connected to Europe. I saw what we were doing was taking over something from France." See Rothenberg's remembrance of meeting Duncan and of what he learned from him in "Robert Duncan: A Memorial" (Rothenberg, *Poetics* 196–99).

3. See Finkelstein, *Not One* 87–111; Meilicke, *Rothenberg*; and Selinger for discussions of Jewish issues in Rothenberg's work.

4. Jed Rasula contends that the Commentaries "are not idle notes, but the real substance of *Technicians of the Sacred*" (*Syncopations* 174).

5. See Paul for an in-depth investigation of Rothenberg's relationship to the "primitive," set in the context of the work of Antin and Snyder.

6. By placing the American poetry and performance art of the sixties and seventies in the expanding contexts first of modern European art and poetry and then of tribal and archaic poetries that represent the widest possible spectrum of human expression, Rothenberg operates within the frame of "deep time" called for by the critic Wai Chee Dimock (3), who contends that American literature must be seen not as confined to the geographical and temporal boundaries of the United States but as a vital participant in "global circuits" that cut across time and space (23).

7. Rothenberg also felt a deep affinity for Berman, whose art graces the covers of *Symposium of the Whole* and of Rothenberg's new work *Triptych* (2007). Rothenberg told me that in 1976 he was on his way out from New York to meet Berman for the first time when Berman was killed in a traffic accident.

8. See Kripal's *Esalen* for a history that ties the postwar arts to the development of the human potential movement.

WORKS CITED

Adamowicz, Elza. *Surrealist Collage in Text and Image: Dissecting the Exquisite Corpse.* Cambridge: Cambridge University Press, 1998.

Adams, Henry. *The Education of Henry Adams.* Boston: Houghton, 1918.

Allen, Donald M., ed. *The New American Poetry.* New York: Grove, 1960.

Alpert, Barry, ed. "David Antin—Jerome Rothenberg." *Vort 7* (1975).

Antin, David. "Some Questions About Modernism." *Occident* 8 (1974): 1–38.

———. "tuning." *Tuning,* 105–42. New York: New Directions, 1984.

———. "Wittgenstein Among the Poets." *Modernism/Modernity* 5 (1998): 149–66.

Artaud, Antonin. *Artaud Anthology.* Jack Hirschman, ed. 2nd ed. San Francisco: City Lights, 1965.

Auping, Michael, ed. *Jess: A Grand Collage 1951–1993.* Buffalo: Buffalo Fine Arts Academy, 1993.

Ayres, Anne. *Forty Years of California Assemblage.* Los Angeles: Wight Art Gallery, 1989.

Baker, Deborah. *A Blue Hand: The Beats in India.* New York: Penguin, 2008.

Banes, Sally. *Greenwich Village 1963: Avant-Garde Performance and the Effervescent Body.* Durham, NC: Duke University Press, 1993.

Bataille, Georges. *Erotism: Death and Sensuality.* Mary Dalwood, trans. New York: Walker, 1962.

Belgrad, Daniel. *The Culture of Spontaneity: Improvisation and the Arts in Postwar America.* Chicago: University of Chicago Press, 1998.

Benjamin, Walter. "The Storyteller: Reflections on the Work of Nikolai Leskov." In Hannah Arendt, ed., Harry Zohn, trans., *Illuminations: Essays and Reflections,* 83–109. New York: Harcourt, 1968.

Berman, Wallace. *Photographs.* With essays by Kristine McKenna and Lorraine Wild, eds. Santa Monica, CA: Rose Gallery, 2007.

Bernstein, Charles. "The Second War and Postmodern Memory." *A Poetics,* 193–217. Cambridge: Harvard University Press, 1992.

———. *My Way: Speeches and Poems.* Chicago: University of Chicago Press, 1999.

Bernstein, Roberta, and Kirk Varnedoe. *Ferus.* New York: Rizzoli, 2009.

Bertholf, Robert. "The Concert: Robert Duncan Writing out of Painting." In Auping (1993), 67–91.

———. *Robert Duncan: A Descriptive Bibliography*. Santa Rosa, CA: Black Sparrow, 1986.

———, and Ian W. Reid, eds. *Robert Duncan: Scales of the Marvelous*. New York: New Directions, 1979.

———, and Albert Gelpi, eds. *The Letters of Robert Duncan and Denise Levertov*. Stanford: Stanford University Press, 2004.

Blaser, Robin. *The Fire: Collected Essays of Robin Blaser*. Miriam Nichols, ed. Berkeley: University of California Press, 2006.

Boon, Marcus. *The Road of Excess: A History of Writers on Drugs*. Cambridge: Harvard University Press, 2002.

Boone, Bruce. "Robert Duncan and Gay Community: A Reflection." *Ironwood* 22 (1983): 66–82.

Bové, Paul A., ed. *Early Postmodernism: Foundational Essays*. Durham, NC: Duke University Press, 1995.

Breton, André. *Nadja*. Richard Howard, trans. New York: Grove, 1960.

Brockelman, Thomas P. *The Frame and the Mirror: On Collage and the Postmodern*. Evanston, IL: Northwestern University Press, 2001.

Brown, Norman O. *Hermes the Thief: The Evolution of a Myth*. Madison: University of Wisconsin Press, 1947.

———. *Life Against Death: The Psychoanalytic Meaning of History*. Middletown, CT: Wesleyan University Press, 1959.

———. *Love's Body*. New York: Random, 1966.

———. "Homage to Robert Duncan." *Sulfur* 7.1 (1987): 11–23.

Bruns, Gerald L. *On the Anarchy of Poetry and Philosophy: A Guide for the Unruly*. New York: Fordham University Press, 2006.

Buber, Martin. *Tales of Angels Spirits & Demons*. David Antin and Jerome Rothenberg trans. New York: Hawk's Well Press, 1958.

Caldwell, Sarah. *Oh Terrifying Mother: Sexuality, Violence and Worship of the Goddess Kali*. New Delhi: Oxford University Press, 1999.

Cándida Smith, Richard. *Utopia and Dissent: Art, Poetry, and Politics in California*. Berkeley: University of California Press, 1995.

———. "The Elusive Quest of the Moderns." In Paul J. Karlstrom, ed., *On the Edge of America: California Modernist Art, 1900–1950*, 21–38. Berkeley: University California Press, 1996.

Cantwell, Robert. *When We Were Good: The Folk Revival*. Cambridge: Harvard University Press, 1996.

Caples, Garrett, ed. *Tau*, by Philip Lamantia, and *Journey to the End*, by John Hoffman. San Francisco: City Lights, 2008.

Cappellazzo, Amy, and Elizabeth Licata, eds. *In Company: Robert Creeley's Collabora-tions.* Niagara Falls, NY: Castellani Art Museum of Niagara University; and Greens-boro: Weatherspoon Art Gallery, University of North Carolina at Greensboro, 1999.

Collis, Stephen. "'The Frayed Trope of Rome': Poetic Architecture in Robert Duncan, Ronald Johnson, and Lisa Robertson." *Mosaic* 35.4 (December 2002): 143–62.

Cowley, Malcolm, ed. *Writers at Work: The Paris Review Interviews.* New York: Viking, 1958.

Creeley, Robert. *Contexts of Poetry: Interviews 1961–1971.* Donald Allen, ed. Bolinas, CA: Four Seasons, 1973.

———. *His Idea.* Photographs by Elsa Dorfman. Toronto: Coach House Press, 1973.

———. *The Collected Poems of Robert Creeley, 1945–1975.* Berkeley: University of Cali-fornia Press, 1982.

———. *The Collected Essays of Robert Creeley.* Berkeley: University of California Press, 1989.

———. *Tales out of School: Selected Interviews.* Ann Arbor: University of Michigan Press, 1993.

———, and Archie Rand. *Drawn & Quartered.* New York: Granary, 2001.

Crow, Thomas. *The Rise of the Sixties: American and European Art in the Era of Dissent.* New Haven: Yale University Press, 2004 (originally published 1996).

———. "Lives of Allegory in the Pop 1960s: Andy Warhol and Bob Dylan." In Charles G. Salas, ed., *The Life and the Work: Art and Biography,* 108–49. Los Angeles: Getty Research Institute, 2007.

Damon, Maria. *The Dark End of the Street: Margins in American Vanguard Poetry.* Min-neapolis: University of Minnesota Press, 1993.

Daniel, Darrin. *Harry Smith: Fragments of a Northwest Life.* Seattle: Elbow Press, 2000.

Davidson, Michael. "A Book of First Things: *The Opening of the Field.*" In Bertholf and Reid (1979), 56–84.

———. *The San Francisco Renaissance: Poetics and Community at Mid-Century.* Cam-bridge: Cambridge University Press, 1989.

———. *Ghostlier Demarcations: Modern Poetry and the Material Word.* Berkeley: Uni-versity of California Press, 1997.

———. "A Cold War Correspondence: The Letters of Robert Duncan and Denise Lever-tov." *Contemporary Literature* 45 (2004): 538–56.

Davis, Erik. *The Visionary State: A Journey Through California's Spiritual Landscape.* Photographs by Michael Rauner. San Francisco: Chronicle Books, 2006.

Dembo, L. S., and Cyrena N. Pondrom. *The Contemporary Writer: Interviews with Six-teen Novelists and Poets.* Madison: University of Wisconsin Press, 1972.

Denning, Michael. *The Cultural Front: The Laboring of American Culture in the Twenti-eth Century.* New York: Verso, 1997.

Dewey, Anne Day. *Beyond Maximus: The Construction of Public Voice in Black Mountain Poetry.* Stanford: Stanford University Press, 2007.

Dimock, Wai Chee. *Through Other Continents: American Literature Across Deep Time.* Princeton: Princeton University Press, 2006.

Dobrzynski, Judith. "Representing America in a Language of Her Own." *New York Times,* May 30, 1999, sec. 2: 1, 30.

Dorn, Edward. *Gunslinger.* Durham, NC: Duke University Press, 1989 (originally published 1975).

Duncan, Michael. *Cameron.* New York: Nicole Klagsbrun Gallery, 2007.

———, and Kristine McKenna, eds. *Semina Culture: Wallace Berman and His Circle.* New York: D.A.P.; Santa Monica: Santa Monica Museum, 2005.

Duncan, Robert. "Taste, Selection and the Ideogram." May 1952, Notebook 11, 39–41. Buffalo: Robert Duncan Archive, University at Buffalo.

———. Letter to Jerome Rothenberg, May 25, 1959. Buffalo: Robert Duncan Archive, University at Buffalo.

———. *The Opening of the Field.* New York: Grove, 1960.

———. *Roots and Branches.* New York: Scribner's, 1964.

———. *A Book of Resemblances: Poems: 1950–1953.* New Haven: Henry Wenning, 1966.

———. *The Years as Catches: First Poems (1939–1946).* Berkeley: Oyez, 1966.

———. "The H.D. Book" [*HD* I.2]. *Coyote's Journal* 8 (1967): 27–35.

———. *Bending the Bow.* New York: New Directions, 1968.

———. *The First Decade: Selected Poems 1940–1950.* London: Fulcrum Press, 1968.

———. "From the H.D. Book" [*HD* I.5]. *Stony Brook* 1/2 (1968): 4–29.

———. "Ground Work." Privately printed by Robert Duncan, 1971.

———. *Caesar's Gate: Poems 1949–50.* Mallorca: Divers Press, 1955; 2nd ed., Berkeley: Sand Dollar, 1972.

———. *Fictive Certainties: Essays by Robert Duncan.* New York: New Directions, 1985.

———. *A Selected Prose.* Robert J. Bertholf, ed. New York: New Directions, 1995.

———. *Letters: Poems 1953–1956.* Chicago: Flood Editions, 2003 (originally published 1958).

———. *Ground Work: Before the War / In the Dark.* Eds. Robert J. Bertholf and James Maynard. New York: New Directions, 2006.

Dylan, Bob. *The Essential Interviews.* Jonathan Cott, ed. New York: Wenner, 2006.

Eliade, Mircea. *Shamanism: Archaic Techniques of Ecstasy.* Willard Trask, trans. Bollingen Series, 76. New York: Pantheon, 1964.

Ellingham, Lew, and Kevin Killian. *Poet Be Like God: Jack Spicer and the San Francisco Renaissance.* Hanover, NH: Wesleyan University Press, 1998.

Emerson, Ralph Waldo. *Essays and Lectures.* New York: Library of America, 1983.

Eshleman, Clayton. "The Lorca Working." *boundary 2* 6.1 (1977): 31–49.

———. "Headpiece Stuffed with Books." *Aufgabe* 5 (2005): 170–77.

Esslin, Martin. *Antonin Artaud*. Harmondsworth, UK: Penguin, 1976.

Evans, Amy, and Shamoon Zamir, eds. *The Unruly Garden: Robert Duncan and Eric Mottram, Letters and Essays*. Bern, Switzerland: Peter Lang, 2007.

Evans-Wentz, W. Y., ed. *The Tibetan Book of the Dead OR The After-Death Experiences on the Bardo Plane, according to Lama Kazi Dawa-Samdup's English Rendering*. New York: Oxford University Press, 1960.

Everson, William. *Archetype West: The Pacific Coast as a Literary Region*. Berkeley: Oyez, 1976.

Faas, Ekbert. *Young Robert Duncan: Portrait of the Poet as Homosexual in Society*. Santa Barbara, CA: Black Sparrow, 1983.

Featherston, Dan. "A Place of First Permission: Robert Duncan's Atlantis Dream." *Modernism/Modernity* 15 (2008): 665–84.

Feld, Ross. "Lowghost to Lowghost." *Parnassus* 4 (1976): 5–30.

Finkelstein, Norman. *The Utopian Moment in Contemporary American Poetry*. Rev. ed. Lewisburg, PA: Bucknell University Press, 1993.

———. *Not One of Them in Place: Modern Poetry and Jewish American Identity*. Albany: State University of New York Press, 2001.

———. "Late Duncan: From Poetry to Scripture." *Twentieth-Century Literature* 51 (2005): 341–72.

Foye, Raymond, ed. *The Heavenly Tree Grows Downward: Selected Works by Harry Smith, Philip Taaffe, Fred Tomaselli*. New York: James Cohan Gallery, 2002.

Frattali, Steven. *Hypodermic Light: The Poetry of Philip Lamantia and the Question of Surrealism*. New York: Peter Lang, 2005.

Fredman, Stephen. *Poet's Prose: The Crisis in American Verse*. 2nd. ed. Cambridge: Cambridge University Press, 1990.

———. *The Grounding of American Poetry: Charles Olson and the Emersonian Tradition*. Cambridge: Cambridge University Press, 1993.

———. *A Menorah for Athena: Charles Reznikoff and the Jewish Dilemmas of Objectivist Poetry*. Chicago: University of Chicago Press, 2001.

———. "Letters on a Reprint of Robert Duncan's *Letters*." *Notre Dame Review* 19 (2005): 97–103.

Freud, Sigmund. *Moses and Monotheism*. New York: Knopf, 1939.

Gelpi, Albert, and Robert J. Bertholf, eds. *Robert Duncan and Denise Levertov: The Poetry of Politics and the Politics of Poetry*. Stanford: Stanford University Press, 2006.

Ginsberg, Allen. *Indian Journals: March 1962–May 1963*. San Francisco: City Lights, 1970.

———. *Deliberate Prose: Selected Essays 1952–1995*. New York: HarperCollins, 2000.

———. *Collected Poems: 1947–1997*. New York: HarperCollins, 2006.

Gizzi, Peter, ed. *The House That Jack Built: The Collected Lectures of Jack Spicer*. Hanover, NH: Wesleyan University Press, 1998.

————, and Kevin Killian, eds. *My Vocabulary Did This to Me: The Collected Poetry of Jack Spicer*. Middletown, CT: Wesleyan University Press, 2008.

Goldstone, Bud, and Arloa Paquin Goldstone. *The Los Angeles Watts Towers*. Los Angeles: Getty Conservation Institute, 1997.

Govinda, Lama Anagarika. *Foundations of Tibetan Mysticism*. New York: Samuel Weiser, 1969.

Greenberg, Clement. "Collage." In Hoffman (1989), 67–77.

Greenham, David. *The Resurrection of the Body: The Work of Norman O. Brown*. Lanham, MD: Lexington Books, 2006.

Grenier, Catherine, ed. *Catalog L.A.: Birth of an Art Capital 1955-1985*. San Francisco: Chronicle Books, 2007.

Grunenberg, Christoph, ed. *Summer of Love: Art of the Psychedelic Era*. London: Tate, 2005.

Gunn, Thom. "Homosexuality in Robert Duncan's Poetry." In Bertholf and Reid (1979), 143–60.

Hadot, Pierre. *Philosophy as a Way of Life: Spiritual Exercises from Socrates to Foucault*. Arnold Davidson, ed., Michael Chase, trans. Oxford: Blackwell, 1995.

Hayles, N. Katherine. "Voice out of Bodies, Bodies out of Voices: Audiotape and the Production of Subjectivity." In Adalaide Morris, ed., *Sound States: Innovative Poetics and Acoustical Technologies*, 74–96. Chapel Hill: University of North Carolina Press, 1997.

Herndon, Jim, to Robin Blaser. In Spicer (1975), 375–78.

Hesiod. *Theogony*. Norman O. Brown, trans. and intro. New York: Liberal Arts, 1953.

Hewett, Greg. "Revealing 'The Torso': Robert Duncan and the Process of Signifying Male Homosexuality." *Contemporary Literature* 35 (1994): 522–46.

Hindus, Milton. "Epic, 'Action-Poem,' Cartoon: Charles Reznikoff's *Testimony: The United States: 1885–1915*." In Milton Hindus, ed., *Charles Reznikoff: Man and Poet*, 309–24. Orono, ME: National Poetry Foundation, 1984.

Hirschman, Jack. *Black Alephs: Poems 1960–1968*. New York: Phoenix Bookshop, 1969.

————. "On the Hebrew Letters." *Tree* 2 (1971): 34–45.

————. *KS: An Essay on Kabbala Surrealism*. Venice, CA: Bayrock & Beyond Baroque, 1973.

————. *Cantillations*. Santa Barbara, CA: Capra, 1974.

Hoffman, Katherine, ed. *Collage: Critical Views*. Studies in the Fine Arts: Criticism, 31. Ann Arbor: UMI Research Press, 1989.

Holsapple, Bruce. "Poetic Design in Reznikoff's *Testimony*." *Sagetrieb* 13 (1994): 123–45.

Homans, Peter. *The Ability to Mourn: Disillusionment and the Social Origins of Psychoanalysis*. Chicago: University of Chicago Press, 1989.

Huxley, Aldous. *The Doors of Perception*. London: Chatto, 1954.

Igliori, Paola, ed. *American Magus: Harry Smith—A Modern Alchemist*. New York: Inanout, 1996.

Iles, Chrissie. "Liquid Dreams." In Grunenberg (2005), 67–83.

Janis, Harriet, and Rudi Blesh. *Collage: Personalities, Concepts, Techniques.* Philadelphia: Chilton, 1962.

Jenkins, Nicholas. "'Running on the Waves': Pollock, Lowell, Bishop, and the American Ocean." *Yale Review* 95.2 (2007): 46–82.

Jess (Collins). *O!* In Rothenberg and Clay (2000, originally published in 1960), 403–22.

———. *Translations by Jess.* New York: Odyssia Gallery, 1971.

Johnson, Ronald. *Ark.* Albuquerque: Living Batch, 1996.

Jung, C. G. *Memories, Dreams, Reflections.* Aniela Jaffé, ed., Richard and Clara Winston, trans. New York: Random, 1963.

———. "Psychological Commentary." In Evans-Wentz (1960), xxxv–lii.

Kadlec, David. "Early Soviet Cinema and American Poetry." *Modernism/Modernity* 11 (2004): 299–331.

Kamenetz, Rodger. "Realms of Being: An Interview with Robert Duncan." *Southern Review* 21 (1985): 5–25.

Kane, Daniel. *We Saw the Light: Conversations between the New American Cinema and Poetry.* Iowa City: University of Iowa Press, 2009.

Kaprow, Allan. *Essays on the Blurring of Art and Life.* Jeff Kelley, ed. Berkeley: University of California Press, 1993.

Kaufman, Robert. "AfterNach: Life's Posthumous Life in Late-Modern American Poetry." In Ross Wilson, ed., *The Meaning of "Life" in Romantic Poetry and Poetics,* 164–90. New York: Routledge, 2009.

Kazin, Alfred. "Introduction." *Writers at Work: The Paris Review Interviews,* vii–xv. Third Series. New York: Viking, 1967.

Keenaghan, Eric. "Vulnerable Households: Cold War Containment and Robert Duncan's Queered Nation." *Journal of Modern Literature* 28.4 (2005): 57–90.

Kerouac, Jack. *On the Road.* New York: New American Library, 1957.

———. *The Dharma Bums.* New York: Viking, 1958.

Killian, Kevin. "Jack Spicer's Secret." Presented at "The Opening of the Field: A Conference on North American Poetry in the 1960s," University of Maine, June 30, 2000.

Kinsley, David R. *The Sword and the Flute: Kālī and Kṛṣṇa—Visions of the Terrible and the Sublime in Hindu Mythology.* 2nd ed. Berkeley: University of California Press, 2000 (originally published 1975).

Kotre, John. *Outliving the Self: Generativity and the Interpretation of Lives.* Baltimore: Johns Hopkins University Press, 1984.

Kramer, Jane. *Allen Ginsberg in America.* New York: Fromm, 1997 (originally published 1969).

Kripal, Jeffey J. *Kali's Child: The Mystical and the Erotic in the Life and Teachings of Ramakrishna.* 2nd ed. Chicago: University of Chicago Press, 1998.

————. *Esalen: America and the Religion of No Religion*. Chicago: University of Chicago Press, 2007.

————. *The Serpent's Gift: Gnostic Reflections on the Study of Religion*. Chicago: University of Chicago Press, 2007.

Krull, Craig. *Photographing the L.A. Art Scene 1955–1975*. Santa Monica, CA: Smart Art, 1996.

Kuspit, Donald. "Collage: The Organizing Principle of Art in the Age of the Relativity of Art." In Hoffman (1989), 39–57.

Lacey, Paul A. "The Vision of the Burning Babe: Southwell, Levertov, and Duncan." In Gelpi and Bertholf (2006), 161–79.

Lamantia, Philip. *Narcotica*. San Francisco: Auerhaun, 1959.

Lawrence, D. H. *Selected Poems*. Kenneth Rexroth, ed. New York: Viking, 1959.

Lazer, Hank. "Remembering David Antin's 'black warrior.'" *Review of Contemporary Fiction* 21.1 (2001): 163–81.

Leland, John. *Hip: The History*. New York: Ecco/HarperCollins, 2004.

Leonard, George. *Into the Light of Things: The Art of the Commonplace from Wordsworth to John Cage*. Chicago: University of Chicago Press, 1994.

Levertov, Denise. *New and Selected Essays*. New York: New Directions, 1992.

Litz, A. Walton, and Christopher MacGowan, eds. *The Collected Poems of William Carlos Williams*, Vol. I: 1909–1939. New York: New Directions, 1986.

Lorca, Federico García. *Poet in New York*. Stephen Fredman, trans. San Francisco: Fog Horn, 1975.

————. *Poet in New York*. Greg Simon and Steven F. White, trans., Christopher Maurer, ed. and Introduction. Rev. ed. New York: Farrar, Straus and Giroux, 1998.

MacAdams, Lewis. *Birth of the Cool: Beat, Bebop, and the American Avant-Garde*. New York: Free Press, 2001.

Mackey, Nathaniel. *Paracritical Hinge: Essays, Talks, Notes, Interviews*. Madison: University of Wisconsin Press, 2005.

Marcus, Greil. *Invisible Republic: Bob Dylan's Basement Tapes*. New York: Holt, 1997.

————. "American Folk." *Granta* 76 (2002). http://www.harrysmitharchives.com/4_news/granta.html.

Marcuse, Herbert. *Eros and Civilization: A Philosophical Inquiry into Freud*. Boston: Beacon, 1955.

————. *Negations: Essays in Critical Theory*. Jeremy J. Shapiro, trans. Boston: Beacon, 1968.

Martin, Susan, and Craig Krull, eds. *Charles Britten*. Santa Monica, CA: Small Art, 1999.

Matt, Daniel, ed. and trans. *The Zohar: Pritzker Edition*. Vol. I. Stanford: Stanford University Press, 2004.

Mayhew, Jonathan. *Apocryphal Lorca: Translation, Parody, Kitsch*. Chicago: University of Chicago Press, 2009.

Maynard, James. "Architect of Excess: Robert Duncan and the American Pragmatist Sublime." Dissertation. University at Buffalo, 2006.

McClure, Michael. Letter to Robert Duncan, ca. 1958. Buffalo: Robert Duncan Archive, University at Buffalo.

———. *Meat Science Essays*. San Francisco: City Lights, 1963.

McDermott, Rachel Fell, and Jeffrey J. Kripal, eds. *Encountering Kali: In the Margins, at the Center, in the West*. Berkeley: University of California Press, 2003.

McKenna, Kristine. *The Ferus Gallery: A Place to Begin*. Göttingen: Steidl, 2009.

McLuhan, Marshall. *The Gutenberg Galaxy: The Making of Typographic Man*. Toronto: University of Toronto Press, 1962.

Meilicke, Christine. "California Kabbalists," *Judaism Today* 14 (1999–2000): 24–30.

———. "Abulafianism Among the Counterculture Kabbalists." *Jewish Studies Quarterly* 9 (2002): 71–101.

———. *Jerome Rothenberg's Experimental Poetry and Jewish Tradition*. Bethlehem, PA: Lehigh University Press, 2005.

Meltzer, David, "The Door of Heaven, The Path of Letters." *Wallace Berman Retrospective*. Hal Glicksman, ed. Los Angeles: Otis Art Institute Gallery, 1978.

———, ed. *The Secret Garden: An Anthology in the Kabbalah*. Barrytown, NY: Station Hill, 1998 (originally published 1976).

———, ed. *San Francisco Beat: Talking with the Poets*. San Francisco: City Lights, 2001.

Michelson, Truman. *The Owl Sacred Pack of the Fox Indians*. Smithsonian, Bureau of American Ethnology, Bulletin 72. Washington, DC: GPO, 1921.

Miller, Barbara Stoller, trans. *The Bhagavad-Gita: Krishna's Counsel in Time of War*. New York: Bantam, 1986.

Moore, Marianne. *The Poems of Marianne Moore*. Grace Schulman, ed. New York: Viking, 2003.

Moritz, William. *Optical Poetry: The Life and Work of Oskar Fischinger*. Bloomington: Indiana University Press, 2004.

Nadel, Alan. *Containment Culture: American Narratives, Postmodernism, and the Atomic Age*. Durham, NC: Duke University Press, 1995.

Neu, Jerome, ed. *In Memoriam: Norman O. Brown*. Santa Cruz, CA: New Pacific, 2005.

O'Leary, Peter. *Gnostic Contagion: Robert Duncan and the Poetry of Illness*. Middletown, CT: Wesleyan University Press, 2002.

Olson, Charles. *The Special View of History*. Ann Charters, ed. Berkeley: Oyez, 1970.

———. *The Maximus Poems*. George F. Butterick, ed. Berkeley: University of California Press, 1983.

———. *Maximus to Gloucester*. Peter Anastas, ed. Gloucester: Ten Pound Island, 1992.

———. *Collected Prose*. Donald Allen and Benjamin Friedlander, eds. Berkeley: University of California Press, 1997.

————, and Robert Creeley. *The Complete Correspondence*. Vol. 1. George F. Butterick, ed. Santa Barbara, CA: Black Sparrow, 1980.

Ossman, David. *The Sullen Art*. New York: Corinth, 1963.

Oudart, Clément. "Les constructions poétiques de Robert Duncan: 'only passages of a poetry, no more.'" *Revue Française D'Études Américaines* 103 (2005): 38–49.

Paul, Sherman. *In Search of the Primitive: Rereading David Antin, Jerome Rothenberg, and Gary Snyder*. Baton Rouge: Louisiana State University Press, 1986.

Pendell, Dale. *Walking with Nobby: Conversations with Norman O. Brown*. San Francisco: Mercury, 2008.

Pennebaker, D. A., dir. *Dont Look Back*. DVD. Pennebaker Hegedus Films, Inc. and Ashes and Sand, Inc., 1967. Distributed by New Video, New York.

Perchuk, Andrew, and Rani Singh, eds. *Harry Smith: The Avant-Garde in the American Vernacular*. Los Angeles: Getty Research Institute, 2010.

Perloff, Marjorie. *The Futurist Moment: Avant-Garde, Avant Guerre, and the Language of Rupture*. Chicago: University of Chicago Press, 1986.

Perls, Frederick S., Ralph E. Hefferline, and Paul Goodman. *Gestalt Therapy: Excitement and Growth in the Human Personality*. New York: Dell, 1965.

Peters, Robert, and Paul Trachtenberg. "A Conversation with Robert Duncan (Part II: May 29, 1976)." *Chicago Review* 44.1 (1998): 92–116.

Phillips, Lisa. *Beat Culture and the New America: 1950–1965*. New York: Whitney Museum, 1995.

Plottel, Jeanine Parisier, ed. *Collage*. New York: New York Literary Forum, 1983.

Poggi, Christine. *In Defiance of Painting: Cubism, Futurism, and the Invention of Collage*. New Haven: Yale University Press, 1992.

Pound, Ezra. *Literary Essays of Ezra Pound*. T. S. Eliot, ed. New York: New Directions: 1968.

Rasula, Jed. *The American Poetry Wax Museum: Reality Effects, 1940–1990*. Urbana, IL: National Council of Teachers of English, 1996.

————. *Syncopations: The Stress of Innovation in Contemporary American Poetry*. Tuscaloosa: University of Alabama Press, 2004.

Reznikoff, Charles. "From 'My Country 'Tis of Thee.'" In Zukofsky (1932), 92–97.

————. "My Country 'Tis of Thee." *Contact* 1.1 (February 1932): 14–34; *Contact* 1.2 (May 1932): 99–108.

————. *Testimony*. New York: Objectivist, 1934.

————. *Testimony: The United States (1885–1915): Recitative*. 2 vols. Santa Barbara, CA: Black Sparrow, 1978–79.

Richter, Hans, dir. *Dreams That Money Can Buy*. 1947. DVD. Produced by Hans Richter and Kenneth MacPherson, New York. Published and distributed by British Film Institute, London.

Robinson, Paul. *The Freudian Left: Wilhelm Reich, Geza Roheim, Herbert Marcuse.* New York: Harper, 1969.

Rothenberg, Jerome, ed. and trans. *New Young German Poets.* San Francisco: City Lights, 1959.

———, ed. *Poems from the Floating World* 1 (1959).

———. Letter to Robert Duncan, May 28, 1959. Buffalo: Robert Duncan Archive, University at Buffalo.

———, ed., with commentaries. *Technicians of the Sacred: A Range of Poetries from Africa, America, Asia, & Oceania.* Garden City, NY: Anchor/Doubleday, 1968.

———, ed., with commentaries. *Shaking the Pumpkin: Traditional Poetry of the Indian North Americas.* Garden City, NY: Anchor/Doubleday, 1972.

———, and George Quasha, eds. *America a Prophecy: A New Reading of American Poetry from Pre-Columbian Times to the Present.* New York: Vintage, 1973.

———, ed. *Revolution of the Word: A New Gathering of American Avant Garde Poetry, 1914–1945.* New York: Seabury, 1974.

———, ed., with Harris Lenowitz and Charles Doria. *A Big Jewish Book: Poems and Other Visions of the Jews from Tribal Times to Present.* Garden City, NY: Anchor/Doubleday, 1978.

———. *Pre-Faces & Other Writings.* New York: New Directions, 1981.

———, and Diane Rothenberg, eds. with commentaries. *Symposium of the Whole: A Range of Discourse Toward an Ethnopoetics.* Berkeley: University of California Press, 1983.

———, ed. with commentaries. *Technicians of the Sacred: A Range of Poetries from Africa, America, Asia, Europe & Oceania.* 2nd ed. Berkeley: University of California Press, 1985.

———, and Pierre Joris, eds. *Poems for the Millennium: The University of California Book of Modern and Postmodern Poetry.* Volume I: *From Fin-de Siècle to Negritude.* Berkeley: University of California Press, 1995. Volume II: *From Postwar to Millennium.* Berkeley: University of California Press, 1998.

———, and Steven Clay, eds. *A Book of the Book: Some Works and Projections About the Book and Writing.* New York: Granary, 2000.

———. *Triptych: Poland/1931, Khurbn, The Burning Babe.* New York: New Directions, 2007.

———. *Poetics and Polemics, 1980–2005.* Tuscaloosa: University of Alabama Press, 2008.

———. Speaking at Kelly Writers House, University of Pennsylvania, April 29, 2008. http://media.sas.upenn.edu/embed_qt.php?x=pennsound/authors/Rothenberg/Rothenberg.

———, and Jeffrey C. Robinson, eds. *Poems for the Millennium.* Volume III: *The University of California Book of Romantic & Postromantic Poetry.* Berkeley: University of California Press, 2009.

Salinger, J. D. *Franny and Zooey*. New York: Little, Brown, 1961.

Sanders, Edward. [Descriptive text.] Harry Smith, ed. *Harry Smith's Anthology of American Folk Music*. Volume Four, 4–30. RVN 211. Austin: Revenant/Harry Smith Archives, 2000.

"San Francisco Scene." *Evergreen Review* 1.2 (1957).

Schaffner, Ingrid, ed. *Jess: To and from the Printed Page*. New York: Independent Curators, 2007.

Scholem, Gershom. *Major Trends in Jewish Mysticism*. 3rd ed. New York: Schocken, 1954 (originally published 1941).

————. *On the Kabbalah and Its Symbolism*. Ralph Mannheim, trans. New York: Schocken, 1965.

Schrank, Sarah. "Picturing the Watts Towers: The Art and Politics of an Urban Landmark." In Stephanie Barron, Sheri Bernstein, and Ilene Susan Fort, eds., *Reading California: Art, Image, and Identity, 1900–2000*, 372–86. Berkeley: University of California Press, 2000.

Seitz, William. *The Art of Assemblage*. New York: Museum of Modern Art, 1961.

Seligmann, Kurt. *The History of Magic*. Reprinted as *Magic, Supernaturalism, and Religion*. New York: Grosset, 1968 (originally published 1948).

Selinger, Eric Murphy. "Shekhinah in America." In Jonathan N. Barron and Eric Murphy Selinger, eds., *Jewish American Poetry: Poems, Commentary, and Reflections*, 250–71. Hanover, NH: Brandeis University Press, 2000.

Sexton, Jamie. "Alchemical Transformations: The Abstract Films of Harry Smith." http://www.sensesofcinema.com/contents/05/36/harry_smith.html.

Shevelow, Kathryn. "History and Objectification in Charles Reznikoff's Documentary Poems, *Testimony* and *Holocaust*." *Sagetrieb* 1 (1982): 290–306.

Silliman, Ron. *The New Sentence*. New York: Roof, 1989.

Singh, Rani, ed. *Think of the Self Speaking: Harry Smith—Selected Interviews*. Seattle: Elbow/Citiful, 1999.

Sitney, P. Adams. *Visionary Film: The American Avant-Garde, 1943–2000*. 3rd ed. New York: Oxford University Press, 2002.

Smith, Harry, ed. *The Kiowa Peyote Meeting*. Recording. Folkways 4601, 1973.

————. "Evensongs of Exstasy." Unpublished poetry, 1977.

————. "(Think of the Self Speaking)." *Film Culture* 76 (1992): 8–11.

————. *Anthology of American Folk Music*. Recording. Reissue SFW 40090. Washington, DC: Smithsonian Folkways, 1997 (originally published 1952).

Smith, Philip. "The Art of Memory." *The Wire* 196 (June 2000): 24–31.

Solnit, Rebecca. *Secret Exhibition: Six California Artists of the Cold War Era*. San Francisco: City Lights, 1990.

Spanos, William V., ed. "Jack Spicer Issue." *boundary 2* 6.1 (1977).

————. "Talking with Robert Creeley." *boundary 2* 6.3/7.1 (1978): 11–74.

Spicer, Jack. *The Collected Books of Jack Spicer*. Robin Blaser, ed. Los Angeles: Black Sparrow, 1975.

———. "[A Plan for a Book on Tarot]." *boundary 2* 6.1 (1977): 25–28.

Starr, Sandra Leonard. *Lost and Found in California: Four Decades of Assemblage Art.* Santa Monica, CA: James Corcoran Gallery, 1988.

Stein, Gertrude. "Composition as Explanation." In Carl Van Vechten, ed., *Selected Writings of Gertrude Stein*, 511–23. New York: Vintage/Random, 1962.

Stickley, Gustav. *Craftsman Homes*. New York: Craftsman, 1909.

Sweney, Matthew. "Deposition: The First *Testimony*." *Sagetrieb* 13.1–2 (1994): 217–24.

Taylor, Brandon. *Collage: The Making of Modern Art*. New York: Thames, 2004.

Taylor, Charles. *Sources of the Self: The Making of the Modern Identity*. Cambridge: Harvard University Press, 1989.

Thompson, Robert Farris. *Flash of the Spirit: African and Afro-American Art and Philosophy*. New York: Random, 1983.

Tomkins, Calvin. *The Bride and the Bachelors: Five Masters of the Avant-Garde*. 2nd ed. New York: Viking, 1968 (originally published 1965).

Trilling, Lionel. "Genuine Writing." In Milton Hindus, ed., *Charles Reznikoff: Man and Poet*, 371–76. Orono, ME: National Poetry Foundation, 1984.

Vescia, Monique Claire. *Depression Glass: Documentary Photography and the Medium of the Camera Eye in Charles Reznikoff, George Oppen, and William Carlos Williams*. New York: Routledge, 2006.

Waldie, D. J. *Holy Land: A Suburban Memoir*. New York: Norton, 1996.

Waldman, Diane. *Collage, Assemblage, and the Found Object*. New York: Abrams, 1992.

Ward, Geoff. *The Writing of America: Literature and Cultural Identity from the Puritans to the Present*. Cambridge, UK: Polity, 2002.

Wescher, Herta. *Collage*. New York: Abrams, 1968.

Whiting, Cécile. *Pop L.A.: Art and the City in the 1960s*. Berkeley: University of California Press, 2006.

Whitman, Walt. *Leaves of Grass*. Sculley Bradley and Harold W. Blodgett, eds. New York: Norton, 1973.

Williams, William Carlos. *In the American Grain*. New York: New Directions, 1956 (originally published 1925).

———. *Paterson*. Rev. ed. Christopher MacGowan, ed. New York: New Directions, 1995.

Wolfram, Eddie. *History of Collage*. New York: Macmillan, 1978.

Yau, John. "Active Participant: Robert Creeley and the Visual Arts." Cappellazzo and Licata (1999), 45–82.

Zukofsky, Louis, ed. *An "Objectivists" Anthology*. Le Beausset, France: TO, 1932.

INDEX

Italic page numbers indicate illustrations.

of, 150; Hindu familial practice and, 150; in Hindu mythology and ritual, 148–49; iconography of, 194n5; as the Other, 148; as salvatory figure, 147; Western appropriation of, 149

Kaprow, Allan, 18

Kazin, Alfred, 33

Kerouac, Jack, 17, 77

Kienholz, Edward, 54

Killian, Kevin, 94, 95

Korean War, 137

Kripal, Jeffrey, 30, 148–51

Kuspit, Donald, 8, 54, 58, 64

Lamantia, Philip, 110, 112–13, 192n5, 192n6

Lawrence, D. H., 137

A Letterbox from Hellgate (Jess), 20–21; pictured, *20*

letters, alphabetical: aleph and bet, 118–22; hieroglyphs, 42, 123; typographic collage, 14

letters, correspondence. *See* correspondence, letters

Letters: Poems 1953–1956 (Duncan), 10, 26, 37, 115–16, 124, 126

Levertov, Denise, 6, 51; Duncan and, 10–11, 126–27, 129, 133, 137–41, 144; as maternal figure, 144; Duncan's depictions of, 147, 159, 163–64; as Kali figure, 11, 147, 163–64; Vietnam War activism of, 138–39, 140–41, 164–65; war poetry of, 138, 140

Life Against Death (Brown), 22, 27

life as art, 8, 46, 108; as anticommercial, 106; Artaud and, 103; assemblage and, 33, 56–57, 98; contextual practice and, 54–55; cultural shift and, 104–5; Duncan's "Grand Collage," 9, 23, 83–85, 88, 116, 125, 165, 173, 176–77; Ginsberg and, 77; "identity in process," 85–86; indeterminacy and, 54–55; interviews and, 33–34; popular interest in artist biographies, 32–33; residence as work of art, 88; self-construction as assemblage, 33; Smith and, 77; uncertainty or chance and, 54–55

limits: Creeley on self-imposed, 34–35, 50; and diminution of life energy, 178–79;

grief and the limits of erotic poetics, 125; mediation and, 64–65; Olson on, 49

literalism, 25, 27

Living Theater, 19, 174

logopoeia, 16

Lorca, Federico García: Duncan and, 10, 142–43, 146; generative loss and desire in works of, 10, 141–44; as progenitor of American poets, 134, 142–43; Spicer and, 94, 96–97, 134

Love's Body (Brown): as aphoristic, 7, 23–24; as assemblage, 13; critical reception of, 25; erotic poetics of, 24–29; Freudian analysis and, 7, 23–24; mysticism in, 7; as poetry rather than academic scholarship, 27; the sexual in, 7

"MACHINE AGE" (Reznikoff), 73

Maclaine, Christopher, 111

Mac Low, Jackson, 22

Mahagonny (film, Smith), 88–89, 92–93

mail art, 10; *Semina* as, 9, 100–101

Manteca (Smith), 62

Marcus, Greil, 69, 71–72, 175

Marcuse, Herbert, 22, 24, 25–26

materiality of text, 15

maternal figure(s): Duncan and, 11, 149, 150–51, 160–61; in Ginsberg's works, 80; homoeroticism and the castrating mother, 150–51; Kali as, 11, 149–51; Mnemosyne as, 160; queer poetics and ambivalence toward, 80, 151

mathematical regularity, 59, 113

Maurer, Christopher, 142–43

Maximus Poems (Olson), 37

McClure, Michael, 10, 19, 102, 107–9, 111–12

McDermott, Rachel Fell, 148

McKenna, Kristine, 107

mediation: anthology as unmediated presentation, 73; presentational immediacy, 64; recording technology and, 51–52, 64–65

melopoeia, 16

Meltzer, David, 6, 111; on Berman and contextual practice, 107; Kabbalah and, 10, 113, 123–24